Vimbuza
The Healing Dance

Published by

Imabili Indigenous Knowledge Publications
P.O. Box 1376
Zomba, Malawi
Published under the auspices of UNESCO

ISBN 978-99908-0247-4 Imabili Text no. IV

Layout and Cover: Josephine KaweJele
Editor: Professor Klaus Fiedler, Mzuzu University

Cover Picture: Kennedy Mvula, Vimbuza Dancer, by Rupert Poeschl

Vimbuza
The Healing Dance of Northern Malawi

Boston Soko

Imabali Text no. 4

A World Cultural Heritage

Foreword

UNESCO must be commended for recognizing the Vimbuza healing dance of the Tumbuka of Northern Malawi. We would like to thank, in particular, UNESCO Malawi for recommending this to their headquarters in Paris. This decision has ultimately led to the promotion and safeguarding of the dance as part of the world's cultural heritage. This book is based on the thesis for a PhD degree presented to the University of Paris III La Sorbonne Nouvelle in 1984 and which was published by the Museum of Man (Musée de l'Homme) on microfiche that same year under the title: "Stylistique et Messages dans le Vimbuza" (Style and Message in the Vimbuza). I am happy to acknowledge the funding of the publication by UNESCO and the editorial work by my colleague at Mzuzu University, Professor Klaus Fiedler.

Prof Pascal Kishindo (University of Malawi), the Author & Ndabazakhe Thole (Curator, Mzuzu Museum (Members of the National Intagible Heritage Committee)

Contents

Introduction

Our readings on and actual experience of Vimbuza possession dances stimulated us to peruse researches already undertaken. As this phenomenon was widespread, we thought that an in depth study could produce some interesting scientific results. In fact, there is enough material in Vimbuza for sociological, historical, medical and ethnological investigations. Moreover, through the richness of the texts and their stylistic features, Vimbuza has a firm place in oral literature.

In the course of our enquiry, we were able to establish that Malawi is a country rich in oral traditions. With a surface area of 118,484 km^2 and an estimated population of 13 million people (2008), researchers have registered more than seventy different dances. It is not by accident that we have so many dances; these traditional dances have diverse functions which can be subsumed under three categories:

> Entertainment dances
>
> Ritual dances
>
> War dances

The Vimbuza dance belongs to the second category.

The phenomenon of possession is recognized everywhere in Malawi. The phenomenon is also known in several of the African countries, of course under different manifestations and names. Our study relates to the districts of Mzimba and Rumphi. The area Mzimba – Rumphi is a crossroads of ethnic groups following the upheaval caused by the Mfecane wars in Zululand. The autochthonous Tumbuka live there in osmosis with a host of other ethnic groups brought there by the Ngoni, formerly the Ndwandwe, running away from Shaka Zulu.

For a whole century these diverse ethnic groups have lived side by side in the area, each one bringing its own kind of Vimbuza, that's why the Vimbuza healing dance is a complex phenomenon.

The Vimbuza dances are rarely performed during the rainy season, as everybody is busy working in the fields. The situation changes after harvest for the people then find time for leisure. Certain men have the habit of making such items intended for sale such as mats, baskets, mortars and pestles. The women, whose routine changes little because of domestic chores, find free time in the evenings, and their distractions are in the form of traditional dances, and particularly Vimbuza which seems to interest them greatly. Thus during the dry season the whole area engages in dancing Vimbuza in the evening.

During the past thirty years Vimbuza has attracted many researchers. We are thinking in particular of the following departments in the Universities: English Department (theatre), African Languages Department (oral literature), Religious Studies Department (traditional religions), and Biology Department (Herbarium). We hope that our book will be of some use in all these different fields.

In the final analysis, the interest of this book is to show that the possession cult of Vimbuza presents itself as an oral genre which is part and parcel of African Oral Literature. The ethnolinguistic study which we undertake will permit us to catch a glimpse of its whole complexity. The analysis has a bearing on four principal aspects:

- historical developments: a certain number of facts concerning the birth of possession among the Tumbuka.

- possession: the study attempts to show how the cult articulates itself with its beliefs and the use of divination.

- the social role: analysis of social functions.

- the style: an analysis of the linguistic procedures which are characteristic of Vimbuza songs. The presence of rhetorical figures would confirm that we are talking about an oral literary genre.

It is our hope that the book will present an adequate representation of the Vimbuza phenomenon.

Chapter 1: Historical Background

Introduction

The history of the Vimbuza healing dance goes back in time to the beginning of Scottish missionary work and the colonial era. It came into the limelight especially when the Nyasaland colonial government banned it in the 1920s following articles presented almost exclusively by missionaries and their local converts of Livingstonia Free Church of Scotland in Northern Malawi. These articles display a systematic prejudice against Vimbuza.[1] After reading these articles, the image one gets of the healing dance seems greatly flawed. Hence the need to retrace the history of Vimbuza with a view to providing an alternative perspective, and particularly elucidating the reasons why the colonial administration decided to prohibit the dance, a move which was doomed to failure, in order to finally arrive at a study of the Vimbuza phenomenon among the Ngoni-Tumbuka ethnic groups.

The historical account will essentially revolve round important events concerning Vimbuza which happened between 1900 and 1963.[2] In this connection, we used two sources of information; the writings of the missionaries and of local converts and the oral sources of our research.[3]

The Arrival of the Scottish Missionaries in Central Africa

It was David Livingstone who, after having visited the shores of Lake Malawi in 1859,[4] had had the idea, on his return to Scotland, of asking the Church authorities to send to those far away lands (Malawi) missionaries and merchants in order to Christianize and "civilize" the local popula-

---

[1]   Available at the National Archives, Zomba.

[2]   This period covers more or less the colonial era.

[3]   Field research for doctoral thesis, 1978–1981.

[4]   David Livingstone named the lake as Lake Nyasa. The British Protectorate later adopted the name Nyasaland.

tions. It was precisely in this part of the African continent that the slave trade was rampant.[5] In response to this appeal, Dr Robert Laws saw himself being entrusted by the Free Church of Scotland with the task of leading the first mission in Nyasaland. After having tried to establish this mission at Cape Maclear and later at Bandawe, along Lake Malawi, he settled definitely on Khondowe Mountain. The mission was later called Livingstonia Mission; with its satellite stations of Njuyu, Ekwendeni and Loudon, it is right in the middle of Vimbuza territory.

The missionaries' first task was to "impose order" in the region through their evangelization. The Ngoni, a break-away group of the Nguni of South Africa, controlled most of this territory, from Dwangwa in the South up to Mwenerondo in Karonga in the North, and up to the Luangwa River (Malambo) in the West. The Ngoni had the habit of living on war booty. During that era, all the neighbouring tribes such as the Chewa, Tonga, Senga, Tumbuka and Ngonde, were subject to frequent raids by the Ngoni in search of food and cattle.[6]

That William Koyi, a South African Livingstonia missionary, had Xhosa as his mother tongue and was therefore easily understood by the Ngoni, facilitated the pacification of the Ngoni.[7] Moreover, the Ngoni accepted the principle that the missionaries be established in their country, known as Mombera kingdom. Many citizens got converted to the new religion and quite a few others benefited from the school education that had been offered to them.

Nyasaland acceded to the status of a British Protectorate in 1891, but the Mombera Kingdom was left out until 1904, when in a special agreement Chimtunga, the Ngoni Paramount Chief, agreed to enter the

---

[5]   J.G. Pike and G.T. Rimmington, *Malawi. A Geographical Study*, London: Oxford University Press, 1965, p. 125. Up to about 1900 Arab slave traders had continued to ferry men to the island of Zanzibar, the "depot of human merchandise."

[6]   Donald Fraser, *Winning a Primitive People*, London: Seeley Service, 1914, p. 215.

[7]   For William Koyi and his fellow missionaries from South Africa see: T. Jack Thompson, "Xhosa Missionaries in Late Nineteenth Century Malawi: Strangers or Fellow Countrymen?" *Religion in Malawi* 1998, pp. 8-16.

colonial state.[8] The first colonial administration arrived in the kingdom in 1904. It was thanks to the advice given to them by the missionaries that the colonial administrators were later able to govern the region without too many difficulties. During this period we learn notably about the abolition of the *mwavi* ordeal, which the society would use in order to identify evil-doers in matters relating to sorcery and adultery.[9] It is necessary to note that the prohibition of the practice of *mwavi* had certain repercussions on the social organization of the Ngoni-Tumbuka. For example, it is about the relations that have existed between the disappearance of *mwavi* as a way of combating sorcery and the development of *vyanusi*, the divination form of *Vimbuza*, which assumes the same functions as *mwavi*.

Without going into any detail, we propose to give a brief account of important moments which have marked the history of *Vimbuza*.

The Situation of Vimbuza in 1900

The official sources as well as local oral sources agree on one point: *Vimbuza* did not proliferate in the area with the arrival of the missionaries. However, people affirm that the old *Vimbuza* did not at all resemble the one that was in full force in the 1920s. Everything leads us to believe, as we have already indicated, that there was a close link between the prohibition of *mwavi* and the rise of *Vimbuza*. Despite the process of evangelization, people had retained their ancestral beliefs and it was no doubt necessary to create an "ersatz" of *mwavi* for the society to continue functioning on its moral and spiritual bases.

It is perhaps necessary to emphasize that in this society, any disease, any death, was always attributed to evil forces: the action of the spirits or the sorcerers. As a manifestation of spiritual possession, *Vimbuza* allowed certain persons to become diviner/healers, specialists of the sacred,

---

[8] A ceremony to celebrate one hundred years of this agreement was held at Mount Hora on 9 August, 2008.

[9] Donald Fraser, *Winning a Primitive People*, London: Seeley Service, 1914, "The poison was administered every week across the Mzimba area and that involved mortal accidents."

capable of thwarting maleficent forces. In response to the rising of this movement, the missionaries did not take long to condemn Vimbuza as a diabolic cult and the colonial administration prohibited it around 1924.

Everything began when representatives of the administration and the missions, intellectuals and traditional chiefs consulted during a meeting at Elangeni.[10]

A number of resolutions were adopted which amounted, practically, to the prohibition of Vimbuza in its twin form as a dance and a possession cult. It is convenient to indicate at this point some reasons among so many others which influenced that decision:

- The activities of the diviner/healers used to set off chain reactions; the villages used to end up disintegrating when an individual was pointed out as a sorcerer or a witch.[11] This was prejudicial to peace in the area.

- The Vimbuza dancers were reputed to move from place to place with other people's wives, which led them to adultery.

- The diviners were accused of being profiteers whose sole goal was to enrich themselves.

- The Vimbuza disease was considered imaginary; the position of the authorities followed from the fact that some "Vyanusi" (diviners) who were called to serve under the flag and went to war against the Germans in Tanganyika showed neither the symptoms of this illness nor the desire to dance.

- The diviners, instead of caring for their clients, administered to them medicines which were putting them under the hold of spiritual possession. This is how the *Vimbuza* "disease" spread.

- Apart from these reasons, the missionaries had other reproaches against the *Vimbuza* dancers. In the first place, the fact that the dance and the other ceremonies which accompany it used to

---

[10] Minute Book of the M'mbelwa Native Association, 8.1.1920.

[11] D.D. Phiri, *Malawians to Remember. Charles Chidongo Chinula,* Lilongwe: Longmans, 1975, p. 40.

take place during the day, would naturally stop people from working in their fields and the children from going to school. From then on *Vimbuza* was performed at night to escape the control of the administrative authorities.[12]

In the second place, it is important to note that the Whites were not unaware of the existence of possession cults around the world. They knew what they were about. It thus seems to us important to see in their maneuvers an attempt to erase everything that connected the people to their ancestral religion in order to bring in Christianity.

We noticed, for example, wherever we went, small temples (*kavuwa*) used for prayers to the ancestors.[13] In this connection, one may even find a reconstitution of the manner in which prayer to the ancestors used to be said among the Tumbuka.[14] It was thus in order to combat the vestiges of the religion of the ancestors inherent in Vimbuza that the colonial authorities had recourse to these draconian measures.

Before applying the law, the authorities determined whether the diviner/healers were authentic or not. The district commissioner in Mzimba, McDonald, locally known as Madondolo, called to this effect several dozens to his headquarters. The test given to the diviners revealed their deceit, for none, except one, found the solution to the riddles posed by the District Commissioner. The latter then dealt harshly with all those who had failed.[15]

After these events, all the traditional chiefs received orders to arrest on sight all those caught red-handed performing Vimbuza. That is how, since 1924, people had witnessed the hunt for Vimbuza dancers and other participants. This policy was in force until after the Second World War. It must be noted nonetheless that the local people did not seem to have respected the law. Avoiding all administrative or missionary locations, the dancing sessions took place during the night in remote areas.

---

[12] Interview Kwenda Phiri.

[13] Cf. Donald Fraser, *Winning a Primitive People*, London: Seeley Service, 1914, p. 215.

[14] S. Gondwe and W. Chinula in *Midauko na Makani gha Wangoni*.

[15] Interview Robert Ziba.

On their part, the traditional chiefs, in order to remedy the situation, used to organize raids from time to time, conducted by guards (*kaphaso*) whose red caps inspired fear:

- the arrests must have been numerous
- the drums must have been confiscated and broken.[16]

It seems other countries experienced similar prohibitions in the colonial era. Bamunoba describes that for the Nyabingi cult, a form of ancestral religion which the administration considered an obstacle to the exercise of power.[17] The novelist Mongo Beti recounts reprisals similar to those undergone by the Ngoni-Tumbuka, for example, the broken drums.[18]

It is fitting to indicate that the authoritarian attitude adopted by the missionaries and the colonial administration with regard to Vimbuza and all its corollary practices had, very quickly, echoes among the local adherents. These latter rendered their support to the attacks, this time through the channel of a bulletin called *Vyaro na Vyaro*, published by Livingstonia Mission. Over a period of ten years, the local people played this role, taking up the same arguments as the missionaries and adding others.

This is how we have been able to put together a certain number of articles having a bearing on *Vimbuza*, divination and other beliefs.

The following themes constituted the most important points of their attacks:

- The diviner/healers were deemed incapable of curing whatever illness there might be. People were therefore taking risks by going to them.

- The diviner/healers behaved like hypocrites. While they demanded that the people should respect the bans with a view to safeguarding society's health, they were the very ones who were

---

[16]   Interview NyamSoli Chiumya and Handwell Nyangulu.

[17]   Y.K. Bamunoba and B. Adoukonou, *La Mort dans la Vie Africaine*, Paris: Présence Africaine – UNESCO, 1979, p. 20.

[18]   Mongo Beti, *Le Pauvre Christ de Bomba*, Paris: Robert Lafont, 1956. (Editions Présence Africaine, 1976), p. 98.

the first to violate these prohibitions, and in the circumstances they were committing adultery.[19]

- Divination was simply a game of trial and error which functioned on the basis of people's credulity.[20]

- Attachment to values of the past had prevented the people from being suitably converted to the Christian religion.[21]

- Vimbuza was not a therapeutic dance but a simple entertainment dance. Dominated by women, it simply testified to the infatuation the women had with the dance. In another connection, people affirmed that Vimbuza, described as a possession dance, served as a place where women had the opportunity of expressing themselves freely. It is important to note that these latter did not have a say, to speak properly, in this society where marriage is patrilineal and virilocal.[22]

- Individuals came to the dance in order to make themselves known to the public.[23] In this connection, we shall examine in Chapter 4 other motivations for participating in Vimbuza.

- People asked themselves, in the end, why Vimbuza was not performed in towns.

On the other hand, while this type of condemnation was multiplying in the bulletin *Vyaro na Vyaro* as well as from the pulpits, people took note of a fact which merits reporting, if only in passing. This fact seems to have played an important role in ensuring the survival of the customs and the dances.

---

[19]   S.G. Chipofya, vol. 2, no. 4, 1933, pp. 6-7.

[20]   T.F. Njunga, vol. 2, no. 7, 1933.

[21]   A. Ng'oma, vol. 4 no. 2, 1935, pp. 19-20.

[22]   A.M. NyamNyirongo, vol. 6, no. 1, 1937, pp. 9-10

[23]   A.S. Mkandawire, vol 6, no. 5, 1938, pp. 96-97.

The Elites Become Aware of their Culture

The realizations of the degradation of the situation on the socio-cultural level took place very quickly. The Reverend Charles Chidongo Chinula, trained at Livingstonia Mission, was one of those who took the first measures to safeguard the cultural patrimony of the Ngoni-Tumbuka.

Having completed his studies at the Livingstonia Teacher Training School in 1907, Chinula served at Loudon Mission Station (Embangweni). It is Chinula in his capacity as secretary to the M'mbelwa Native Association who wrote the report condemning *Vimbuza*. Later, nevertheless, Chinula noticed that the prohibitions of dances and other traditional practices that were taking place right across the country were impoverishing the cultural patrimony.[24] Serman Chavula wrote as follows in 1974 in relation to Chinula's positions:

> Even when he was Headmaster at Loudon, he believed that African customs should be purified and preserved rather than neglected and destroyed. He had therefore secretly encouraged pupils to take part in the dances while at Loudon.[25]

Other people shared the attitude adopted by Chinula. In this way, the Christian converts went back to participating in Vimbuza in secret. Numerous dances also served to turn the Christians from the right path. As the séances took place at night, the faithful, who took part in them, went unnoticed, and could not be denounced as everybody was implicated.

Indigenous Religion

The Ngoni-Tumbuka practised the cult of the ancestors up to the beginning of the 20th Century. The dead were the source of laws and customs which were perpetuated from generation to generation.

We are thus in the presence of a system of values which rests on past references. It is to these models that every individual spontaneously

---

[24] Equally prohibited was *Gule Wamkulu* in the Central and Southern regions.

[25] Serman Chavula, "The History of Loudon Mission: 1902–1973", History Seminar Paper, University of Malawi, 1974, p. 18.

submits himself by introducing them without modification into his cultural patrimony. Here is a glimpse of the way the Tumbuka paid homage to their ancestors and the spirits.

Long before the arrival of the missionaries the Tumbuka knew that there was "someone" who influenced the important events of their daily lives such as famines, harvests, wars, the rain and a host of other things besides.[26] They thought that this spiritual entity was represented by a great mountain from which came rain and mist, or by a great tree.[27] This representation could equally take the form of a river with strong flow of water. The fear of talking directly to this "unknown" led the Tumbuka to use the privileged interpreters who were their dead relatives (grand-father, grand-mother, father or mother). Nevertheless, any other individual, who incarnated a dead person (*chibanda*) could be used. But preference went particularly to the late traditional chief (*Themba*); for according to belief, he continued to be concerned about his subjects from beyond the grave.[28] Such has been the case for the Chikulamayembe lineage whose intercession was often solicited in difficult times. Prayers were said principally at the tomb of one of them.

Today vestiges of these beliefs can be found in the *kumeta* practice, whereby members of the family set a date when to meet after the death of a relative to "cut the hair" (*kumeta*).

The house in which the remembrance ceremony takes place must have a room which is reserved to the spirit of the defunct. During the ceremony, all the members enter the room and the leader of the group speaks on their behalf for a long time evoking the spirit of the deceased narrating the life in the village, events that have taken place and how much they miss him or her. This practice is apparently widespread in Rumphi and some parts of Mzimba district.[29]

---

[26] *Midauko na Makani gha Wangoni,* Blantyre: Hetherwick Press, 1961, pp. 28-33.

[27] Nyakwa Mountain was a centre of such prayers (Donald Fraser, *Winning a Primitive People*, London: Seeley Service, 1914).

[28] *Midauko na Makani gha Wangoni*, Blantyre: Hetherwick Press, 1961.

[29] This we witnessed when a colleague invited us to such a ceremony, when the family celebrated *kumeta* of his late brother.

In the past small prayer altars called *kavuwa* were found everywhere. These *kavuwa* were built under a Msoro tree (Pseudolachnostylis mapronneifolia Euphorb), to show their respect to their ancestors and to seek their pardon in cases where these latter were offended. The Tumbuka had the habit of making offerings of beer (*moba*) which they used to place in the *kavuwa* or even at the cemetery. Occasionally people made sacrifices by killing domestic animals (goats, cows). Traces of these practices, which were opposed by the missionaries, are still found in the Vimbuza.

Chikanga

A problem for the missionaries was to prevent their followers from consulting Vimbuza diviner/healers. This problem became especially serious from around 1957 when a man called Chikanga arrived on the scene.[30] With Chikanga, divination assumed a new dimension. All villages in Mzimba district were ordered to send men to Thete, the headquarters of Chikanga, to be screened for witchcraft. The Church was against this because it did not want its members to be involved in witch hunting. The Vyanusi songs that served as a base when the diviner was smelling out the sorcerers and their objects in the past, were to all intents and purposes replaced by religious hymns, in the circumstances those of the local Protestant church and some Catholic canticles.

We noted especially two new elements in the development of divination. On the one hand, the diviner no longer wore the habitual costume of the Vimbuza cult, but dressed himself in Western manner, wearing a necktie. On the other hand, the Bible was used: prayers were said at the beginning and the ending of séances. These took place at the end of the afternoon and extended late into the evening. The choir was composed especially of women, then boys and girls, who came to be treated or to get some information on the cause of their misfortunes.

---

[30] Boston J. Soko, *Nchimi Chikanga. The Battle against Witchcraft in Malawi*, Zomba: Kachere, 2002.

Chikanga consulting

The new type of divination impressed the churches, which at a certain point had believed that Chikanga was the potential founder of a sect.[31] People thought the more of it considering that similar phenomena were being produced around the same time in neighbouring countries. Among the Lunda-Bemba in Zambia, a woman called Elenshina had apparently died and after her resurrection had founded a powerful sect. This sect stood in the way of the missionaries as well as the administrative authorities.

Talking about sects, François Soudan and Kumanda Kasombo give some reasons for their origins:

> Historically, the African sects were born, between 1880 and 1920, in quite a precise context: the colonial situation. At the beginning of these movements, there is always a founding "father" or "mother", declaring himself or herself suddenly enlightened by the revelation of a divine mission. Very quickly, all those who, in one way or another, oppose the colonial order, come to swell the ranks of the faithful ... the syncretist religious ideology moreover made it possible ... not to lose contact with the animist foundation, while adapting this ancestral faith to modern imperatives.[32]

---

[31] A. Redmayne, "Chikanga", National Archives, Zomba, 1968, p. 7.

[32] *Jeune Afrique*, "Culture et Vie. L' Afrique des Sectes", no. 938/939 (27.12.1978), pp. 67-70.

Although the *makwaya* of Chikanga and other diviners had nothing comparable to religious sects, Vimbuza seems nevertheless to be akin to these movements, as I. Lewis observes on different types of possession:

> Peripheral cults of the sort we have examined are only a few steps removed from those thoroughly moralistic and thrusting messianic religions which so often arise in circumstances of acute social disruption and which frequently employ possession as a supreme religious experience.[33]

We are tempted to affirm, under the guise of a conclusion, that since the beginning of Christianization, there has been tension between the teaching of the missionaries and the desire of the indigenous people to live their ancestral beliefs. This explains why despite the draconian measures taken against Vimbuza, the administrative and missionary authorities have not succeeded in stamping it out.

The Present Status of the Dance and the Possession Cult

The position of the Malawi Government after independence has favoured the revival and preservation of the socio-cultural patrimony of the country. Appropriate institutions such as the Museum of Malawi, the National Archives, Malawi Television, Malawi Broadcasting Cooperation and the Department of Culture, are endowed with facilities to record and disseminate the arts to the general public. A lot of dances which had previously been have been reintroduced and recognized, among them Vimbuza. It is fitting to specify, in this regard, that Vimbuza dancers are often invited to participate actively during anniversary celebrations. There are many Vimbuza dancers these days, but the most famous entertainment dancer is still Siyayo Mkandawire of Mzimba. In addition, divination is now recognized. The diviner/healers practise their trade under the aegis of the Traditional Healers Association of Malawi.[34]

---

[33] I.M. Lewis, *Ecstatic Religion. An Anthropological Study of Spirit Possession and Shamanism*, Harmondsworth: Penguin, 1971, p. 128.

[34] MANA, *Daily Times*, 27.4.1981. See also "This is Malawi", Dec. 1980, p. 17.

Chikanga and witchcraft implements (nyanga)

Researches on Vimbuza

As has already been said, it is only after independence that people saw the arrival of another attitude regarding traditional dances in general and Vimbuza in particular. Before this date, no serious research had been undertaken[35] and this situation was not peculiar to Malawi as Judith Hanna underscores:

> African dance has rarely been the focus of research ... African dance is usually given a place quite unworthy of its social importance. The typical report on African dance is either a limited, vague description without reference to context, or a discussion of the context of a dance without explicit reference to its function, style and structure.[36]

Today it is established that dance can, in fact, offer a rich terrain in the study of the socio-cultural elements of societies.[37]

---

[35] Only Western scholars were interested in folklore or ritual dances, works by local researchers were rare.

[36] J.L. Hanna, "The Status of African Dance Studies", *Africa*, vol xxxvi, no. 3, 1966, London: Oxford University Press, p. 303.

[37] G.P. Kurath, Remarks at the 1954 and 1964 Annual Meetings of the Society of the Ethnomusicology, in J.L. Hanna, "The Status of African Dance Studies."

Research work on Vimbuza started from 1969. It is really a matter of a small collection of three traditional dances where A. Chilibvumbo gives, in a few pages, the outline of what was to constitute, twelve years later, the basis of our research on Vimbuza for our doctoral thesis.[38] This collection was followed by an article published in South Africa.[39] Since then a lot of work has been done on its different aspects, which underlines the importance of Vimbuza as a field of research,[40] and Vimbuza also achieved recognition by international organizations such as UNESCO.

UNESCO officials attending a Vimbuza dance festival, 2004, Rumphi

Conclusion

The early missionary was frightened of the dances without ever coming near them ... Thus, while there may have been a kind of voyeuristic

---

[38] A.B. Chilibvumbo, "Some Traditional Malawi Dances, Preliminary Account", 1969.

[39] A.B. Chilibvumbo, "Vimbuza or Mashawe. A Mystic Therapy," 1972.

[40] E. Kalipeni, "Traditional African Healing of Mental Illness as Compared with Western Psychiatry, (Clinical Psychology)," 1957.

appreciation of African dance, an objective report was psychologically and socially difficult.[41]

The analysis of the situation has shown that during the whole colonial era, Vimbuza was considered as a dance harmful to evangelization and modernization. The missionaries as well as the administrators shared this view, to the point where they found it necessary to ban it. Despite all their efforts, the faithful could change nothing, for, Vimbuza had entered into secrecy, thus becoming more difficult to uproot. When the country gained independence, there was a change of policy tending to encourage the maintenance and the revaluation of the cultural patrimony by all means possible.

It goes without saying that the historical account raises numerous questions which it will be necessary to answer. In fact, the interest of this introduction is twofold. In the first instance, we evoke events which have been analyzed in a profound manner. In the second instance, we hope to have brought a contribution to the knowledge of the history of Vimbuza about which a lot has been said without much being truly known.

Finally, all we have to do is underline two important points which we are holding back from the indictment against Vimbuza. In the first place, it will have been observed that Vimbuza was of a recent origin in the area. On this score, we think that it will be necessary to shed light on its origins.[42] In the second place, people will have expressed doubts on the real nature of the disease called Vimbuza. This will lead us to study the reasons which were at the source of "profane" Vimbuza.[43]

---

[41] Kalipeni, E., "Traditional African Healing of Mental Illness as Compared with Western Psychiatry, (Clinical Psychology)," 1957.

[42] Chapter 2: "Vimbuza as a Possession Cult."

[43] Chapter 4: "Style in Vimbuza Songs"

Chapter 2: Vimbuza as a Possession Cult

This chapter deals with the stages through which a Vimbuza dancer passes. The information is essentially that which obtained in the 1970s and 1980s. Latest additions have been included although they do not change much the general outlook.

The Vimbuza "Disease"

Vimbuza can be defined as a disease caused by the presence of spirits within an individual. The name "Vimbuza" is a generic term which is used to indicate three types of dances: Vimbuza, Virombo and Vyanusi. Thus the same term is used to indicate the presence of spirits in the body of the possessed individual and for the dance which is performed to appease them. It seems that the term adopted by numerous researchers to indicate the spirit which leads to spirit possession is *genie*. This could be justified in part by the affirmation of the Jinetigi of Mali (specialists of the Water Drums possession cult): "They all say that, if the names of the spirits differ from one people to another, the identity of the spirits remains the same from one end of Africa to another, and of the world.[1] It is commonly admitted that *Vimbuza* started in Zambia among the Bemba and the Bisa.

In attempting to verify this information, we first observed that the form of possession which exists there has a different name: Ngulu[2] and that it does not present itself after the manner of Vimbuza, for the social organization of the Bemba is different from that of the Ngoni-Tumbuka. While the Bemba are matrilineal and matrilocal, the Ngoni-Tumbuka are patrilineal and virilocal. We then observed that the only connection that exists between Vimbuza and its country of origin seems to reside in the term itself: "Vimbuza." According to Makasa Kasonde, there are three

---

[1] J.M. Gibaal, *Tambours d'eau*, Paris: Le Sycamore, 1982:169.

[2] Interview Makasa Kasonde, Kalabwe Village, Chief Mumpolokoso, Mporokoso District, Northern Province, Zambia.

words which approximate to Vimbuza on the phonetic level; the first is *imbusa*, then *bana-chimbusa*, and finally, *ifimbusa*. Now, these three terms are not applied to the possession cult *Ngulu* of which we have taken note above.

> *Imbusa* signifies a collection of clay items (pots, jars) which may go beyond fifty in number; this collection is used in initiation ceremonies for girls known as *Chisungu*.
>
> *Ifimbusa* and *bana-chimbusa* are the matrons responsible for the education of the girls during the initiation, and while they are at the hearth, the matrons sing a lot during these ceremonies and according to Makasa Kasonde the music would perhaps be the connecting line between the name *ifimbusa* and *vimbuza*.
>
> We only note that there has been a deformation of the word at the phonetic and semantic level. The distance which the word has covered can explain this evolution. Moreover, the Bemba and the Tumbuka are separated by another ethnic group, the Senga.

There are two principal types of possession. The first type is the one where the possessed person is severely convulsed and loses consciousness, perhaps after the manner of the Haitian Voodoo. In the second type, the victim seems to remain mistress of her body, at least in so far as the utilization of her limbs and her voice are concerned. This is precisely what happens in the Vimbuza of the North of Malawi and in the Malombo in the Central Region of the country.

After having worked on possession dances in Zambia, W. Brelsford gives a description of the two types of possession which may throw some light on what we are saying:

The inharmonious dance is also subdivided into 'pure' convulsive dances in which all control is lost of the limbs, which jerk and twitch until the dancer gets into a state of extreme nervous excitement accompanied by wild paroxysm. The 'weakened' convulsive dance involves the same movements, but the limbs are always under control, and this dance does not end, as does often the pure one, in unconsciousness…the latter if often characteristic of the travelling exhibition dancer who stands for long

24

periods twitching his buttocks and ceaselessly shaking his rattles and rustling his skirts.[3]

We are thus led to say that Vimbuza is to be considered as a dance of "mild possession." Nevertheless, it is fitting to draw attention to one exception: the *Vyanusi* type does not correspond to this definition. We shall return to it later.

Another remarkable characteristic of Vimbuza consists in the fact that the spirits which give rise to this possession are never attributed to the direct ancestors of the victim.[4] All our informants were categorical on this point. C.M. White describes a similar situation among the Luvale (Western Zambia) from which we draw surprising parallels, for example:

Mahamba ... the term has for several decades been applied to affliction derived from other sources. Such other sources are in many instances said to be contacts with other tribal or racial groups. Contact with the Ovimbundu is said to cause the afflictions of Chimbuli and Tundumbu, with the Kasai Chokwe to cause Viyaya, with Europeans to cause Vindele and with mulattoes to cause Vasando.[5]

In fact, the Ngoni wars known as *Mfecane* across the whole of Southern Africa, mixed even the population in the area inhabited by the Tumbuka.[6] The contact between the Ngoni from KwaZulu-Natal and the other ethnic groups gave birth to *Vyanusi*; the contact between the Chewa and other groups including the Ngoni gave birth to *Virombo*, and the contact between the Bemba/Bisa and the other ethnic groups gave birth to *Vimbuza*. On the historical level, that explains why these phenomena are relatively recent in the area.

---

[3] W.V. Brelsford, "African Dances of Northern Rhodesia", in Rhodes-Livingstone Museum Occasional Papers, no. 2 (1948), p. 4.

[4] According to research carried out in the 1970s.

[5] C.M.N. White, *Elements in Luvale Beliefs and Rituals*. The Rhodes-Livingstone Occasional Papers no. 32, Manchester University Press, 1961, pp. 49-50.

[6] J.G. Pike and G.T. Rimmington, *Malawi. A Geographical Study*, London: Oxford University Press, 1965, pp. 125-127.

It is interesting to note that since the last research carried out in the 1970s and 1980s on Vimbuza in Mzimba district, new developments have taken place. It concerns spirits which are responsible for the onset of Vimbuza possession. Most informants we have come across (2007 – 2008) attribute these spirits to their defunct parents, a mother, a grandmother or a grandfather, etc. This means that we are no longer dealing with wandering spirits only, but as well with those of the same lineage with the patient. Furthermore, we have noted the appearance of red and white crosses on the uniform worn by the dancers. This indicates some departure from the old Vimbuza. These white and red crosses are there as a result of a directive from the spirits. We will look at them later. Finally, we should report that there are many diviner-healers born of the Vimbuza nowadays, most of them new recruits. Here, too, there is need to find the reasons why.

The Principal Types of Vimbuza

All alluded to above, the Vimbuza phenomenon is a composite dance which can be divided into three major types.
Vyanusi of Ngoni origin.
Virombo of Chewa origin
Vimbuza of Bemba, Bisa and Senga origins.

Denomination of Possession (of the olden days)

We shall present the classification which the Ngoni-Tumbuka make of possession at home. To carry out this classification we have three criteria:
the geographical origin of each type of possession. (See table and map which follow.)
the nature of the disease at the moment when the spirits enter an individual's body.
the language the spirits use

THE THREE PRINCIPAL TYPES OF VIMBUZA

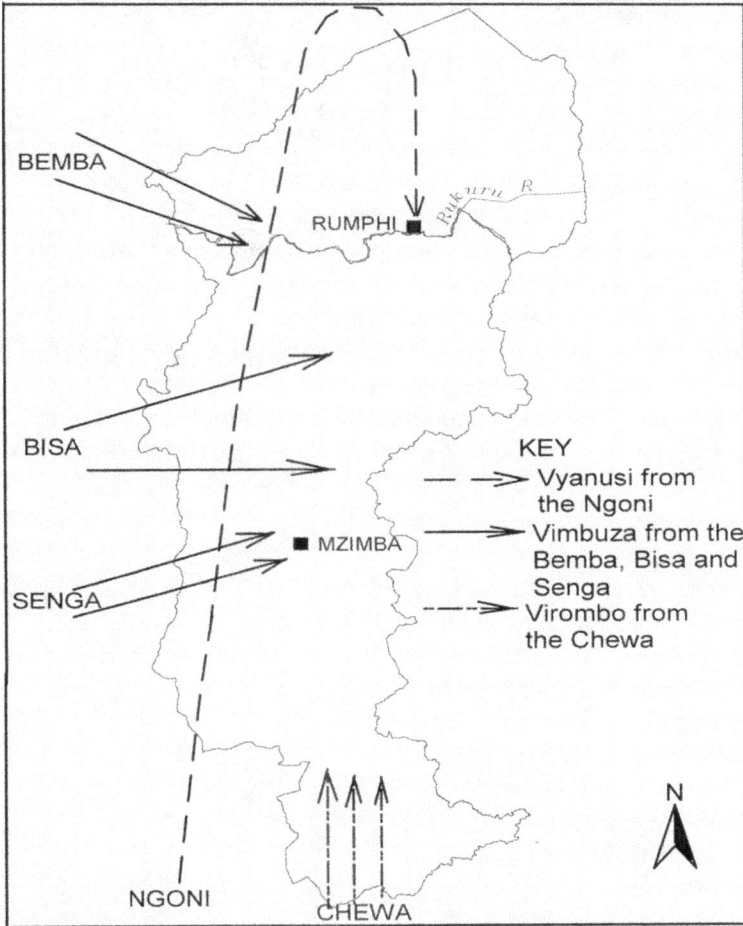

BEMBA

RUMPHI ■

Rukuru R.

BISA

KEY

- - - ➤ Vyanusi from the Ngoni

■ MZIMBA

➤ Vimbuza from the Bemba, Bisa and Senga

SENGA

- · - ➤ Virombo from the Chewa

N

NGONI

CHEWA

0 — 30 Kilometers

The table below illustrates our point.

The Three Principal Types of Vimbuza

Possession	Nature of Disease
Vimbuza	Pains of the "fever" type. Generalized pains in the body. Loss of appetite.
Virombo	Severe head pains at the peak of the cranium. Palpitations at the level of the heart. Loss of appetite.
Vyanusi	A form of mental illness, the victim behaves in an abnormal way. If not attended to, the patient can run mad. Loss of appetite.

Vimbuza

The Vimbuza has specific names given to the spirit that possesses somebody or enters into someone. When asked who the spirit is, the following are some of the names, usually belonging to dead chiefs or other important personages from the Bemba, Bisa, Lunda and Senga ethnic groups:

Chota Muliro
Chanda
Chibesakunda
Chitimukulu
Jandalala
Mazabamba
Mwiza
Kafwimbi
Kakota
Kota
Kawuswe
Kazembe
Njekulala

It is important to note that each name represents a number of spirits. For example; "Chota Muliro" is described as genies:

Chota Muliro	Chota Muliro
Chota Muliro mvibanda	Chota Muliro are genies

Buki Banda, a leading Vimbuza dancer,[7] affirms, in this connection, that once possessed, one sees a multitude of genies, "after the manner of the crowd that Jesus exorcised" (Mark 5:1-15).

Certain genies do not have individual names but a common name and act together. This is the case with the following type:

Virombo

Groups of genies that have common characteristics:
    BaRondo
    BaSenga
    BaChewa
    Mam'phanda
    Mavundura
    Makhabango
    Ukhazi

Vyanusi

    Mngoma
    Mhalule
    Mthwasi – a form of possession which leads to divining and
        healing
    Majelemani

Possession can manifest itself under diverse forms, among which are the following:

---

[7] Of T.A. Kabunduli, Nkhata Bay, 1979.

Momentary Manifestation	Permanent Manifestation
1. Singo (stiff neck)	Chadoroka – possession which makes people go blind
2. Jikamalalo (dancing on the knees)	Uchumba – sterility
3. Vifusi (madness)	Repeated miscarriages
4. Crisis at the sight of blood	Refusal to eat beef
5. Paralysis of limbs or body	Lasting paralysis

Dancing on the mortar

Stiff neck "Singo"

Climbing on to the roof "Katantha"

It is important to determine the place of the genies in the belief system of the Ngoni-Tumbuka. The Tumbuka believe in the existence of spirits (*vibanda*) in general, as discussed above under "Indigenous religion." We think that the arrival of these foreign spirits did not entail a change in their conception of the action exercised by the spiritual world on the living. Moreover, we can suppose that their presence is felt as a tangible demonstration of the spiritual presence of the ancestors.

Ordinarily, when somebody falls ill, he/she takes medicine provided by a healer. If the illness persists, it is attributed to the action of either sorcerers or spirits. One thus goes to consult a diviner who eliminates sorcery for it may be the case of the anger of an ancestor avenging himself on the victim. But very often it is more a matter of the 'disease' of possession. Whatever its source, an attack by an ancestor or by a foreign genie seems to be felt the same way, that is, it will become necessary to appease the spirits through the dance and sacrifices.

Like the spirits of the ancestors, the Vimbuza genies are not always malevolent. They can be beneficent as in the cases of illness due to bewitching where they save people from certain death. On the other hand, the world of Vimbuza genies seems to be peopled by a multitude of genies of various kinds: humans, animals, birds, reptiles, natural phenomena. Below we present some forms which the spirits take in the Vimbuza dance sessions.

The Forms which the Genies Take: Incarnation

During séances of Vimbuza which have as their goal healing by therapeutic means, sometimes extraordinary things happen. Through the songs and the gestures, the possessed gives the portrait of the genie or the genies that possess him or her. The first type of possession which we are going to consider is that of lightning. Here the individual is visibly afraid and he sketches the gestures that are made by a man when lightning strikes. Lightning is called *Leza* in Tumbuka.

Generally people relate that lightning appears in the form of a bird, a pigeon, to be precise. There is a belief among the Luwale of Zambia which goes in the same direction:

When lightning strikes a tree, Kalunga is visible in the form of a bearded he-goat.[8]

Often, the apparition of lightning to the afflicted person is accompanied by a song like *BaLeza* (no. 97).

BaLeza bali ng'ang'a	Lightning falls
Tichite uli apa baLeza aba?	What to do in its face?
Mwe BaLeza bali ng'ang'a	Watch the lighting fall
Tichite uli apa?	What do we do now?
We tizingirire nawe nkhu?	Where should we take you?
Para ndiwe M'Biza, M'bemba	If you are Bisa or Bemba
Panji Makhabango	Or Makhabango[9]

We can interpret this song as signifying that the possessed person is not sure whether the genies are Vimbuza or Virombo (*Makhabango*).

Sometimes the possessed person behaves as if she/he is hearing the roars of lions, from which comes the following song (no. 98) in which the genies disguise themselves as lions:

Nkhalamu yalira jaraniko (2x)	The lion has been roaring, shut the door (2x)
Jaranikomwe nkhalamu yalira	Shut the door please, the lion has been roaring?
Ndatenge ndi nkhalamu	I would say that it is a lion
Kweni ndi Vimbuza	But it is Vimbuza
Mwe penjani munkhwara	Go seek the remedies
Penjani penjani mwe	Search please

In another song the victim specifies the place where the "lions" are. This place is under the *Msoro* tree [pseudolachnistylis mapronneifolia Pax (Euphorb)] under which the Tumbuka ancestors used to build altars in honour of the spirits. Naturally we are led to observe that there is here a

---

[8]   C.M.N. White, *Elements in Luvale Beliefs and Rituals*. Rhodes-Livingstone Occasional Papers no. 32, Manchester University Press, 1961, pp. 49-50.

[9]   The first three lines are uttered by the afflicted who is apparently very fearful. The next four lines are uttered by the participating audience which does not know how to help, surmising that this lightning is the manifestation of Bisa, Bemba (Vimbuza) or Makhabango (Virombo) spirits.

reconciliation between the foreign genies (Vimbuza, Virombo, Vyanusi) and the spirits of the Tumbuka ancestors; for all seem to be united under this same sacred Msoro tree.

Nkhalamu zalira ku Msoro	The lions are roaring under the Msoro
Para zikujuma muniwuske	If they start again wake me up
Ku Msoro nkhawoneko	I shall go to see them under the Msoro

At other occasions the genies present themselves as birds. When it is the guinea-fowl, for example, the afflicted appears to incarnate it by imitating its gestures. She starts scratching the soil with her fingernails and occasionally she hops in the manner of the guinea-fowl. In addition, the possessed person feels a strange pain due to the fact that the bird or genie is actually scratching her heart:

Jopilo, kuli nkhanga zikupala (2x)	Jopilo, there are guinea-fowl scratching
Kasi nthenda iyi yitimare?	This illness, will it ever disappear?
Apa nkhanga zikupala	Since the guinea-fowls have not done well
Jopilo jopilo	Jopilo jopilo
Nkhanga izi mwe zananga	There are guinea-fowls scratching
Jopilo kuli nkhanga zikupala	Jopilo there are guinea-fowls scratching

An extraordinary scene unfolds when the possessed person suddenly places herself on all the four limbs; people immediately bring her a large basket (*chihengo*) which she is going to hold between the teeth in order to represent the way in which a type of mole digs its hole. They are in fact *mnjiri* (moles) which dig deep holes along valleys. Then she sings (song no 109).:

BaMnjiri	You Mnjiri
Jimani BaMnjiri jimani	Dig Mnjiri dig
BaMnjiri	You Mnjiri
Oh oh le jimani BaMnjiri jimani	Oh oh, Mnjiri dig, Mnjiri dig

A similar spectacle is presented when the possessed person incarnates the insect known as *Mazombwe*.

Still on all fours, the possessed person moves after the manner of this insect, that is, so slowly that one would say that he is immobile. Our informant told us that the afflicted is supposed to be climbing a hill: hence the complaint: "how can I climb, I am Mazombwe" (song no. 32).

Kwera kwera	Climb, climb
Nikwere uli nili Mazombwe	How can I climb, I am Mazombwe
Kweru kweru	climbing, climbing
Nikwere uli	How can I climb
Nikwere uli kuchanya kwerukweru	How can I climb to the sky
Nikwere uli	How can I climb
Kuli kunjira vibanda kwerukweru	Over there are already the genies
Nikwere uli ku mdima ine	How can I climb in the dark
Nili Mazombwe yayayiwe	I am Mazombwe, yayayiwe
Mwana wali kumsana amama	I have a child on my back, mother
Katundu wali pa mutu	I have a load on my head
Manyi nikwere uli amama	I don't know how to climb, mother

We could without doubt multiply these examples but the essential point is to know that the genies manifest themselves to the possessed persons in a variety of ways. To end this section we would like to give a particular example which shows to what point possession may be diversified. We know a type of possession in which the dancer behaves like a soldier. It is in the middle of a frenetic dance that the dancer stops suddenly to demand a baton and a whistle. He begins to march, shouting "one, two, one, two," and "left, right, left, right." Everything happens as if in the inspection of a military parade and he visibly gives the impression of commanding a squad. He can even show the drummers how to beat the drums to the rhythm of his "military march."[10]

Although its origin is recent, this type of possession seems to have spread throughout the whole area. It seems to be the result of contact between the African world and the Western world represented by towns. In this connection, C. White presents an even more spectacular example than our own; for the possession emanates here from mechanical sources:

Still more removed from kinship are the afflictions of *sitima* (train) and *ndege* (aeroplane) ... The ritual of the former mimes a railway with

---

[10] This could be spirits referred to as "Jelemani" relating to the First World War in Tanganyika where many Tumbuka had served as porters under the British. See John McCracken, *Politics and Christianity in Malawi 1875-1940. The Impact of the Livingstonia Mission in the Northern Province,* Zomba: Kachere, [2]2008, pp. 266-276.

pounding poles laid as the track along which the patient shuffles emitting puffing noises and dragging behind a series of long baskets tied end to end as trucks.[11]

These phenomena are indicated in many possession cults. According to G. Rouget, this type of dance belongs to the dances described as figurative or dumb shows "which have as their function to manifest the state of possession."[12]

Among the Songhay, when the possessed person obtains the complicity of the god whom he incarnates, he gives himself up to stereotypical mimicry.[13] Among the Wolof, the *Ndop* dance presents the possibility of "identificatory conduct."[14] There is a similar phenomenon in the South of Italy in the Tarantella.[15]

Conception of Spirits

The Ngoni-Tumbuka distinguish five types of spirits but the distinction sometimes seems to lead to confusion. Nevertheless, we briefly describe two important types.

(a) Muzimu (pl. Mizimu)

This is the spirit which leaves the body after death and goes to wander in such remote places as mountains, valleys and the bush. In relation to what we have evoked above, the Ngoni-Tumbuka believe that the spirits of chiefs and other personalities return to the village. From this fact, some of these latter are buried in the villages.[16]

---

[11] C.M.N. White, *Elements in Luvale Beliefs and Rituals*. Rhodes-Livingstone Occasional Papers no. 32, Manchester University Press, 1961, pp. 49-50.

[12] G. Rouget, *La Musique et la Transe*, Paris: Gallimard, 1980, p. 170.

[13] Jean Rouch, *Religion et la Magie Songhay,* Paris: Press Universitaires de France, 1960, pp. 147-148.

[14] A. Zempleni, "La Dimension Thérapeutique du Culte des Rab." *Rites de Possessions chez les Lebon et les Wolof,* 1966, p. 402.

[15] Ernesto de Martino, *La Terre du Remords*, Paris: Gallimard, 1966 p. 35.

[16] The practice is disappearing today.

b) Chibanda (pl. Vibanda)

These are entities that are considered the double of human society, capable of being perceived by the living. They are the spirits which the possessed persons incarnate during the dance. In the songs, for example, people always talk about some *vibanda* doing this or that. However, a number of people interviewed convinced us that they are incapable of distinguishing the *Mizimu* from the *Vibanda*.

The *Vibanda* have diverse ways of manifesting themselves, sometimes they call a person by his or her name without making themselves seen. They imitate the whistling of herd boys when these latter call out to their friends in the forest. When one is at a graveyard or in the mountains the noise of a branch being broken clean would indicate the action of *Vibanda*. When a *Chibanda* is nearby the hairs seem to stand on end on the head.

Diagnosis of the Disease

Usually, a person who falls ill is cared for at home; for a lot of people know which medicinal plants to use for simple illnesses. When a disease becomes serious, the family approaches a healer. Today, the tendency is to go to the clinic, health centre or hospital for treatment. However, the sick man who is also possessed cannot stay in a hospital; for to him the hospital ward has a certain odour. There have been a number of cases where sick persons have fled almost as soon as they have been registered and have gone back to the village.

The possessed man or woman sometimes claims that the bed in which he had slept was bad because someone died there and the bed sheets had not been changed. Moreover, the hospital does not seem to be in a position to cure the Vimbuza disease. Donald Fraser, a Scottish missionary, had already observed this problem at the beginning of the 20th Century, basing his conclusions on the fact that the Ngoni-Tumbuka believe that a 'disease' has supernatural causes: if it's not magic, then it's the genies. He says thus ironically:

> They have this great advantage over you that they have learned long time ago a fact never taught in your medical schools... that magic of some sort

36

is at the back of nearly all sicknesses. Therefore magic must fight the battle.[17]

Chirombos are spirits and are divided into four or five classes each requiring special treatment, and in all the shelves of the mission dispensary there is no medicine which deals with evil spirits. After all, what influence can a little pill have on an evil spirit? It requires more special treatment and a special language. [18]

After running away from the hospital, there is no doubt for the relations of the sick person that it is the *Vimbuza* disease. The people take care to go and consult a diviner who will tell them the exact nature of the 'disease' as well as the causes. It's only after this step that preparations are made in order to determine the type of possession that torments the individual and its treatment.

The Symptoms

To the question "can you describe the way in which one catches the disease (onset of the disease, signs, etc.), we received a wide variety of answers.[19] To say the truth, there don't seem to be any specific causes which one would take as symptoms of the 'disease'. As C. White notes, talking about causes in Mahamba:

They are invisible, transient like wind and liable to be picked up by accident like germs.[20]

---

[17] Donald Fraser, *African Idylls,* London: Seeley Service, 1925, p. 188.

[18] Donald Fraser, *African Idylls,* London: Seeley Service, 1925, p. 193.

[19] For my articles on Vimbuza see: Boston Soko, "An Introduction to the Vimbuza Phenomenon", *Religion in Malawi* no. 1, 1987, pp. 9-13; "The Vimbuza Possession Cult: The Onset of the Disease," *Religion in Malawi* no 2., 1988, pp. 11-15; "The Vimbuza Phenomenon: Dialogue with the Spirits," *Religion in Malawi* no 3, 1991, pp. 28-33.

[20] C.M.N. White, *Elements in Luvale Beliefs and Rituals.* The Rhodes-Livingstone Occasional Papers no. 32, Manchester University Press, 1961, pp. 49-50, p. 50.

A certain person had a pain in the throat which degenerated into coughs. She coughed for over a year, neither healers nor the hospital had been of help. While trying to treat the disease by therapeutic means, they discovered that it was a case of *Vimbuza*. Another person had eaten a sauce of *Kabata* (Bidens pilosa Comp.), a wild legume, and immediately afterwards she started hiccupping continually and later fell ill.

Occasionally it is during a wedding that the 'disease' begins. That is the case of a woman who fell seriously ill as soon as she had consummated her marriage. The death of a child or an abortion can cause the 'disease' in one of the couple. A man whose wife had aborted after three months of pregnancy, had the misfortune of catching the 'disease'.

Another person had pain in the teeth but the pain transformed itself into the 'disease' of Vimbuza. If one has a high fever and refuses to eat, it's also Vimbuza. Nchimi Chikanga explained that *Vimbuza* should be considered as a normal disease in the body of an individual, dormant for a time, but that attacks him suddenly through various forms.[21] At first the person may feel a headache or heart palpitations or even malaria. In a nutshell, there are many ways in which one can catch the 'disease'.

Finally, there are cases of hallucination where people talk of *kubwebweta*. We can multiply these examples, but the essential point is to know the 'disease' can appear in the form of somatic or mental problems. It is also reported that in the past some people started to 'feel' they had Vimbuza through a dream one night. They suddenly started to shiver. The people around woken up had to clap hands in order to appease the spirits. There were no drums at that time for the phenomenon.[22]

It is important to note that the 'disease' often occurs during the season when trees are producing shoots. This period, which is locally called *nyengo ya nyambwani* and precedes the season of the "rains which put out bush fires" *(vula za chizimya malupya)*. This appears in the months of August and September.

---

[21] Interview Nchimi Chikanga, 28.3.1989.

[22] Interview Nchimi Chikanga, 28.3.1989.

The great rains begin in November. It seems that it is the smell which the leaves release which causes this discomfort. In this connection, M. Leiris describes a similar situation among the Abyssinians of Ethiopia:

> The two most critical moments are the one in which the yellow flowers which mark the beginning of spring appear and the one in which the first clouds of the season of rains show forth.[23]

In another connection, the phases of the moon seem to determine the moments in which most crises are revealed. During the period of the new moon the séances are more frequent than usual. Similar phenomena can be found among epileptics.

We can say that the Vimbuza 'disease' is indeed imbued with mystery in so far as its real causes are concerned. People catch the 'disease' without any apparent reason. Certain people caught the 'disease' as a means of running away from the death that was lying in wait for them. That often happens when one has had a spell cast on one or has been bewitched. The Vimbuza genies in this case are considered as benevolent forces since they have protected an individual from dying. Elsewhere, there might be bad genies who push people to become wizards and witches.

Phase 1: The Test

The people need to know if the sick person has really contracted the Vimbuza disease despite the symptoms that they have been able to observe and the diagnosis that the diviner has made. In order to administer the remedies intended to relieve Vimbuza it is important to be very sure of the disease; for whoever takes them without a good reason runs the risk of going completely mad, even of dying of them. This séance (*kubunyisela*) takes place in a hut, big enough to accommodate a large audience.

The sick person sits on a mat placed in the middle of the hut. He or she is covered from head to feet with a blanket or a wrapper because of the fear that may be caused in the audience by the grimaces of the patient during the 'descent' of the genies. A small empty gourd (*nkhombo*) or a

---

[23] M. Leiris, "La croyance aux génies 'zar' en Ethiopie du Nord", *Journal de Psychologie Normale et Pathologique*, Paris 1938, p. 112.

gourd full of grains of j*ungu*[24] is placed in front of the patient. The audience stands or sits all round, leaving a small space behind the patient for the drummer. Later on the drummer places a drum above the head of the patient and beats the drum. Sometimes, instead of doing this, people put small bells on the head of the patient.

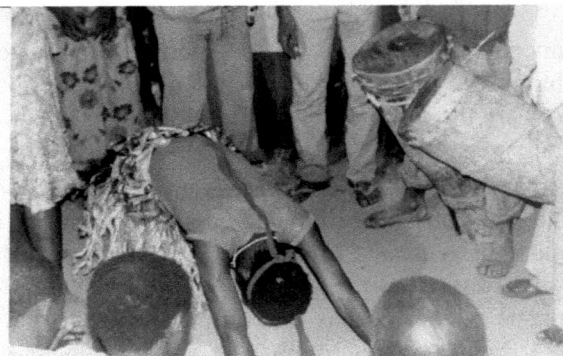
Drum's above the head of a patient

It is not always the diviner who busies himself with the patient during this phase. It may be anybody of the same sex as the sick person and he/she is called a *musamu*. At the beginning people of the opposite sex could play the role of *musamu* but that did not go down well with the missionaries, leading them to think of the practice as the prelude to sexual relations. This role is all the more important as it allows the assurance of order as the séance unfolds and a little like among the Vezo of Madagascar, this person "is not a specialist but the most capable person the most exalted. On the basis of a simple melody, the choir master improvises certain words or phrases aimed at qualifying and flattering the god."[25]

It seems there are three ways of preparing for the 'descent' of the genies. Sometimes it is done without drum accompaniment. The essential element is to put small bells on the patient's head and the small gourd before him. The audience begins singing. The song is accompanied by a special clapping of the hands in which the palms cross at each stroke

---

[24] Cucurbit maxima Duch. or Lagenaria sicraria (Molina) Standley.

[25] G. Rouget, "Possession à Madagascar", Collection Musée de l'Homme.

producing a mute and discrete sound (*kuchaya vikufi*). This kind of clapping ordinarily symbolizes the respect which the society owes to its paramount chief, M'mbelwa of Mzimba district, at the moment when he was standing up, sitting down, approaching or taking leave.

The following song (no. 31) is used to welcome the genies, repeated several times:

Tiwonjele fumu	Let's greet the chiefs,
Zawela weluwelu	They have returned.

The 'descent' may take place immediately but at times the waiting may go up to a good half an hour. Everything depends on the nature of the genies and on their number.

At other occasions, drums are used. People start beating, with full force, the principal drum, which is placed in a standing position just close to the head of the patient. The audience intones one of the numerous songs from the welcoming repertoire.[26]

In the song that follows (*Msekeleni*, no. 89) it is a question of receiving the genie with joy along with all the honours which are due to a friend or an important person:

Uyo wawela	Here he is coming [back]
Sekelelani wawela sekelelani	Be happy, he is present, be happy
Uyo waphuma	Here he is coming [back]
Sekelelani wawela sekelelani	Be happy, he is present, be happy

The 'descent' of the genies is accompanied either by movements of the head, which go from front to back, or by the noise: *hi! hi! hi! hi! hi!*. Contrary to what is the case in other types of possession, the 'descent' of the genies among the Ngoni-Tumbuka is not brutal. The patient does not undergo convulsions or lose consciousness.[27]

---

[26] Cf G. Rouget, *La Musique et la Transe*, Paris: Gallimard, 1980, p. 108: "Thus the music intervenes here not to trigger the crisis but to the contrary to put an end to it, by establishing communication with the god who is responsible for it."

[27] G. Rouget, *La Musique et la Transe*, Paris: Gallimard, 1980, notes certain types of brutal cases.

The third option is that the diviner uses plants to 'force' the 'descent' of the genies. We have already drawn attention to this problem in relation to the accusations which the colonial administration made against the diviners. The procedure consists in placing the leaves of a certain plant on a potsherd which is called *dengere* from the fireplace and putting it before the patient by slipping it inside the blanket with the intention that he should inhale. The effect is immediate for the patient instantly begins shouting *hi! hi! hi!* or shaking his head. But what is inconvenient about this method is the fact that other persons in the audience run the risk of "catching" the genies by sniffing and in this way contracting the Vimbuza disease. The old accusation that Vimbuza is a 'disease' manufactured by diviners seems to be confirmed in this practice. In this connection, I. Lewis notes a procedure which is close to the one we have just described.

Here the aim is to strip the body of its soul so that the strange genies can enter it freely:

> The Akawaio Caribs of British Guiana ... believe that in trance, which is induced by chewing tobacco, the Shaman's spirit (or soul) becomes very small and light and is able to detach itself from his body and fly with the aid of "ladder spirits" into the skies ... At the same time, his body which is left behind as an empty receptacle, is filled by various forest spirits. It is these which now possess his body and speak through it.[28]

This practice of inducement seems to be quite widespread. M. Leiris observed it in Ethiopia where it sometimes happens that an adherent voluntarily contaminates one of his relations with a view to initiating him into the cult.[29]

Preparation to 'induce' the genies

[28] I.M. Lewis, *Ecstatic Religion. An Anthropological Study of Spirit Possession and Shamanism,* Harmondsworth, 1971, p. 47.

[29] G. Rouget, *La Musique et la Transe*, Paris: Gallimard, 1980, p. 112.

In all three approaches the *musamu* gives himself the task of praying to the genies to show themselves very quickly and to ease their grip on this suffering person. His plea may be summarized as follows:

Tikuyowoya kasi ndiwe wakoma munthu uyu? Yowoya delele ili wakoma ni delele lako. Sono para muli nthenda yikwenerera kuti yiyowoye. Yowoya, ufume, munthu wachile.

Translation:

We are talking to you. Who are you? You have killed this man. Speak, this *delele* [okra] sauce is all yours. If there is the Vimbuza 'disease' in this man, it should speak, show yourself, this man should recover his health.

To this the genies respond favourably by beginning to give their names one after the other through the mouth of the sick person who is still under the cover.[30]

The order in which these genies arrive is not always the same. If to the question "who are you?" the answer is "I am Mazabamba", the *musamu* knows that there are other types of genies beside this one such as Kakota, Jandalala, Kazembe and so many others from the "Vimbuza family." However, the *musamu* is not satisfied with one class; for often behind Vimbuza hides "Virombo" with genies such as: Mavundula, BaRondo, or Mam'phanda. Finally, in exceptional circumstances, one can come across *Vyanusi* which we shall consider in greater detail later on.

The *musamu* is satisfied when all the genies have shown themselves, then the blanket cover is removed and the sick person is led outside for the dressing up phase.

Phase 2: Dressing

The dressing up séance takes place on the veranda behind the hut. If the dancing is going to take place in an open space, the dressing may be done just outside the arena. It's the *musamu's* role to dress up the patient. It is fitting to recall that a man is dressed up by a man and a woman by a fellow woman. While one could notice the same manner of dressing

---

[30] From now onwards, the dancer assumes the name of either Chimbuza, Chanusi or Chirombo. See also M. Leiris on this phase.

43

among the dancers thirty years ago, today the costume comes in a variety of forms as shown by the accompanying pictures. However, the following items constitute the essential clothes of the costume of Vimbuza dancers.

Men wear, on the head, the *njukula*. It is in the form of a crown of feathers arranged in a certain way.

Kazuba Mkandawire, Rumphi, wearing a ndlukula

Originally, the *njukula* was worn by *Ngoni Ingoma* dancers or on the battle field.

Kennedy   Mvula,   Embangweni   ,Mzimba (ndlukula)

The *njukula* strikes a good balance between the movements of the body and the head.

The women wear a doek (*duku*) around the temples. Apparently this takes the place of the *chibelebeza*, a band of beads worn around the head, quite popular among the Ngoni women of the past.

44

A man performing the Kulamba, lying low in respect of the Chimbuza dancer

A man with a doek being attended to by two musamu

The men wear feathers on the arms while women put on handkerchiefs.

The men prefer an uncovered torso, wearing a pair of shorts (*kabudula*). For their part the women have a tee-shirt to hide and to hold a bracelet (*kachingabele*). Moreover, they have a skirt (*sketi*).

Around the waistline the dancers wear the *madumbo* which are also called *zamba* or *nyisi*. It is actually a piece of goatskin arranged so that when the dancer jumps or turns, the *madumbo* amuses the audience by turning and by causing the flaps to fly in all directions.

The most expensive of these *madumbo* are made from beads as shown in the picture.

Madumbo of beads

It is indispensable to wear small bells around the ankles. These are locally called *mangenjeza* or *mangwanda* (see picture below)

Mpaparika wearing bells (mangenjeza)

These iron bells seem to have a rhythmic effect which chimes with those of the drums. The hand clapping and the whistle are used in order to produce the characteristic rhythm of Vimbuza music.

It would not be superfluous to add that other persons such as the diviners of both sexes wear amulets on the chest, handkerchiefs or amulets around the arms, and that in the end they have marks painted on the face, the body and the arms with clay or ash.

Kennedy Mvula with his amulets

During the Vimbuza 'dance' proper the dancer holds in the right hand a small symbolic hatchet which is called *mphomphwe*.

Goat skin flaps (madumbo or zamba on Nyisi) carring flywhiske

It hasn't been possible for us to establish the significance of this practice; it would be necessary to go back to the sources in Zambia in order to understand it.

In the Vyanusi dance, there are two objects to carry. The genies of Mngoma require that one should carry a spear (*mkondo*) in the right hand. This is increasingly being replaced by a stick of the same size (*mchiza*) which the old men ordinarily use as a cane. To carry such a weapon signifies that one is a warrior. On the other hand, for the genies of

47

Mthwasi, one has to carry a spear in the right hand and a flywhisk in the left. The flywhisk seems to be the insignia of diviner healers.

The recent addition to the Vimbuza costume is the white or red cross. The cross came with the donning of white or red uniforms.

To put on the uniform, one dreams the colour of the uniform, the colour of the cross, and the number of crosses. If one does not conform to the wishes of the genies or ancestral spirits, one falls seriously ill. One will get well when one has satisfied all the demands of the genies.

White cross on red uniform

Here is an example of a woman who bought uniforms right at the beginning of her possession:

> A cloth which was shown to me in a dream. The uniform was worn by somebody with a lot of beads and a cross. At that time a song for divination was sung. I woke up and that was the beginning of my entrance into the Vimbuza.

The white uniform means that the spirits should be cleansed. The red uniform means that the spirits have already worn the white uniforms. There is usually a special occasion when the uniforms are officially offered to the spirits. In this connection, Mrs Chikanga is quoted thus, addressing the spirits.

> Here are the uniforms which you desired, and we are offering you today: BaBiza, BaRondo, BaMphanda and all of you I have not mentioned. We

are dressing you these uniforms today. Therefore please do not trouble this person anymore.[31]

The addition of the uniform and the cross to the Vimbuza costume will require further study.

Before going to the next phase, we would like to indicate in passing that the dressing up phase is not modified for the people already initiated into the dance. These wait until their genies descend before they go to put on the costume. The 'descent' of the genies is aided by some songs while someone else is dancing; as G. Rouget has observed: "the already initiated people do not enter into a trance until they hear the call of the song of the rhythm proper to the god who should live in them."[32]

Phase 3: The Dance

As he or she dances, the patient starts with the simple stages. It is to be understood that each stage means specific genies with their own specific songs. The more able the patient is to dance to the songs of each stage, the greater is said to be the hold of the disease and his expertise in dancing. We can list the stages in their order as follows:

1. Vimbuza

2. BaMphanda

3. BaRondo

4. Vyanusi

Very few patients are capable of dancing to the music of all these stages - which may last long moments.

The moment he is returning into the hut, after dressing up, the audience greets the dancer with some welcoming songs such as indicated above. After these songs, the dancer herself or himself has to start other songs under the influence of his or her genies. The séance runs without a programme, for everything depends on the caprices of the genies

---

[31] Interview Editha Chikanga by Rupert Poeschl, 17.05.89.

[32] G. Rouget, *La Musique et la Transe*, Paris: Gallimard, 1980, p. 108.

The Composition of the Audience

The majority of the audience is made up of women. The men are not, ordinarily, enthusiastic about this dance. There is, therefore, a tendency by women to also occupy a preponderant place as dancers. The number of people who take part in a séance can vary depending on the population in the village and that of neighbouring villages invited to participate. In rough figures it can be groups ranging from thirty to a hundred persons. The smallness of huts influences us to say that the last figure marks the maximum. We recall, nevertheless, that certain people prefer to stay outside. It might happen that there are more people outside than those within. Increasingly, the séances take place in the courtyard and this audience is not only there to be entertained. It seems its participation is linked to the sympathy which these people feel with regard to the person who is suffering from the Vimbuza 'disease'. Their presence, apart from the fact that it testifies to the solidarity which exists between them and the patient, is also a form of therapy in its own right. The informants told us unambiguously that they attend these séances in order to help the patient rather than for their own personal satisfaction. Naturally, there are some occasions on which one can permit oneself such leisure, after the fashion of profane Vimbuza or other entertainment dances.

The audience fulfills several functions during the séance:

the principal role of the women is to sing and to clap hands.

the men are by obligation drummers.

the *musamu* busies himself of herself with the patient while the diviner-healer directs the ceremony.

Contrary to what is the case in the West, the audience in Vimbuza séances is active. It is nevertheless submitted to certain rules while it is in the hut. There is no age limit in order to take part in a séance. From the description which Ruth Finnegan makes of the "participatory audience" we shall retain, in what concerns us, the following extract:

It is clear that audiences do often have an effect on the form and delivery of a poem. Of course, the nature of the likely audience influences all literature, but with oral literature there is the additional factor that members of the audience can take a direct part in the performance. This is obvious in the case of a participatory audience, or in the fairly frequent

50

situation where a basically specialist solo performance is supplanted by the audience joining in the choruses' responses.[33]

In effect, the Vimbuza dance is a dialogue. While the dancer takes the solo part, the audience plays the role of the choir. The relationship between the *Chimbuza* and his audience is very important.

If the latter for an instant neglects its participation, for example, by clapping hands wrongly or amiss, or by singing poorly, the *Chimbuza* gets angry and strikes the big drum.

Afterwards the *Chimbuza* reproaches the persons concerned. The sanctions go as far as throwing some fire in their direction or forcing them to leave. On the contrary, if everything goes well, the dancer thanks the people. That happens when the dance attains its peak and the dancer increases his frenzy in his jerks (*kuteketeka*) and gesticulations. He pauses for a moment to press the hands of those who excell in their participation. Those may be, depending on the case, good drummers (*vilimbi vya ng'oma*) or ladies who lead the songs. In all that the goal sought is to have musical harmony which permits the spirits to enjoy the dance fully. Then, people believe, the spirits will release their grip on the *Chimbuza*.

Duration of the Dance

There is no limit to the duration of the séances. Everything seems to depend on the number of genies who "descend" and also the time which each one wants to pass on the scene. A séance may last all night. We witnessed this at Hewe where there were seventeen dancers in all and the dancing went on for twelve hours. But sometimes it may not go beyond several hours, and occasionally it may last only a few minutes.

All the same, the Vimbuza songs have variable length. There are cases where a song goes on for some fifteen minutes. A song may be repeated several times following the wish of a genie, although the repertoire of songs might be extensive. It is worth noting that older people do not generally take long in their sessions.

---

[33] Ruth Finnegan, *Oral Poetry. Its Nature, Significance and Social Context*, London: Cambridge University Press, 1977, p. 231.

The Women

Apart from the tasks of *musamu* which we have already described, the women are indispensable during the séance for two reasons. First of all they are singers. Then, they help in the clapping of hands which is done with the hands flat in order to produce a dry sound. They use sometimes thin planks to supplement the hands; these are in some way easier to use for long hours than hands.

The Men

The men sing, too, but their presence is desired for playing the drums. Not every man becomes player of the big drum (*ng'oma yikulu*); for it is normally necessary to follow a kind of apprenticeship over the years. It is fitting to add that a drummer is often rewarded (this payment is not demanded by him but it is a sign of gratitude) in the form of a chicken or some money. The drummer is a specialist who often comes from a distant village. As for the small drums (*mboza* and *mphiningu*), most boys already know how to play them.

The Drums

Drums are the only instruments used in Vimbuza. Two or more drums are necessary to give the rhythm. In the same manner this is what happens among the Ntandu in the Democratic Republic of the Congo, these membraphones are known by the generic term *ng'oma*.[34] In Mzimba people normally use two types of drums of different sizes. The *ng'oma yikulu* (big drum), as the name indicates, is the biggest. The small drum is called *mphiningu* and it is used to vary the rhythm (*kubitiza* or *kubitika*: from the English word 'beat') given by the big drum. A third type exists in some places, particularly in the Rumphi area. This third drum is called *mboza* and its rhythm is slow and invariable.

---

[34] UCLA, *Africa Arts*, vol XI., no. i, p. 35: "A Kongo Drum Stand."

As is usually the case in this part of Africa, the drum is made from light trees[35] and in Mzimba it is a tree known as *Mubale*.[36] The size of these tom toms varies depending on the type of drum: *Ng'oma yikulu* (the biggest), *Mboza* (medium) and *Mphiningu* (the smallest). The diameter varies around 30 cm and their length between 70 and 100 cm. The drum takes this form:

A drum

The range of the drum sound is of the order of 7 or 10 km in the absence of wind.

The making of the drum is surrounded with mystery. Our informants did not say anything on this matter but it appears that the choice of this tree is not exclusively guided by its quality of lightness, but also by its association with the spirits.

The proof seems to be that this tree is also used as a remedy for those who speak or walk during their sleep (*vigharaghandu*). According to the beliefs, speaking during one's sleep can only reflect the work of the spirits, as it is recorded:

---

[35] J. Williamson, *Useful Plants of Malawi*, Zomba: University of Malawi, 1975, p. 108.

[36] Erythtrina abyssinica (Kaffin Boon).

An infusion of the bark is drunk by those who suffer from the affliction of calling out in the night.[37]

Let's indicate in passing that the drums are vulnerable to attacks by sorcerers and to the presence of a woman who has her monthly period during a séance. They say the drums stop producing sound. As a precaution, the makers take care to protect them at the end of the production process by using amulets.

In the past the drum was not used in the Vyanusi ceremony. The Ngoni had a particular instrument which they called *ingubhu*.

> Two to three men who use sticks beating an especially designed Vyanusi drum, the *ingubhu*, as the drum is called, which is made from the dried hide of a bovine which, after it has been rolled, has the form of a basin or half-cylinder. During performance the *ingubhu* is laid with the concave side facing down.[38]

The *ingubhu* had definitively been replaced for reasons of simplicity by war shields (*vihlango*). The technique consisted in clashing two shields in order to produce a sound which more or less resembled that of the *ingubhu*. The rapid rhythm which one may compare to the sound made by a galloping horse had been retained. When the tribal wars were over, the making of shields was reduced. That explains the reason why these were quickly replaced by the drum.

Communication with the Genies

It happens sometimes that the people want to enter into contact with the genies of Vimbuza; that takes place often when there are deaths in the village. After a frenetic dance, the procedure consists in interrupting the dance when people judge that the *Chimbuza* has performed it long enough. The condition of this interruption depends on the goodwill of the genies who live in the body of the dancer. At that moment, the drums are placed on the floor, and the possessed person sits on one of them. Later,

---

[37] S.M. Shirokogoff, *Psychomental Complex of the Tungus*, London: Kegan Paul, Trench, Trubner, 1935, p. 256.

[38] Steven Moyo, A Linguo-Aesthetic Study of Ngoni Poetry, PhD, University of Wisconsin, 1978, p. 230.

one of the drummers slowly strikes his instrument with his right hand flat, producing a simple rhythm: *ta ta ta ta ta*. At the same time a diviner or *musamu* addresses the genies, in a measured and very polite fashion. Everything takes place in an atmosphere of great gravity. The following extract is from of a speech a diviner made during our enquiry:

A Ng'ona, pepani tachedwa kumumanyiskani, (Angana) bala mukabamanyanga bali kuluta. Na (Angana) nabo bali kuluta. Tachita kuti mungazizwanga, ivi ndivyo viliko. [39]

Translation

Mister Ng'ona, we regret not having been able to inform you earlier. (One such) whom you knew passed away, (one such) is also dead. We are letting you know of the bereavements that have struck us so that you should not be surprised one day.

Usually, the genie answers through the dancer either by means of animated sobs or by mumbling. The genies have to be kept up to date in this way each time there are deaths, illnesses and even miscarriages. If not that runs the risk of provoking their anger and reprisals on the possessed individual. She will fall seriously ill and won't recover until the situation has been regularized by a sacrifice. At the end of the intervention, the dancer raises himself up and the dance resumes its pace.

Pauses

Strictly speaking, there are no pauses. But one does notice stops during the séance. Occasionally the drums stop so that the skin can be stretched again; in order to rediscover the sharp sound necessary for the dance. The drummer then warms the instrument above the embers of the fire place in circular movements. He stops from time to time to verify the tonality. Other pauses may be necessary to put back in place the small bells (*mangenjeza*) worn by the dancer when these have fallen off, and also to put back the handkerchief correctly.

---

[39] Recorded at Chaponya Village, Perete Phiri, Mabilabo.

But there are also moments when the dancer wants to refresh himself. He then demands something to eat or drink. We shall give some examples:

1. The dancer can claim water which has to be brought to him in a covered plate. Having uncovered it, he passes it on to the audience, who wash their hands in it, but above all, the drummers pour in their sweat as well. At the end of this collective cleansing, the possessed person swallows the contents in big mouthfuls.

2. The second example is less spectacular. The dancer gulps down a raw egg presented similarly in a covered plate. In that case it is not habitual food.

3. The third example is about the respect one must show others. In this case there are several ways demonstrated in the dance. The first one is known as *kulamba*. Here the dancer prostrates in front of his or her diviner-healer, makes two movements, to the left and the right. The dancer may also do this to the drummers if they perform well. This is also done to important visitors. Other people, such as Vimbuza

4. The fourth example is when the dancer, in his or her possessed condition, goes to welcome visitors. Usually coins are put in a plate.

The latter is covered with another plate. The plate is then taken to the visitor by the dancer.

It is believed that this action shows that the spirits welcome the visitors and acknowledge the cordial relationship that exists between them and the people.

There are also other things that the dancer can do; everything apparently depends on the state of the genies. Alifeyo Chilivumbo affirms that that is part of the ritual.[40]

Prohibitions

There are a number of prohibitions. First of all, women who are menstruating must not attend the séance without having taken preliminary precautions. The practice would have it that when these indisposed women enter the hut where the séance is taking place, they should take some ash from the fireplace in order to rub it on the high part of the drum, where the drummer beats it. When this prohibition is violated the instruments become blocked, and do not produce any sound. It is then necessary that this ritual be effected so that the sound may come back. This usage is not a reflection of the taste of the persons concerned; for everything happens publicly. Men and children are in this way informed of the particular state of these women who otherwise have the habit of keeping it secret. They suffer some discomfort from it which they have to surmount in order to help the patient.

Other individuals, namely wearers of amulets (*vinthumwa*), are subjected to a prohibition. Their presence disturbs the proper functioning of the drums, and the dancer may himself be stopped in his or her task. Nevertheless, this last one quickly observes the introduction of these intruders into the séance and does not hesitate to chase them away. This attitude can be explained by the fact that these amulets may be the source of evil, and thus block the drums; on the other hand they represent possible rivals, ready to replace the dancer. Entrance is also barred, on the one hand, to anyone who smokes, but not to snuff-takers who are

---

[40] Alifeyo Chilivumbo, "Vimbuza or Mashawe, A Mystic Therapy", p. 7.

tolerated, and, on the other hand, to those married or otherwise, who have just had sex. Drunkards are also barred.

Nevertheless we observed the lifting of certain taboos. As a rule nobody should sit on a mortar. This applies on a daily basis to women, men and children. To stop the last category from being tempted to effect such an act, a rumour explains to them that if they do not respect the taboo, their future marriage partner will die an early death. The drum and the mortar symbolically represent the woman. The action of pounding evokes the sexual act. The form and movement of the pestle relate to the penis. The mouth of the mortar represents the female sexual organ. Elsewhere one notes that the movements the women make while pounding seem to be thoroughly erotic.

As for the drum, the action of holding it between the legs is analogous to that of possessing a woman. Let's note in passing that the form of the mortar resembles that of a drum. Finally, in a sense, the act of beating the drum recalls pounding. On the evening of the séance, the drummers contravene these principles. All the same women are not allowed to play drums. Now, during the séance this rule does not apply to the possessed dancer; for she has to show the different drummers the harmony sought when the drummers seem to him or her to be incompetent. It's solely during these séances that the women, in communication with the genies, have the power to use these instruments.

The diviners show themselves to be extremely strict when it comes to enforcing respect for the prohibitions.

We could multiply examples of prohibitions but the point seems to have been made about these.

The Problem of Glossolalia in Vimbuza

Having little information on the subject, we do not at all have the intention of studying glossolalia.[41] Nevertheless, we want to give here some

---

[41] Ntole Kazadi, Essai d' Etude Ethnolinguistique des Chants du Butembo et des Mikendi (Chez les Bahemba et les Baluba du Zaire), PhD, Université de Paris III, 1982, p. 202, pp. 82–87. He has made a much deeper study in the songs of the Butembo and the Mikendi of the Congo.

58

expressions frequently encountered during the dance. Most of the time it is a question of syntagmes composed of two of three morphemes only. This has given us the impression that these possessed persons do not come up with phrases, properly speaking, but rather produce a series of words. These words or syntagmes come essentially from the languages of the ethnic groups that have provided the possession. These are the Bisa and Bemba from Northern Zambia. The ease with which these terms are assimilated is explained by the heterogeneous nature of Ngoni-Tumbuka society.

Contacts exist between the diverse ethnic groups thanks in particular to the numerous Malawians in all the adjacent lands. Malawians work in places like the Copper Belt of Zambia and in Lusaka, where they are exposed to the languages spoken there.

The following table gives the words and the expressions which relate to Vimbuza possession:

Tumbuka	Bemba	Bisa	Word used in a possessed state	English
kuvina	ukuchina	-	nichine	I want to dance
kukhumba	ukufwaya	-	mfwaya/ndefwaya	I want, I seek
maji	amenshi	twizi	mezi/menshi/twizi	water
kudumula	ukuputula	-	kuputula	to cut
ndopa	umulopa	-	chilopa	Sacrifice of an animal where blood is drunk
kuchimbira	Ukubutuka	-	nibutuke	I should run away/end of dance
chiwawa	ichongo	-	chongo	Noise (used to stop noise)
ng'oma	itumba	-	kamango	Drum

We have not taken into account Ngoni or Chewa vocabulary.

The interpreters of the possessed persons are people in the audience who know these foreign languages. There are those who have travelled and have had the opportunity to learn a foreign language. Others have learned a certain number of words or expressions simply by attending dance séances. As for the Ngoni language, a lot of people still speak it, notably in the chiefdom of Mpherembe in the northwest of Mzimba.

The Parting Scene

At the end of the séance, the dancer does not leave the hut abruptly. He takes care to inform his audience by saying *nibutuke* (let me go away). To this, there are a number of songs one can pick to say goodbye. Here is one of the songs (no. 130) which announce the departure:

Malayilano (3x)	Good-bye (3x)
Malayilano sono tikuwela	Good-bye now we return (home)
Malayilano malayilano	Good-bye good-bye
Malayilano sono tikuwela	Good-bye now we return (home)

Dancing all along, the dancer goes out walking backwards (*chitunutunu*).[42] This symbolically signifies that the genies remain among the audience. A person touched by the disease of Vimbuza keeps its traces till the end of his life.

After this first dance, the diviner sets the date for the next meeting where the rite of *chilopa* will take place. While waiting, he asks the parents of the sick person to get either a chicken or a goat, following the diagnosis he has made.

The Remedies

On the day after the first dance, our dancer starts taking medication. The aim is to calm the genies and to alleviate his suffering. It was difficult for us to obtain all the names of the plants which the diviner utilizes to this effect, for fear, so it would seem, of reprisals from the genies. The following list gives some names which we have been able to record:

Name in Tumbuka	Scientific name
Chitongololo	Acacia Macrothyrsa Harms
Mphangula	Dichrostachys glomerata Forsk ("Chinese Lantern Tree")
Mpumba	Rothmannia whitfieldii (Lindl.) Dandy

---

[42] See G. Rouget, Record Collection, Musée de l'Homme: "In general, the medium notifies through words of good-bye ... the séance ends with the departure of the *tsuumba*."

Mpungaviwanda	Ocimur Canum ("Holy Basil")
Msindila	Turraea nilotica Kotschy & Peyr. (Meliac)
Msoro	Pseudolachnostylis mapronneifolia Pax (Euphorb)
Murwivyi/Mtanthanyelele	Cassia petersiana/Cassia Singueana
Muwuka/Mzura	Pavetta crassipes K. Schum
Nchika	Friesodielsia Obovata (Benth.) Verdc
Ngwivi	Randia sp.
Ntekanjiwa	Strychnos pottatorum L.

The plant which has been mentioned a lot is *chithundu* of which we do not know the scientific name. It is used generally at the beginning of the 'disease'. Afterwards, the variety of plants used as remedies seems to reflect the diversity and the seriousness of the 'disease' which one encounters. It is fitting to give an idea of the treatments which people practice in a general manner.[43]

1. Msindila + Murwivyi + Nchika
   a. Cook their roots; give a teaspoonful of the beverage to the sick person.
   b. Pound the leaves; cook; rub the hair with; wash the face with

2. Chitongololo
   a. Cook the roots; give three teaspoonfuls of the beverage to the patient.

3. Muwuluka
   a. Cook the roots; give three teaspoonfuls of the beverage to the patient.

4. Mugulura or Mzura
   a. Cook the roots, give two small teaspoonfuls to a child; a cup for an adult.

5. Mpungaviwanda + Mkozana*
   a. Cook the roots; give five spoonfuls of the beverage to the patient.

6. Mkanamajaha + Ngwivi + Msindila + Mphangula
   a. Cook the roots, give one teaspoonful of the beverage to the patient.

7. Murwivyi + Mpungaviwanda
   a. Cut four roots each, give one teaspoonful of the beverage to the patient.

8. Mtekanjiwa + Mpumba

---

[43] One takes these medicines either with food (porridge, sauce) or as a bath or as purification fumigations, or through the absorption of beverages.

a.   Peel the bark, pound to powder, put a quarter of a teaspoonful in a cup of water, give all of it to the patient.
b.   Pound the roots; allow to soak in a jar; take as a bath from time to time.

It is fitting to state, finally, that it is important to take treatments with prudence; for we do not know which particular disease they are supposed to be for, given the fact that there are three of them: V*imbuza, Virombo* and *Vyanusi.*

Phase 4: *Chilopa*

The rite of *Chilopa* is indispensable for a patient. It is in some way the principal ingredient in the remedies. The word *Chilopa* comes from the Bemba word *umlopa* (blood) as we have presented it in the table above. People think that here again we are dealing with the distortion of the original word.

Vimbuza people dance the whole night, several persons can take turns all the way till cock crow. Afterwards they prepare for the rite of *Chilopa.* There is a hierarchy in this rite; the importance of the sacrifice accords with the seriousness of the "disease": for a serious 'disease' the sacrifice is that of an animal; for a lesser 'disease', the sacrifice is that of a bird. While the *Chilopa* of a cock (*tambala*) or of a pigeon (*nkhunda*) takes place at three in the morning, that of a goat (*mbuzi*), of a sheep (*mberere*) or of a cow (*n'gombe)* is performed at sunrise, between six and seven.

The *chilopa* of a cock or pigeon takes place very quickly, under a blanket. The patient places herself under the blanket and the cock is brought there. The patient holds it with his hands. The rite consists in cutting its neck with the teeth and in sucking all its blood. Song no. 17 (*Tambala kwanahekeya*) normally accompanies this ceremony:

Luluwe luluwe a Nyirongo luluwe	Luluwe luluwe Mr Nyirongo luluwe
Tambala wakanangachi	What (wrong) did the cock do
kwa Mahekeya	at Mahekeya's
Ahe luluwe	Ahe luluwe
Pakumudula mutu nangoda zake?	To have his head cut off with the feathers?

The patient continues dancing after this rite. Quickly people pass on to the plucking and cutting up of the chicken which will be prepared, later, along with the remedies the diviner has prescribed. It's from this moment that one sees the action of the diviner. First of all he takes the head of the cock and its feathers and puts it on the head of the patient who has just drunk the blood. It's considered funny to behold, especially while he is dancing, hence the song above in which one asks oneself why people play with the cock in this way. Later the diviner discretely buries the head and the feathers in the neighbouring wood. The *Chilopa* of a pigeon is done in a similar manner. The only difference is that instead of carrying the head of the bird, the patient swallows the raw heart of the pigeon.

The *Chilopa* of a cock is performed for the disease due to the genies of Vimbuza; for the genies of Vyanusi it is the *Chilopa* of a cow or a goat. The *Chilopa* of a goat proceeds in the following manner:

> The patient sits on the mat. People put in his mouth medicine which gives him a strange strength. He is later covered again with a blanket. Then people slide in a goat by holding strongly its four feet which are held together. Then the patient climbs onto the back of the beast and emits a guttural sound before putting the muzzle of the goat in his mouth. He then begins sucking the blood of the animal which, according to certain testimonies, comes out through the nose. After a little time and with the blocking-up of its respiratory system, the animal, which has been struggling, dies. For his part, the patient falls unconscious. He is taken to his home in this state. He regains consciousness only a few hours afterwards.

According to our informers, the rite of *Chilopa* signifies a transfer of the life of the animal to the man. They say that the patient truly regains his health when he has taken the *Chilopa*. But others have assured us that it is the genies who require such or such type of *Chilopa*. When their wish has been fulfilled, it is normal for the patient to recover. That coincides with the observations made by Leiris among the Ethiopians :

> When the genie manifests itself, it is because it requires a sacrifice or, as people say, a 'blood'. It is in the person of his 'horse' that he will receive the sacrifice.[44]

---

[44] M. Leiris, "La croyance aux génies 'zar' en Ethiopie du Nord", *Journal de Psychologie Normale et Pathologique*, Paris 1938, p. 114.

In fact blood seems to be the preferred offering of the genies in a general fashion. For example, following the death of an important person, it is necessary to kill either a cow or a goat. Custom has it then that blood be poured in honour of the dead. The meat is shared out by the people who buried him, these latter are called *bazukulu* (grand-children). This rite is called *kuruma* (to bite). If this rite is not performed in time, the soul of the deceased returns, so people say, "to look for someone," that is, another death will take place in the village.

Elsewhere, we asked ourselves the question why the rite is performed at dawn or at sunrise. Our interpretation has been inspired notably by the work of G. Calame-Griaule, in which appears an analysis having a bearing on the oppositions night/day and life/death in African oral literature.[45] We can say that among the Ngoni-Tumbuka, night is associated with diseases. If it is not the moment at which one falls ill, it is the one at which the suffering is accentuated, in contrast one feels better during the day, which seems to bring some life.

With this observation, we think that the choice of this hour is not arbitrary; it would symbolize the final passage from the "disease" to life; which corresponds to the passage from night to day. This draws the appeasement of the genies to a close. The Ngoni-Tumbuka themselves speak of *kujara nthenda* (closure of the disease).

Afterwards the goat is cut up, and the *Chimbuza* (dancer or patient of Vimbuza) will wear skin belts from it on the arms and as straps on the shoulders. The last rite is known as *kuvwarika machowa* (to wear skins); it signifies that the *chimbuza* is placed in quarantine for one month.

During this time she will have to observe a certain number of prohibitions in order to safeguard her health. For example, she should not have sexual relations,[46] for that would provoke the wrath of the genies and the disease would resume with a vengeance. He is equally prohibited from

---

[45] Geneviève Calame-Griaule, "Pour une étude ethnolinguistique des littératures orales africaines", in *Langage* no. 18, Didier/Larousse, Paris, 1970, p. 30. Most adherents of Vimbuza catch the 'disease' at night.

[46] V.W. Turner, *Lunda Rites and Ceremonies*, Rhodes–Livingstone Museum Occasional Papers no. 10, 1953, p. 52. For the possession of Chihamba, Turner describes three prohibitions just like the way they apply to Vimbuza.

talking to people without in the first place having received a gift called *mboni*. This practice of *kuwongozga* is current in the other rites, such as the initiation of young girls after their first menstruation (*kukura umwali*).

During the colonial era people used to give as *mboni* coins with a hole in the middle. The *Chimbuza* or dancer would attach them to the belts (*machowa*: strips of goat skin) which he wore with the beads (*mukanda* or *buhlalu*). That would give him the appearance of a madman.

The goat meat is distributed among the people who have participated in the séance all night. One front leg of the goat is reserved for the patient who will eat it with remedies. The diviner, for his part, takes the chest (*nganga*) and one thigh (*mlenze*).

The final ceremony, *kuputula,* takes place one month after the rite of *Chilopa* (people wait for the new moon: *ukuthwasa kwa mwezi*). The *Chimbuza* will get rid of the skins (*machowa*) which he had worn.

Phase 5: *Kuputula*

During the ceremony of *kuputula* the diviner cuts and removes the skin belts which the *Chimbuza* was wearing. These skins are burnt and buried in the wood. We are talking about a final rite, for from that moment onwards the *Chimbuza* is free in so far as the spirits/genies are concerned. He has satisfied their demands by carrying out all the rites necessary. The genies should thus release their grip on the *Chimbuza*, and the prohibitions are lifted.

It happens often that the *Chimbuza* continues suffering. In this case, the solution is to perform again the rites of *Chilopa* and *kuputula*, making the sacrifice of a more important animal than the previous one. For example, that of a cow instead of a goat. This rite of *kuputula* corresponds to the funeral rite of *kumeta masisi*. After this ceremony life returns to normal.

The diviner also becomes free, for he has cured the *Chimbuza*: *kulapha*. It is also the day on which he is paid. Apart from the chicken and the goat which he will take home, he gathers together the gifts (previously the coins attached to the skin belts) which people have given to the *chimbuza* as *mboni* during the quarantine period.

We recall, finally, that possession is never cured.[47] The individual will continue to undergo moments of passion, even relapses of the disease. This situation of a *modus vivendi* is known in other types of possession:

> The treatment of a person afflicted by the *zar* will thus be a very complicated matter, it is important to consider that in the case of non cure, of relapse or of new disease, it will always be possible to incriminate a new *zar*.[48]

Having studied the disease of Vimbuza and its treatment, we are now going to consider the aspect of this possession cult which leads people to become diviners.

Possession generates divination

There are close links between the cults of possession and divination. Our study of possession would be incomplete if this aspect was missing from it. Essentially it will be a question of giving a brief idea of the manner in which one becomes a diviner in the service of the society.

Healers and Diviners

Usually people distinguish healers from diviners. The healers are people who have learned the job of healing by following an apprenticeship lasting years in order to know medicinal plants. Such training often passes from father to son.

But it is also true that any individual can buy this knowledge. As for the diviners, they assume tasks which are more important and diversified than those of the healers, for that we refer to what C. White has to say:

---

[47] The symptoms of the disease can disappear but not the 'disease'. — Different from this there are reliable reports that some women who underwent Christian exorcist prayers have never returned to *Vimbuza* dancing.

[48] M. Leiris, "La croyance aux génies 'zar' en Ethiopie du Nord", *Journal de Psychologie Normale et Pathologique*, Paris 1938, p. 111. – For a recent treatment of the *zar* phenomenon in the Near East in the context of similar phenomena see: William O. Beeman, "Religion and Ritual Performance", *Interkulturelle Theologie,* vol. 39, 4/2013, pp. 320-341, esp. pp. 329ff.

Although some medicines are common knowledge and may be used by anyone, a great many more being of an esoteric nature require the services of a 'doctor'. Just as medicines can be applied to other conditions than diseases, so a doctor may treat diseases, provide lucky charms, diagnose and treat troublesome spirits, provide a client with *wanga* (medicine for killing or detecting witches).[49]

The diviner (*ng'anga*)[50] thus distinguishes himself by the fact that his science is essentially based on esoterism, which places him at the juncture between the natural and supernatural. He operates in the occult. The *ng'anga* is in part tied to the invisible, cosmic powers, the *basiki* or the dead.

The functions of healers and diviners can be considered as being complementary, at least in so far as the curing of diseases is concerned. We do not at all want to go into a study of divination as such, but our interest is rather to see how one becomes a diviner through possession.

Vyanusi Possession as a Basis of Divination

A lot of people catch the disease of vyanusi but it is not everyone who becomes a diviner.

The majority of these people are struck by the genies which are called *mngoma*,[51] which confer on people the secrets of divination. People believe, in this connection, that it's a form of selection which the genies operate in order to maintain equilibrium in the face of the misfortunes which society undergoes.

The *Vyanusi* 'disease' begins with a violent attack, which even can lead to death. Apart from the symptoms, which we have already described, one may note other symptoms:

---

[49] C.M.N. White, *Elements in Luvale Beliefs and Rituals*. The Rhodes-Livingstone Occasional Papers no. 32, Manchester University Press, 1961, pp. 49-50.

[50] The translation of ng'anga is traditional doctor. This term is employed almost throughout the entire extent of Central Africa, from Malawi to the Congo, with phonetic variations.

[51] The root "*ngoma*" generally signifies dance and music.

he may have convulsions

he has tears in the eyes which flow ceaselessly

he issues cries of pain

when he sees blood or a dead body the 'disease' becomes
aggravated

he runs all over like a mad man (*munthu wavifusi*), people say that
if he goes towards the East and loses himself, he will return
home a little after. But if he goes towards the West that means
he will never return, for that leads him to death.[52]

there was a man who ran away into the bush and was missing for a
number of days. The man hunt which followed led the villagers
to a place where they saw him 'perched' in a tree. He refused to
descend from the tree. But upon singing a Vyanusi song and the
clapping of hands, he quickly came down and started to dance.
Thereafter he accepted to return home.

The therapeutic of this 'disease' is performed in the same way as Vimbuza
or Virombo. But it requires a rite of *Chilopa* which is more important than
those of the other two. Moreover, for there to be spiritual communion
between the genies and the individual, there has to be a lot of music. To
respond to this need, songs consisting of two or three lines are repeated
interminably and in such a monotonous fashion that they seem to be
propitious to collective trances. A typical example of these songs is no.
106 (*Uthwasile*) which marks the 'descent' of *mthwasi* genies into
somebody's body.

Uthwasile eh yanh hoyi hoya	He is being born
Wathwasanga	He has just been born
Uthwasile eh yanh hoyi hoya	He is being born
Wathwasanga	He has just been born
Eh uthwasile ha uthwasile ha	Eh, he is being born
Wathwasanga	He has just been born

---

[52] Frank Melland describes a similar situation among the Kaonde of Zambia: "If
a man dreams that he is walking East it is good, but if he dreams he is going West
it is bad, since it signifies that the spirits of the departed are calling him to join
them" (F.H. Melland, *In Witch–Bound Africa. An Account of the Primitive
Kaonde Tribe and their Beliefs*, London: Frank Cass, 1967, p. 245).

The individual afflicted by the *mthwasi* disease is followed closely by his diviner. Steven Moyo sees a constant element in the course of this 'disease':

> a developmental design in which an individual moves from his unaffected wholesome state, through the critical transitional phase wherein the individual is ill morbid and has the appearance of someone who is moribund. The third stage is that the person seems to be well again. The direction of this entire development is not simply to get the afflicted back to normal health. The individual who has undergone such trying experience graduates to become his society's *isanusi* diviner and practitioner of medicine.[53]

The ethnologists seem to be unanimous in considering the 'disease' to be the only way of becoming a diviner. Thus P. Wilson affirms:

> A practitioner only becomes qualified to deal with illness involving possession if he or she has herself been ill and been possessed, usually by the same spirit.[54]

Finally, I. Lewis describes a similar situation in Haiti:

> Possession and initiation into the cults of the Ioa mysteries often follow a serious illness or other affliction.[55]

Usually people call the diviner *ng'anga* as we have already indicated above, but he is equally called *chanusi* or *nchimi*. A *nchimi* is someone who is capable of prophesying (from the Tumbuka verb *kuchima* to prophesy). The areas of Mzimba and Rumphi have many *nchimi* and *vyanusi*. The greatest among them has been Chikanga whom we described in Chapter 1. The number of these diviners seems to correspond to the needs of the society. We can cite Marcel Cohen who attempts to define the place of the diviner in a society:

---

[53] Steven Moyo, A Linguo-Aesthetic Study of Ngoni Poetry, PhD, University of Wisconsin, 1978, p. 231.

[54] P.J. Wilson, "Status Ambiguity and Spirit Possession," *Man*, 1967, pp. 366–378 [375].

[55] I.M. Lewis, *Ecstatic Religion. An Anthropological Study of Spirit Possession and Shamanism*, Harmondsworth: Penguin, 1971, p. 67.

The act of the magician, sorcerer or diviner, accomplished either solitary or in the presence of a person or an assembly is essentially individual, but it has no raison d'être except if the personality and his activity are socially recognized.[56]

The role of the diviner among the Ngoni-Tumbuka is to resolve the problem of evil which is posed by sorcerers and dangerous forces. His principal tasks are:

to diagnose the causes of diseases

to find the remedies

It is fitting to emphasize that the diviner does not follow a period of probation as is the case in Ifa divination in Nigeria.[57] Each diviner is guided by his own genies in what concerns divination and the treatment of diseases. From this fact one can expect that each one has his own methods of divination. The most widespread methods are the following:

a stick replies either by standing erect or by falling according to the questions which the diviner asks;

the diviner looks into a mirror and he seems to read the answers to problems;

the diviner reads the Bible during the consultation;

a hide which responds either by pasting itself on the wall or falling to the ground according to the question asked;

small calabash attached to the wall which speaks (apparently it is the diviner himself who is a ventriloquist);

a block of wood is moved to and fro on the ground to provide answers;

like Chikanga, the diviner does not use any instrument but just speaks to the person who has come for consultation.

We can multiply the examples.

The enthronement of a diviner was normally crowned by a symbolic act which consisted in catching a python. After having danced for several hours the diviner would leave the hut and go into the bush from which he

---

[56] M. Cohen, *Matériaux pour une Sociologie du Langage*, Paris: Maspéro, 1971, vol ii, pp. 12-13.

[57] Wamde Abimbola, *Ifa Divination Poetry*, New York, London, Lagos: Nok Publishers, 1977, pp. 12-13.

would return with a python which he had killed with his bare hands and rolled round his neck. This person having seen the snake in the night was considered as capable of becoming a great diviner who would know how to explain the mysteries and the enigmas that society would encounter. The python was thus the symbol of clairvoyance and of the aptitude for traditional medicine in the area. There is a song titled *Ndimwe anzathu* (no. 64) which evokes this snake which the diviner captures. Today pythons are rare due to deforestation. The future diviners bring back remedies from the bush at night instead of a python.

Diviners and Sorcerers

Consecrated intercessors and defenders of the weak, the major role of the diviners is to stop sorcerers from continuing their destruction of human lives. The diviners are not only capable of identifying sorcerers, they equally give themselves the task of discovering where these latter hide their dangerous implements. The problem of sorcery is vast and includes, with the exception of the Vimbuza disease, all the diseases and all the deaths which people systematically attribute to it.

In each generation, the struggle against sorcery has been organized. Since the prohibition of *mwavi* which we described in Chapter 1, we can evoke notably Bangeya NyaLongwe (the 1930s) and the movement of *BaMucape* (literally: those who wash) reported by Omoyajowo:

> One group operated in Nyasaland (in South East Africa) round about the year 1934. They were called the BaMucapi, and this was their method: Their members toured the country in groups of two or three. In every village they visited they made the people stand in rows according to their sex. Everyone then had to pass in turn behind the witch-hunters who tried to catch their reflections in a mirror. A suspect was asked to submit her or his horn of witchcraft. If she denied, her house would be searched and in fact some objects might be found. Every accused person was made to drink certain mixtures prepared in bottles. This, it was believed, would clear the whole area of witchcraft.[58]

---

[58] J.A. Omoyajowo, *Witches. A Study of Belief in Witchcraft and of its Future in Modern African Society*, University of Ibadan, 1965, p. 23. For a source closer to the events see: J.C. Chakanza, "*Provisional Annotated Chronological List of*

Kusecha or *musecho* is the term which indicates the séance where the exorcism of sorcerers takes place. The Ngoni call this operation *imihlalo*. On the day of the exorcism, all the villagers must assemble. The diviner dances to the rhythm of the drum and the music suitable for *Vyanusi*.

Once he places himself in a state of possession, he begins to smell out people with a view to identifying the sorcerers. One of the songs that accompany this ceremony (no. 16) is called *Zinyanga*:

Ore yaya vinyanga yayawe ore	Horns [charms]
Orewe yayawe vinyanga mwa Tegha	Horns in the village of Tegha
Holewe yayawe	Holewe yayawe
Vinyanga pamuzi uno hole	Horns in this village

Having taken all the witchcraft implements and amulets in the village, the diviner burns them in the public square. Among the Ngoni-Tumbuka the objects utilized by the sorcerers generally present themselves in the form of horns of wild animals of various sizes.

After burning the objects, the custom is to make incisions on the faces of the sorcerers, which prevents them from returning to sorcery. *Kumeta* is its rite. As the fact of being a sorcerer is hereditary, it is not easy to get rid of it. It is thus a matter of purifying the blood. A. Redmayne summarizes for us the rite of *kumeta* (to cut the hair).

> Once a person has obtained and used evil medicines if he wishes to change his ways and live once more as an ordinary person it is not merely enough for him to destroy all his evil medicines or implements of witchcraft, he must confess and be shaved. This process does not consist of shaving the hair but of making a series of little cuts on the temples, down the sides of the face and possibly also on the throat and hands as well and then rubbing medicine into the cuts.[59]

Very often this practice is not efficacious as the people who have been 'purified' return instantly to sorcery.[60] The situation has been different

---

Witch-finding Movements in Malawi 1850-1980," Journal of Religion in Africa, Vol. 15/3 (1985), pp. 227-243.

[59] A. Redmayne, "Chikanga", National Archives, Zomba, 1968, p. 4.

[60] There is some evidence of sorcerers and wizards who did leave their craft and became even Christian evangelists.

with Nchimi Chikanga. It is he who introduced the kind of divination in which one needs neither divination objects nor drums. His main stay was a choir composed of people who had been purified, some women and some children.[61] This group was called *makwaya* (choir). It would sing modern songs of exorcism, canticles or some hymns sprinkled with strange utterances. The following song is an example among others which the oral tradition has adopted. One hears it especially during the drinking of the local beer, *moba*, when some people, after the manner of the *makwaya*, sing the same song (*Pelekani kwa Chikanga*, no. 79) over a long period:

Pelekani, pelekani	Hand over, hand over
Pelekani para muli nazo pelekani	Give them if you have them
Pelekani kwa Chikanga	Give to Chikanga
Pelekani para muli nazo pelekani	Give them if you have them (2x)

It seems this music promoted the mental concentration of the great diviner.

Conclusion

The study of the possession cult known as "Vimbuza" has enabled us to extricate a certain number of points. In the first place, we observe that the genies who form the base of these cults are not those of the direct ancestors of the Ngoni-Tumbuka. All the followers deny being in touch with their dead relatives. Nevertheless, we have seen that the society does not make any distinction, strictly speaking, between foreign genies and the spirits of the ancestors. The appearance of these cults has not involved any change in local beliefs. In the second place, the arrival of the 'disease' and its treatment oblige an individual to undergo a series of tests and to offer some sacrifices. Each phase seems to represent a stage in the unfolding of the whole ritual. These phases are in their turn linked in a regular and logical fashion. Each phase seems to have a precise goal following the system of beliefs and cultural practices. In this connection, we have given brief descriptions of rites outside Vimbuza with a view to being able to

---

[61] There are many today who copy this approach.

compare. Finally, we have noted that the third type of Vimbuza, Vyanusi, confers upon an individual the faculties of seeing what is hidden and of treating diseases.

This individual who is called *ng'anga*, *chanusi* or *nchimi*, seems to enjoy great respect, especially since he is the only one to serve as an intermediary between the living and the genies. Speaking about these diviners, Steven Moyo cites three important services which they render to society:

> First, these *isanusi* or *izangoma* serve as their people's ultimate interpreters of omen and dreams. Secondly, they are endowed with power to diagnose causes of many a misfortune and natural disaster. Finally, the *izangoma* provide medicines and methods of treating illnesses.[62]

One can therefore say that the diviner is indispensable in a society such as that of the Ngoni-Tumbuka where plagues and death are almost always attributed the maleficent forces of sorcery. It is the diviner who fights sorcerers as well as other obscure powers which bring about misfortunes among people. Formerly he used to play the role of counselor before traditional chiefs. Today his services have taken another turn since it is city dwellers who, in discreet fashion, come to see him in order to resolve their problems.

---

[62] Steven Moyo, A Linguo-Aesthetic Study of Ngoni Poetry, PhD, University of Wisconsin, 1978, p. 236.

Chapter 3: Vimbuza as a Social Fact

The preceding chapter presented two social functions. It concerned, in the first place, the therapeutic of the Vimbuza dance. Secondly, we described the role played by diviner/healers in the struggle against sorcery. Apart from these two functions, it is important to include several others. The great value of Vimbuza is without doubt its aptitude to embrace qualities which one ordinarily attributes to other genres of oral literature such as the tale. From the analysis by G. Calame-Griaule of oral literature in Africa, we shall retain, in what concerns us, the following extract:

> The social role played by oral literature in Africa remains in effect considerable. Permeated with cultural realities, it constitutes an irreplaceable testimony on the institutions, the system of values, the vision of the world belonging to a society.[1]

It seems that its capacity to play several social roles is due to the birth of a Vimbuza which we shall qualify as "profane." According to Kwenda Phiri, the difference between the "sacred" dance and the "profane" dance resides in the composition of the songs and the way the dance is performed. Furthermore, he affirms that this type of dance is of recent origin.

In the analysis which follows we shall endeavour to study the six principal functions which Vimbuza comprises in its role as a "profane" dance. We insist, in this connection, on evoking as many as possible of the elements which characterize them. Finally, it is fitting to underline the fact that we shall use some songs as supports for the ideas advanced.

Kwenda Phiri calls the songs with a satirical tone in Tumbuka *nyimbo za vigerembo* or *nyimbo za vigetyo* (satirical songs).[2] This type of songs is, as we have just mentioned, associated with profane Vimbuza. We are not in a position to give the exact date of its birth, but we estimate that it was

---

[1] Geneviève Calame-Griaule, "Pour une étude ethnolinguistique des littératures Africaines," p. 25.

[2] Interview Kwenda Phri.

in the 1920s. We have already seen, in this connection, that Vimbuza dancers were accused by the authorities of spreading the disease. People believe, in fact, that this rumour was well founded. It was then a question of false possession. There is a plant known by the generic name *seketela* which serves as an antidote to a possible attack by abused Vimbuza spirits. In this way, a person may dance as if he is under the influence of real possession. This plant also makes it possible for the person not to feel tired even if the performance lasts so many hours without interruption. The plant, which is also called *mphelele*, was at first used in the Malambo area, in eastern Zambia, among the Senga. Siyayo Mkandawire, professional dancer at the national level; is without doubt one of those who have recourse to it in our day. This practice is not unique in Africa. G. Rouget reports a similar situation:

> Among the Hausa, the non-initiated young girls undergo crises of possession owing to the taking of a drug, the datura metel.[3] This 'profane possession' presents all the signs of the normal possession crisis, except that 'the gods do not evidently show themselves'. These false possessions are produced when the young girls want to imitate the followers of the bori and swallow to this effect grains of datura.[4]

The introduction of this plant constitutes an important turning point in the history of Vimbuza. It is, in fact, from that moment that the functions which we present in this chapter start appearing.

One of the characteristics of this "false possession" is the fact that there are more women than men. People believe that women seized the opportunity to express a profound malaise which concerns their status as spouses. They feel heavily crushed by the patrilineal and virilocal system of marriage. In this way, benefiting from the "sacred" nature of the dance, these women understood that they could question the position of the man in Ngoni-Tumbuka society. Speaking of a situation which corresponds well to the one we are describing, I.M. Lewis reports the following:

> For all their concern with disease and its treatment such women's possession cults are also, I argue, thinly disguised protest movements

---

[3]   Also called "Devil's Trumpet."

[4]   G. Rouget, *La Musique et la Transe*, Paris: Gallimard, 1980, p. 108.

directed against the dominant sex. They thus play a significant part in the sex-war in traditional societies and cultures where women lack more obvious and direct means for forwarding their aims. To a considerable extent they protect women from the exactions of men, and offer an effective vehicle for manipulating husbands and male relatives.[5]

In the course of the dance they could from now on mount a fundamental critique, without nevertheless provoking misunderstandings in the families or in their circle. One such phenomenon exists also among the Banem during the funeral weeping which they call *imbey*.

> The women who are usually passive while men are talking nevertheless record and keep in their memory a whole series of observations which are occasionally very pertinent. Also the day on which they sing *imbey*, they don't miss the opportunity to reveal maliciously what they have learnt on these or those people. But on that day nobody takes umbrage over what has thus been made public; on the contrary, it is customary that the victim makes a small gift for the lady singer as a way of saying: 'I have heard, but I am not bothered!'[6]

As a conclusion to these preliminary remarks, one can say that profane Vimbuza offers society another form of therapeutic. Although in this dance the dancer is not possessed, he may feel at the end of the performance the same effect of calmness as in the sacred dance. Anthony Nazombe describes this situation:

> The social strain is dramatized in the spirit possession performance and is reflected in the dominant themes of the accompanying songs. The combined effect is primarily that of catharsis at the level of the performance itself and ultimately that of a perceptible social readjustment in respect of the patient.[7]

---

[5] I.M. Lewis, *Ecstatic Religion. An Anthropological Study of Spirit Possession and Shamanism*, Harmondsworth: Penguin, 1971, p. 31.

[6] *Jeune Afrique*, 5.3.1976, p. 50.

[7] Anthony Nazombe, "Spirit Possession Songs and Social Tension: A Comparative Study of Vimbuza and Nantongwe" Conference on Literature in Society in Southern Africa, University of York, 8–11.9.1981, p. 1.

Through the songs that we will have the opportunity of analyzing, we shall see, among other things, women's preoccupations in Ngoni-Tumbuka society.

Social Critique

The study of the songs reveals that Vimbuza is a genre, which acts as a vehicle for social critique. It seems that it is satire or caricature which is the procedure used to this effect. One of the sources of inspiration comes from the *pathuli* (the pounding of maize) where the work is usually accompanied by songs. Here women allow themselves to compose, in all tranquility, songs which reveal the defects and the traits of people without giving offence. The *pathuli* has become a veritable platform for social criticism. The links which exist between the *pathuli* and Vimbuza depend on two facts. On the one hand, among the women who pound maize, some suffer from the Vimbuza disease. It is thus understandable that they come to the dance with songs created during pounding. On the other hand, the men who listen to these chants full of satirical couplets use them, too, during the séances of the dances.[8]

The critique we are considering has a bearing on the loss of a social institution. This is the "council of men" (*mphala*) fallen into disuse, but the observance of which subsists in certain rural areas. Through this example we wish to indicate that Vimbuza bears witness on such institutions as marriage, polygamy and the hunt.

West Africans have the habit of referring to the tree under which the men discuss matters of the village or even the country as "palaver tree." Among the Ngoni-Tumbuka this place has also existed and it used to be situated near the *isibaya* (the cattle kraal), occasionally under a tree, but this condition was not obligatory. It was not rare to find there a construction, a kind of shed, to protect the men from rain and wind. That's where men passed their day outside of other daily activities such as the hunt, fishing and field work. The *mphala*, as people used to call this place, was a veritable master place for the education of men. Firstly, it had a

---

[8] E.S. Timpunza-Mvula, The Pounding Song as a Vehicle of Social Consciousness", Conference on Literature in Society in Southern Africa, University of York, 8–11.9.1981, p. 7.

unifying role; for all the men of the village met there every day. Secondly, it was the place where people used to learn the various crafts. People found there forges for the makers of hoes and axes; there people constructed granaries (*nkhokwe*), and there they learned to make traps, and so many other things besides. It was there, too, that one imbibed traditional wisdom passed on from generation to generation, on listening to tales, legends, myths and proverbs. The *mphala* also used to serve as a tribunal for resolving conflicts which arose in the group. On such an occasion even the women could participate in the debates. As for the travellers, this was the place through which they transited, either to take refreshment or to demand lodging.

The song which we present below deplores the disintegration of the *mphala*. According to our informants one can attribute its degradation or disappearance to modernism. Two factors seem to have been at the origin of this situation. It would seem, at first, that some people who had received an education at school were refusing to sit at the *mphala* with their fellow men. Through pride they preferred staying at home i.e. at their house. Afterwards, migrant workers, after their return, also had a tendency to neglect the tradition as they had become 'personalities'. In the eventuality that they were obliged to go to the *mphala*, they used to give instructions to their spouses that the latter should put on one side the best portions which they used to eat in secret on their return. From then, people began to notice that the quantity of food sent to the *mphala* had diminished and that the quality had gone down. The women lectured in this way sent to the *mphala* nothing but legume sauce, keeping the meat for the husband alone. The following song bears testimony

> I commiserate with Yowoyani at the council of men (*mphala*)
> A very meagre dish of *sima*[9] always leaves a bad impression
> That leaves a bad impression at the council of men (*mphala*)
> She who has a baby (2x)
> Must send to the council of men (*mphala*)
> A copious dish of *sima*

---

[9] A sort of solid gruel, with a flour base, be it of maize, millet or manioc.

In this song, Yowoyani is the name of any man whose wife sends a meagre dish of *sima* to the *mphala*. The critique relates to the fact that this man as well as his son profit from what other hearths bring to the *mphala*.

The fact that one also wants to underline here is that the abandonment of the *mphala* by certain families brings with it supplementary charges to the households which have remained loyal to the institution as the following song (no. 126) says:

Sima niphikire uku niphikire uku	I cook *sima* for this side and for that side
Mama	Mother
Dende nigabire uku nigabire uku	Relish I must share this side and that side
Mama	Mother
Ine ziyendere	Must I go
Ziyendere uku ziyendere uku mama	Must I go here and there, mother?
Ine ziyendere	Must I go
Ziyendere uku ziyendere uku mama	Go here and there, mother
Ine navwara	I am just running around,
Mayinga yinga mayinga yinga	This way and that way

Kennedy Mvula in a critical mood

It is fitting to add that the distance which the man maintained with regard to his wife thanks to his stay at the *mphala* had a profound significance. [10] The man ought not to immerse himself in the world of women at the risk of losing himself there. People believed that a man who passed his time beside his wife would lose virility. People mocked him by nicknaming him *chidolola-nkhali* (he who breaks cooking pots/he who makes himself a woman/he who is at the beck and call of his wife). In order to prevent men from falling under the domination of women, the society had created stories. The storytellers at the *mphala* warned the men about the dangers and the risks they were running, as the following story shows.

> A long time ago, some men went to hunt in the bush. They left very early in the morning. Over there, there was neither water to drink nor fruit to eat. These men were very hungry.

> By accident, someone discovered tens of snake's eggs, eggs which were truly white! He called his friends so that they could partake of the eggs with him. His friends were very happy about this discovery because they were very hungry. One of the men broke an egg to taste. He exclaimed: these things are good!

> The others followed his example and all were satisfied by it. The sun was soon going to set. Someone warned the others that it was necessary to return and not take an egg back to the village, for the snake would be angry. Still someone took an egg and hid it in his bag. He loved his wife so much that he wanted her to taste the eggs also.

> The man who had brought the egg said to his wife "here is what we ate during the hunt. I wanted you to eat it too. The woman ate and exclaimed: "Ah! Ah! Ah! you have eaten good things! Why did you not bring me more of them?" The man told her that his friends had been strict in that

---

[10] See Denise Paulme and Monique Gessau (eds), *Femmes d'Afrique Noir*, Paris: Mouton, 1960, p. 67: "It is completely out of place to show oneself during the day beside one's husband and to show one's affection for him in public. Returning from a journey, the husband receives under a tree the men of the camp but he does not hasten to go and greet his wife ... the socio-moral code requires this reserve between spouses throughout life." See also Donald Fraser, *African Idylls,* London: Seeley Service, 1925, p. 195.

regard; nobody was supposed to bring eggs to the village and that he himself had broken this order by hiding the egg.

Before going to bed, the woman placed the egg shell full of water under the mat. When the man lay on the mat, he broke the shell. The woman told him: "You have broken my egg." She insisted that he should go and search for another one. "How can I go there," answered the man, "my friends have prohibited it!" She said, "That's your own business, you will leave at dawn and no one will see you."

The next day the man left at dawn. On arriving at the same place as the previous day, he noticed that the snake was sitting on the eggs. It asked him what he was looking for. He answered that he was searching for eggs. The snake told him to take some for the last time and never to return. When he returned to the village, he explained to his wife what the snake had told him.

They ate, they were full, but the woman said this time we shall go together to look for other eggs. The man refused by saying that the snake was terrifying. The woman said "I'm going to keep myself busy. We are going to sing and it is going to let us take some eggs."

When they arrived, the snake was seated on the eggs and it lifted its head while looking at them with angry eyes. The man said to the woman, "You see, I had forewarned you." They sang a song hoping that the serpent would pardon them:

> Vimalangalanga
> My beauty is crying
> Give a little to my wife

The serpent replied: "As you say Vimalangalanga, your wife is crying, I permit you to come and take some eggs if you are truly a man." The man approached and as he was going to take an egg, the snake bit him. He died of his wound. Afterwards the snake produced a great wind which took the dead man and his wife to the village. It followed them, but told the people not to run away because it had a message to convey. "I pardon you because I wanted to kill everyone in this village. This man I have killed him because he took all my eggs. Now you are going to bury this man and his wife in the same grave." Then they took the living woman and buried her with her husband because it was she who had pushed him towards death.

When the snake had left, the hunting comrades of the deceased said "Ah! Ah! Ah! There, it is always important to listen to what others say. Our friend had hidden an egg for his wife. He has killed himself while trying to please his wife."[11]

This tale has a largely symbolic significance, in the circumstances; man should not violate the secret of initiation.[12]

We wanted to talk about the *mphala* in order to show how an aspect of traditional life has given way to modernity, thus initiating the disintegration of the social organization of the village. The importance of the *mphala* is reflected nowadays in the extent to which society currently uses the term to denote the tribunal. The boys' dormitory also carries this name among the Ngoni-Tumbuka.

The Resolution of Social and Family Conflicts

We have collected a great repertoire of songs intended to resolve social conflicts. The number of these disputes is such that we can only analyze some of them. To better understand the nature of these disputes we propose to study two aspects which one can consider as being representative of conflicts. Firstly, it is a matter of social conflicts due to jealousy between co-wives in polygamous marriages. Secondly, we shall speak of family conflicts in the widest sense of the term.

---

[11] This tale has been published by A.H.C. Mkandawire in *Mahara gha Bana* [Wisdom for the Children], Lusaka and Blantyre: Publications Bureau, 1975. (1957), pp. 27-30.

[12] This problem is more highly developed in Geneviève Calame-Griaule, *Le Théme de l'Arbre dans les Contes Africains*, Bibliothèque de la SELAF, Paris: Klincksieck, 1969–1974, vol. 1, p. 50: The ornaments with which the heroes return to the village remind one of those worn by the initiated when they return from the bush and are reintegrated into social life. The negative hero, the one who has taken an evil route, only finds anti-ornaments ... and even death, whereas the truely initiated ones accede to life.

Social Conflicts

A certain number of Vimbuza songs transmit the messages of wives addressed to their co-wives. The tenor of these songs is often aggressive. The efficacy of this approach seems remarkable. People believe that the messages "get through well." According to certain people, after a séance where such complaints or inquiries have been communicated, the fault is rectified.

Polygamy is a widespread practice in the areas of Mzimba and Rumphi, as well as in other parts of the country. *Mitala*, as one calls it in Tumbuka, is an old tradition. In the first place, people attach economic importance to polygamy.[13] In the second place, it is invested with a social character; for the woman needs protection. For the man, the wives and their children represent capital. There is a Tumbuka proverb which says: *Kamunwe kamoza ntha kakutinya nyinda* (One fingernail cannot kill a louse).[14] In this way, they can produce enough food for the entire family.[15] If a man has five wives, he has five times the labour force and productive land. Each woman has her own reserves of grain which increase the man's resources.

As for the women, so many among them have understood that without a husband in this society they are nothing. They thus need a man who will give them a piece of land to till, a house to live in and some children; for a woman without children is brought into disrepute.

According to our informants, the number of spouses and children reveals the prestige and the important status of the husband. The children, as they marry, will make numerous links with other clans. The dowry brought by his numerous daughters will enrich the polygamist. Moreover,

---

[13] P.J. Wilson, "Status Ambiguity and Spirit Possession," *Man*, 1967, pp. 366-378 [375].

[14] To that one may add a Tsonga proverb which justifies polygamy: "One woman does not constitute a village" (T.F. Johnston, "Conflict Resolution in Tsonga. Co-Wifely Jealousy Songs," *Africana Marburgensia*, vol. xi, no. 2. 1978, p. 23.

[15] That comprises all the dependents of a man, the extended family.

the marriages, by creating a solid family, kill in the bud family quarrels and possible lineage contestations.

It is thus in the context of these functions, so it would seem, that the Ngoni-Tumbuka conceive of the merits of polygamy.

In reality, the situation is quite far from this ideal, as is underlined by this Tumbuka proverb: *Kanarume kamitala kuthongomala! Chitengo chake ndi mbavi, jiso ku mulyango* (A polygamist squats! His seat is the handle of his matchet; his look is always turned towards the door).[16] This proverb is all the more significant as it comes from experiences, and it is in real life that one should seek the accord between the use of proverbs and educative principles. In fact, a polygamist is not a happy man from the fact that his wives are always in full discord.

The arrival of the new wife is not generally accepted by the older one. G. Calame-Griaule reports that the major problem of the husband is to assure good understanding between the old spouse and the new one: "The women have in fact a terrible jealousy, each one thinking that the other is the husband's favourite." This is what happens in the following song, the old spouse treats her co-wives as mistresses no doubt because her husband spends most of his time with them. According to her, their place is elsewhere and they are there solely to profit from the goods acquired (song no. 27 *Dyera*).

Banyake ndiwo yayi	Certain people are not much
Banyake ndiwo yayi	Certain people are not much
Kuchipinda mwawonako?	What have you seen in the bedroom?
Eh eh bakhalira dyera	Eh eh. They just stay there, coveting
Banyake ndiwo yayi	Certain people are not much
Banyake ndiwo yayi	Certain people are not much
Kubanalumi babene	The husbands of other women

Chorus

Oh oh bakhalira dyera	Oh oh they stay there coveting
Yebili dyera we	Yebili, coveting, we
Eh yayawe	Eh yayawe

---

[16] A.H.C. Mkandawire, *Mahara gha Bana* [Wisdom for the Children], Lusaka and Blantyre: Publications Bureau, 1957, p. 46

Dyera ilo	Coveting that
Eh eh bakhalira dyera	Eh eh they have remained there coveting
Kankhali kwetekwete[17]	Scratching the small pot, kwetekwete
Kankhali kwetekwete	Small pan ,kwetekwete
Kubanalumi babene	Coveting other women's husbands
Yo oh bakhalira dyera	Yo oh they have remained there coveting
Kankhali kwetekwete	Small pan, kwetekwete

It is common that the husband has more love for one of his spouses than for the others. We take another example from G. Calame-Griaule with respect to a husband's timetable among the Dogon:

> He must not favour anyone and should scrupulously share his nights between the two. The women watch his comings and goings and she whose turn it is does not permit him to go to the other.[18]

This situation is illustrated among the Ngoni-Tumbuka by the song below (no. 10) in which one spouse attacks the children of her co-wife to show her impatience to see the husband again. She considers that one week of waiting is simply too long. The spouse whose children are the victims charges:

A Nyirongo 'mwe!	Mr Nyirongo,[19] you!
Awoli binu balero bosina mwana	Your new wife pinches my child
Bosina[20] mwana	She pinches the child
Bosina mwana chifukwa cha imwe	She pinches the child because of you.
Chifukwa cha imwe[21]	Because of you

---

[17] Onomatopoeia.

[18] Geneviève Calame-Griaule, *Ethnologie et Langage: La Parole chez les Dogons*, Paris: Gallimard, p. 33.

[19] Nyirongo is a name that carries all the shortcomings of men in *vimbuza* songs.

[20] bo: third person plural used here as a mark of respect

Chifukwa cha imwe mugona mwane	Because of you who sleeps in my house
Chorus	
Wayowoyenge, wayowoyenge	Let her talk, let her talk
Wayowoyenge he sabata yindamane	Let her talk the week it is not yet finished

The situation between wives becomes intolerable when the children grow up. They find themselves in an inferior position according to whether such or such a spouse has big children. Despite the love that the husband can feel for her, a woman who has beautiful children and especially boys is sure to attract most of his attention. This can naturally provoke the jealousy of the others. It's the case of one wife in the song below (no. 53): she is desperate for she has only given birth to girl children:

Mwana wane Tamala	Tamala, my child,
Wabenge mwanalume	If only she had been a boy
Eh yayi lero	Eh, no, today [It's not the case]
Mwana wane Zifa	Zifa, my child,
Wabenge mwanalume	If only she had been a boy
Eh yayi lero	Eh no today

As a girl leaves her village of birth after marriage in a patrilineal and virilocal system, people prefer a boy to her. Through his patronymic name, this latter assures the perpetuity of the lineage of his father. Therefore a spouse can lose her husband's affection if she only has girl children.[22] People believe that certain women go as far as to take medicines in order to "produce" boys.

Elsewhere, the conflicts are due to the fact that the childless women beat up those of their co-wives as it is the children who reinforce the love of the husband for their mother. So in order to provoke the co-wife, it is enough to beat her child. The co-wife replies through the song *Jesinala* (no. 55).

---

[21] The woman uses the respectful form of 'you' for her husband while this latter uses the less respectful form to address her.

[22] Despite the bride price which the man obtains from his daughter's marriage.

Bear your own [child], bear your own, Jesinala
Bear your own [child], so that I can cradle
Bear yours, Jesinala, bear yours

To raise a child is difficult. One cannot then stand the idea of someone hitting it. As she has no child, she does not have, people say, maternal sentiments. However, in other societies, that happens in a different way. Speaking of sterile co-wives among Bororo women, Denise Paulme notes that they attach themselves to the children of one co-wife despite the misunderstandings that may reign among them.[23]

In this manner the rivalries of co-wives sometimes lead them to dangerous practices of which here are two examples:

> One night, one of the women had gone to sit up in front of the door of her co-wife's hut, where the husband was to spend the night. The aim of this step was to discover the reasons why the man loved this woman better than herself. Towards midnight a hyena, which was passing by, saw the woman. Thinking that it was a dog, the hyena threw itself on her and removed the nose. The woman shouted for help, but it was too late to get the nose back. Because of the disfigurement, the husband repudiated her.[24]

The other story is about a woman in her fifties who had placed her niece at the disposal of her husband as a second wife. This institution, whereby one gives a sister, a niece or any other young woman from the same village as the wife to the husband, is called *kupeleka mbirigha*. It is a means of preventing the husband from marrying a stranger and in this way assuring oneself of succession without quarrels.

> Now this woman had demanded that the niece should share her hut so that she should be able to control the situation. One night, as she was finding it difficult to sleep because of what was happening in her face, she discreetly put a saucepan full of water on the fire. Without hesitating a moment she threw the hot water on the couple, seriously burning their lower stomachs.[25]

---

[23] Denise Paulme and Monique Gessau (eds), *Femmes d'Afrique Noir*, Paris: Mouton, 1960, p. 69.

[24] A story commonly told among the Ngoni-Tumbuka.

[25] A story commonly told among the Ngoni-Tumbuka.

In the form of a conclusion we can affirm that, through the songs, is drawn the image of marriage in a polygamous regime. Distancing itself from the ideal where this type of conjugal union would be beneficial we observe, on the contrary, that there are a lot of conflicts which render it negative. In addition to the disputes which revolve round the position of each woman with regard to the husband, the children, and sexual exigencies, we can add other sources of dispute: the way in which the husband distributes clothes; sorcery between co-wives, the use of amulets in order to obtain favour from the husband; the husband's contribution to field work; if he has gone to work in town, how does he distribute the money he sends to the village. We could cite numerous instances. The most important point is to underline the difficulty of living in a polygamous household.

Family Conflicts

Family conflicts are produced more or less on the scale of those described above. But it is a matter here of misunderstandings which tear up family links between husband and wife; between brothers; between sisters; between mothers-in-law and daughters-in-law, etc. It is necessary to underline that the problem of family relations occupies a very big place in Vimbuza songs. We hope to catch a glimpse of the complexity of the problem through the examples that follow.

The importance and the necessity of the child in the home is translated by the following song in which, by means of a play on words, the child is compared to a blanket which the couple shares on the mat. Without the blanket, at night, one feels cold. In the same way, without a child in the home relations between husband and wife are tensed up. One is always quarrelling and accusing the other of banal faults: Song no 38 *Bulangeti*.

Zawona ine zawona ine	They [the problems] have seen me
Zawona ine zawona ine	They [the problems] have seen me
Bulangeti munyumba mulije	There is no blanket in the house
Nizgokere uku	If I turn this side
Kuli chibowo kuli chibowo	There is a hole, there is a hole
Chibowo chalutilira, asweni bane	The hole continues [to grow], husband of mine

Through the slant of this song the woman explains to the public that there is a problem in her household. According to the informants, it is sterility which is at the root of this problem, and everything leads one to believe that the husband "is somehow to blame." By making the matter public, she desires that the husband should find a solution to the problem.

Usually, when the family is poor, it is the woman who feels the effects most. In the following song (no 26 *Mwana mubapire weya*), she expresses her humiliation before other women. The verbal sanctions are addressed as much to her husband as to men in general.)

> In this modern world,
> Can one continue to carry one's child in a goat skin
> I not only use the meat of the animal
> But I also use its skin to carry my child

Before the arrival of the Whites, the Ngoni-Tumbuka did not wear clothes as they do today. Their clothes were loin-cloths and slips. The Tumbuka used to make loin-cloths from the bark of a tree of which the material was known by the name *nyanda*. When the Ngoni established themselves in the country, they brought the loin-cloth made from animal skin which was called *nguwo*. As pastoralists, the Ngoni used the skin of their domestic animals as mat and as loin-cloth. The man used to wear two pieces of skin attached to the belt, one in front and the other at the back.[26] The women would use the skin for carrying their babies on the back.

The Ngoni-Tumbuka adopted the western manner of dress after the arrival of the colonial administration. The change has been rapid, for since the beginning of the 20th century people have been wearing European clothes. But, as the above song shows, certain people still did not have the means of obtaining them and so continued using goat skins. In this song, the woman criticizes her husband who doesn't evolve. She protests because she is still carrying her baby on the back with the help of a goat skin while the other women use Western cloth bought in the shops. Consequently, she feels ashamed of it.

We note that there has been a change of attitude with regard to traditional values. The goat skin had been, for example, a luxury item

---

[26] *Chitewe* was the name given to a piece of skin; plural form *vitewe*.

compared with tree bark cloth (*nyanda*), for only the stock-breeder and those who had objects for exchange could procure them.

It's not for nothing that a woman criticizes her husband through a Vimbuza song. We often meet irresponsible men, who spend their lives drinking *moba*, the local beer. These men depend on their wives for survival. In this way the situation becomes intolerable for the woman, and sooner or later she begins to make the problems she encounters public. One woman alone cannot balance her budget. In the following song (no. 125 *Kasaru kafuma kwadada*) she thus takes draconian measures against her husband with a view to, so it seems, putting him back on the right track.

Yayi nakana	No I refuse
Kasaru kafuma kwa dada	The little cloth, it comes from my father
Oh ving'unu pera	Oh such impundence
Nidikiskeko NyaLongwe	Cover me NyaLongwe
Yayi nakana kasaru	No, I refuse the little cloth
kafuma kwa dada ako	It comes from my father
Oh ving'unu pera	Nothing but impudence
Analumi imwe, mwakhutapo moba	You man (husband), you are drunk with beer.
Chinthumbo babarara kwa ine, he	The big belly shakes towards me, he
Mwaluwa naku Joni	You have forgotten even (going to) Johannesburg
Oh ving'unu pera	Oh such impundence

Alcoholism, which is also addressed in this song ("you are drunk with beer") brings numerous misfortunes to families. It serves as a bulwark to the man who doesn't want to work.

Nevertheless, if the husband does not want to work in the fields, he can do so elsewhere. The last line of the song suggests that he leave for Johannesburg in South Africa, where he will be able to find some work and in this way send some money to his family. This money could even be used to pay someone who will work the land at this place, or in order to start a business. That way he will no longer be despised.

This song shows us that the woman, in an embarrassing situation, is obliged, in order to preserve her dignity, to return to her village of birth, to solicit help from her father ("my cloth, it is my father who gave it to me"). Such examples are numerous among the Ngoni-Tumbuka:

> The woman has the right to refuse the sharing of the cloth with her husband; for, according to our informants, it is scandalous for a man to utilize a cloth or a blanket given by his parents-in-law; this is close to the taboo which consists in not touching their clothes. This also signifies that the man, not being capable of assuming his responsibilities, is not mature.[27]

We have to underline the importance of norms in this society. A son-in-law or a daughter-in-law has to, usually, keep his or her distance towards the parents-in-law.[28] In this regard, we must mention the fact that one is not supposed to speak to them or to sit at table with them. Everything must be done through intermediaries. Nevertheless, the prohibition is lifted when one buys the right to speak to them by offering a *mboni* (a chicken or a sum of money). And even in this case, there is no question of eating together. There are yet other prohibitions and it appears that their aim is to maintain the respect of one for the other across this social distance. Also, the parents-in-law are considered as sacred and one cannot play with what is sacred.

Sterility is one of the problems resulting from sexually transmitted diseases; it can be the cause of misunderstandings in the bosom of the household. But it is always the woman who is blamed even if the husband is responsible for it. In this way many women compose songs in order to defend themselves publicly. It is this truth which is translated in the following song (song no. 49 *Mphapo yamala a Nyirongo*).

> You do not know what has happened to Nyirongo?
> Guess what has happened to Nyirongo!
> He has contracted syphilis, oh yes
> The syphilis has eaten his seed
> And it's the syphilis which has made him sterile

---

[27] G.R. Chirambo, *Kugomezgeka* [To be responsible], Lusaka/ Blantyre: University of London Press in association with The Publications Bureau, 1956, p. 36.

[28] Especially in what concerns parents-in-law with regard to their sons-in-law or daughters-in-law.

This song is addressed to many other men; Nyirongo is but one example.

Elsewhere, the mothers-in-law complain about the conduct of their daughters-in-law. Spokespersons for the clan, they condemn the attitude of their daughters-in-law, opposed to the norms of the society.[29] In the following song we see drawing itself a form of segregation (Song no. 42 *Dende palije*):

Bakwawo	Those from her home
Mbwambwambwa	"Welcome, welcome!" (Ideophone)
Bakwawo	Those from her home
Mbwambwambwa	"Welcome, welcome!" (Ideophone)
Bakuchanalume	Those from the husband's side
Dende[30] palije ehe dende palije	"There is no relish, ehe, there is no relish."
Bakuchanalume	Those from the husband's side
Dende palije ehe dende palije	"There is no relish, ehe, there is no relish."

While the mother-in-law expected from her daughter-in-law help in day-to-day work, this help was only a supplementary charge. In fact, according to the Tumbuka tradition, a good wife is obliged to receive at her home, as a matter of priority, all the members of her husband's clan and only afterwards those of her village of birth. But sometimes people abuse the service of the woman. There are many cases where her husband's parents, the brothers, sisters and cousins, come endlessly to borrow some objects which they later keep, or to demand some services from her, reducing her in this way practically to the status of a slave. This attitude of the husband's family towards the wife has other drawbacks; for example it encourages parasitism.

Certain women are accused of practicing a policy which tends to divide the men. Quite often they provoke conflicts which end in the disintegration of villages. In the following song one woman has succeeded in sowing discord between her husband and her brother-in-law. In lamenting, the brother-in-law informs the public of what is happening between his brother and himself (Song no. 58 *Waziroya*).

---

[29] With age, the women identify themselves with the patrilineal system.

[30] *Dende* refers to all relish: fish, chicken, vegetables.

Waziroya, hole
I don't understand what is happening in the neighbouring house[31]
It causes me sorrow
I have pain in enduring it
I have stopped talking about it

But sometimes the women are used as scapegoats, that's why they end up saying it. In this way, in the following song (no. 29 *Nkhwerekwere*), in which a daughter-in-law reveals her true problem, her hosts are never happy:

Bamuzi uno nanga unozge	Those of the village even if you do a good thing
Nkhwerekwere, nkhwerekwere	Slander, slander [ideophone,]
Nanga unozge	Even if you do good
Nkhwerekwere, nkhwerekwere	Slander, slander
Ine lero nanga unozge	Even if I do good today
Nkhwerekwere, nkhwerekwere	Slander, slander
Bamuzi uno musinjilo	Those of the village, they despise
Nkhwerekwere, nkhwerekwere	Slander, slander

For their part, the mothers-in-law are not of the same view as the daughters-in-law. These latter seem to pass their time criticizing their mothers-in-law. Thus in the following song (no. 67 *Ntchito nkukagozga*) one of them attacks her daughters-in-law.

The woman of this house
She went to her village
That of the second one
She went to her village
That of the third one
She went to her village
But when they go home
It's nothing but gossip[32]

---

[31] He does not say that the matter concerns his brother, but according to the alignment of houses in the village, the public understands the message.

94

The mothers-in-law are perhaps not right; for it happens that a daughter-in-law can no longer tolerate life in the village. That is why it is necessary for her to return to her own village with a view to finding someone who can reconcile her with her parents-in-law and her husband. Usually the matter is resolved through intermediaries from both sides.[33] Thus talking about a problem of this nature, song no. 65 (*Mwana kumunena yayi*) makes a demonstration of it.

> Do not insult my daughter
> Do not mistreat my child?
> Let her live in peace
> I pray you, brother-in-law, don't mistreat my child
> I pray you, parents-in-law of my daughter, don't mistreat my child
> I pray you, Mr Go-Between, don't mistreat my child

When a young man has married a young woman, the woman's parents and those of the husband greet one another through the term *sebele* ("in-laws of our child"). As it is in other societies, the marriage serves as a mark of union between two families. They visit one another to consolidate the relationship, from now on considered as emanating from blood links. The parents of the newly wed young woman are the first to pay a visit to their *sebele*. They think naturally about the bride price which their counterparts have paid to them. After the birth of children, they go there to make themselves known by them. Therefore the marriage assumes great significance for the young married people and for the entire family. The understanding between the *sebele* plays a beneficial role, it is a factor of unification in the bosom of the family and the ethnic group.[34]

---

[32] The translation given here differs from the translation in chapter 5. Both are warranted by the original text.

[33] These are mediators who, from the start, have been involved in negotiations concerning the marriage. This type of negotiations has been described for the Ngbaka in the Central African Republic (Luc Bouquiaux, "L'arbre *ngbé* et les relations amoureuses chez les Ngbaka", in *Langages et Cultures Africaines*, Etudes réunies et présentées par Geneviève Calame-Griaule, Paris: Maspéro, 1977, p. 109).

[34] Mkandawire, A.H.C. (1965) cf A.H.C. Mkandawire, *Mahara gha Bana* [Wisdom of for the Children], Lusaka and Blantyre: Publications Bureau, 1975.

When the situation of the women in the village does not promote good relations, the links between the *sebele* become tense. If attempts at reconciliation do not work, the daughter-in-law has no other alternative than to divorce. In this way, in the following song (no. 66 *Mukatore ng'ombe zinu*), the war of words is transformed into acts, the over-taxed woman pleads with her intermediary to contact his intermediary so that they can break the marriage.

Odi athenga adada b̠akumuchemani	Excuse, my go-between, my father calls you
Mukatore ng'ombe zinu	Go and collect your cows
Odi atatavyara athenga b̠akumuhemani	Excuse me, father in law, the go-between is calling you
Mukatore ng'ombe zinu	Go and collect your cows
Ati nkuyimanya yayi	People say I don't know it [marriage]
Nkuyimanya yayi nthengwa iyi lero	I do not know this marriage anymore, [even if that finishes the marriage]

This song, marking the definitive departure of a woman, is sung only rarely. First of all, because the society has always been against divorce. In the case where the husband dies, that is made concrete by the intermediary who intimates to the widow not to leave the village, and to marry someone from the family or the clan. This system of inheritance of women is known as *kuhara chokoro* and has as its goal to ensure the continuity of the house of the deceased man.[35] The children born into this second marriage necessarily carry the name of the first husband. The above song is often sung by women whose marriage is in trouble.

The recourse to this type of song serves, in some way, as an alarm signal in order to draw the attention of the public. In many cases such songs produce positive results, as the concerned parties take note of the seriousness of the situation and try to resolve the problem.

---

[35] There was the same custom in Israel in the days of old, see Deuteronomy 25:5-6.

Transmission of Information

One of the functions of Vimbuza songs is to transmit information. We can affirm that it is an oral literary genre which is truly open to everything. Thus, the migration of men in search of work towards neighbouring countries and historic events find their place in these songs.

The Migrant Workers

The history of migrant workers is a very important subject about which Western researchers have spoken. The problem of migrant workers has concerned, during close to half a century, all the countries of Southern Africa from Tanzania to Lesotho. Donald Fraser indicated this situation at the beginning of the century in these terms:

> Husband and wife cannot always be together in this land. The labour market is far away, and money must be found to pay the taxes, and to buy more bright clothes for the pretty wife, and to provide the luxuries which make life more dignified. So the husband has taken his load of meal [maize flour and dried relish] and some extra clothes, and is off to the plantations. A year, at least, will pass before his wife will see him again[36]

To that it is necessary to add the words of M. Harris who gives the reasons of this emigration:

> Labour migration into the Union has for many years been a general phenomenon springing from the high tempo of development of its mining and secondary industries which offer the highest wages paid in the whole of Africa south of the Sahara. The high percentage of males absent from their traditional communities in Bechuanaland, Swaziland and especially Basutoland and Nyasaland, seems very significant.[37]

In several regards, this migration has brought advantages to the families concerned. First of all, it has permitted the migrant workers to remit part of their wages to pay the school fees of their children. In this way a great

---

[36] Donald Fraser, *African Idylls,* London: Seeley Service, 1925, p. 196.

[37] M. Harris, "Labour Emigration among the Mocambique Thonga", *Africa*, vol xxx no. 2, 1960, London: Oxford University Press, p. 149. See also Jeune Afrique, *Grand Atlas du Continent Africain*, Paris, 1973, p. 284.

number of them have received a good education. The families have also profited on the level of agriculture. They were the only ones able to buy fertilizer and to employ labour, managing thereby to increase their harvests considerably.

The return of a migrant worker aroused envy in the village; for he brought not only money but also clothes and other products which he distributed generously. Finally, the colonial government had important earnings of foreign currency. We give below two tables in order to underline the volume of this emigration and the sums of money brought back home.

As the borders of Southern Africa were not altogether open, during several decades, Malawians left for South Africa on foot, a perilous journey which lasted months. Later two recruitment companies for workers were created. They were the South African Company Witwatersrand Native Labour Association which the Malawians called WENELA by adding a vowel after each initial, and the Rhodesian African Labour Supply Commission known by the name of *Mthandizi*. These companies used to transport people by air.

Male beneficiaries of identity cards of the country of destination and distribution between the countries of destination (1958–1967).[38]

All destinations				South Africa		Rhodesia		Zambia
Year	Total	Re-cruited	Not re-cruited	Re-cruited	Not recruited	Recruited	Not re-cruited	Not-recruited
1958	68,945	27,492	41,453	18,037	1,578	9,455	35,408	3,961
1959	68,294	97,785	40,509	19,985	2,037	7,800	32,452	5,155
1960	73,505	32,743	40,769	25,981	3,630	6,762	29,662	7,448
1961	72,584	37,461	35,123	31,988	2,395	5,473	23,514	8,521
1962	55,739	23,029	32,710	20,396	1,469	2,633	23,296	7,126
1963	62,373	34,088	28,285	28,894	1,594	5,194	20,825	5,151
1964	62,931	34,099	28,832	29,180	3,046	4,919	19,488	4,080
1965	62,293	41,603	20,690	37,424	1,890	4,179	17,659	171[39]
1966	40,905	28,879	12,026	25,260	1,827	3,619	9,807	63
1967	51,339	39,538	11,801	36,254	2,788	3,285	8,734	

Summary of net capital inflow (in £) derived from labour emigration by source country (1965 –1967)[40]

	1965	1966	1967
South Africa	1,905,389	1,824,978	1,717,349
Rhodesia	310,642	271,503	272,337
Zambia	173,029	333,548	323,446
Total (in £)	**2,389,060**	**2,430,029**	**2,313,132**

Hazlewood and Henderson commented on these figures:

---

[38] According to the report of the Ministry of Labour, 1963–1967, p. 23 cited in R.B. Boeder, The Effects of Labor Emigration on Rural Life in Malawi", in *Land and Labor in Rural Malawi*, Part I (Spring 1973), Michigan State University, p. 43.

[39] From 1965 Malawian nationals had to have passports in order to enter Zambia, which has greatly reduced the number of migrants.

[40] Report of the Ministry of Labour, Malawi, 1963–1967 The Effects of Labor Emigration on Rural Life in Malawi", in *Land and Labor in Rural Malawi*, Part I (Spring 1973), Michigan State University, p. 44.

There can be few countries so dependent on the opportunities open for employment outside their borders; and despite the undoubted social evils of migration, and the retarding effect which it may also have on economic development in Nyasaland, there is no doubt that a marked reduction in the number of migrant workers would greatly worsen economic conditions within the country.[41]

According to our enquiry, we obtained two attitudes relative to the migration of the men: the idea that each young man should go to South Africa at least once in his life and that someone who returns from South Africa arouses envy among those who remained in the village.

If by chance a man refuses to leave, he is despised by everybody. Thus, in the following song (no. 48 *Ku Joni bakopakochi?*), some women incite the men to go in the form of jokes.

Ku Joni mukopakochi?	What do you fear in Johannesburg?
Banalume bamuzi uno?	The menfolk of this village?
Ku Joni bakopakochi?	What do you fear in Johannesburg?
Bali komako mu Zungu?	Have they killed a White man there?

This type of language used to place the men under the obligation to make the journey. These women envied the couples whose husbands had brought back dresses, shoes, bracelets and so many other things.

The other attitude revealed by the enquiry consists in fearing the departure of the men for South Africa, for these do not want to return to the country to rejoin their families. The consequences are baneful for the couple and for family life; the victims are naturally the women and the children. According to our informants, the reasons for this protracted stay in South Africa are diverse, but frequently family problems, like misunderstandings in the clan, make these men to extend their stay in this distant country as a refuge.

The return of a villager used to provoke, most of the time, envy and hatred on the part of those who stayed in the village despite the presents he brought them. Because of this envy he was often bewitched. Inversely, if there was a death in the village soon after his return, he was

---

[41] A. Hazlewood and P.D. Henderson, *Nyasaland. The Economics of Federation,* Oxford: Basil Blackwood, 1960, p. 81

automatically accused of being a sorcerer. To run away from these disappointments, the men simply got married where they were. Numerous testimonies appeared in the 1930s confirming what our informants reported through the songs.[42]

A stay of two to three years in South Africa could be agreed to by the woman, especially when the husband left soon after confinement. This corresponded with the period of abstinence during which the woman had to avoid sexual relations with her husband in order not to have another child. To become pregnant while a child is still suckling is viewed negatively in this society; for the first child risks having fragile health which the Tumbuka call *unthumbirwa*. This problem is pointed out by G. Calame-Griaule who reports: "after two winter seasons, the mother, suckling still, can conceive again, and her milk would become bad, which would risk killing the child."[43] Beyond three years the woman started worrying about her husband. The people around her felt compassionate towards her, as song no. 40 (*Ine lero namtengwa* - Today I am going to remarry) tells us.

A Nyirongo lero naliwona ine	Mr. Nyirongo, I am suffering
Fumbani mwana winu	Ask your son
Mwana wino wachona lero	Your son has stayed away too long
Ine lero namtengwa	Today I am going to remarry

Mr Nyirongo is the fictitious father-in-law who should arrange for his son's return. This spouse threatens to leave, given the fact that her husband's absence has placed her in a position of need.

The following song (no. 23) takes into account the reason why a man has abandoned his family in the country of origin, for the benefit of a woman in the great city of Johannesburg.[44]

There in Johannesburg
Yes, I am listening
Who is going to inherit me?

---

[42] *Vyaro na Vyaro*. vol. 1, no. 6, July 1937, pp. 2-4.

[43] Geneviève Calame-Griaule, *Ethnologie et Langage: La Parole chez les Dogons*, Paris: Gallimard, 1965, p. 336.

[44] For a more literal translation see chapter 5.

You have married NyapaGiro[45]
You have had a modern house constructed[46]
With a door with a padlock
But you, who will replace you?

The woman who composed this song seems to have lost all hope of getting her husband back. In saying that she wants to remarry, she hopes to incite him to come back to the country. It is in fact a last ditch attempt. At the same time she accuses her husband of having abandoned her, leaving her in a difficult situation, while he, in Johannesburg, is spending his money needlessly on other women. She doesn't understand the reason why he has married a strange woman. Should she think that he has been attracted by her wealth? (Line 4: the woman NyapaGiro). In her view this other woman must be prettier than her to be preferred. The fact that he has built her a modern house while she, in the village, still lives in a hut, proves it.

T. Mhango in *Vyaro na Vyaro* does not think that the *machona*[47] have for spouses girls from good families. He himself, a *muchona*, affirms on the contrary that these men led a debauched life, that the girls took their money and were as a consequence preventing them from returning to their country.[48]

Moreover, the woman whose husband is in South Africa, suffers from the incomprehension and the bad treatment of her parents-in-law. The money which she receives from her husband provokes their jealousy. Custom demands that he simultaneously sends a little money to his wife and to his parents, failing which the daughter-in-law ends up being kept in the background.

---

[45] NyapaGiro is a name derived from the name Gill. Mr Gill, a businessman of Indian origin, had built several shops in the country. He was considered as being very rich. Then every rich man was nicknamed Giro and for the women NyapaGiro.

[46] The rectangular houses are recent.

[47] A term for migrant workers who stay abroad without returning home.

[48] *Vyaro na Vyaro*, vol. 6, no. 5, 1938, pp. 98-99.

The following extract summarizes well what one can expect in such a society where the kinship system demands that an individual should share his possessions with his (extended) family:

> The property and the labour of a man are not only utilised to satisfy his own needs and those of his household, but must occasionally be placed at the disposal of others ... Relatives by blood or by marriage are entitled of right not only to hospitality but also to gifts of various kinds and to labour assistance.[49]

Such a system has the inconvenience of producing many profiteers. The situation becomes dramatic for the daughter-in-law when the parents-in-law intervene directly, as is shown by this song (no. 50 *Apongozi mbaheni*)

My mother-in-law is a bad woman
She has robbed me of the letter my husband sent me
My dear, return
I plead with you, my dear, return from Johannesburg

Mother in-law complaining

The mother-in-law stole the letters addressed to her daughter-in-law in order to prevent her from having news of her husband. But rumours travel

---

[49] M. Harris, "Labour Emigration among the Mocambique Thonga", *Africa*, vol xxx no. 2, 1960, London: Oxford University Press, p. 142.

fast and the daughter-in-law can thus publicly denounce her mother-in-law.

From their side, the mothers-in-law have their own version of facts in response to the accusations made by their daughters-in-law. In the first place, they suspect them of having illicit relationships with men. They have the proof, of course: (Song no. 18 *NyaMtonga*).

Ha! Ha! Ha! NyaMtonga
How have you done to close the door, NyaMtonga
A man has just come out through it, NyaMtonga

Adultery is an offence punishable by the law in society. One of the reasons for their interdiction is based on a belief that adultery would bring in its wake catastrophes like epidemics, famines, or even death. We mention here, as an illustration, an illness attributed to adultery.

Vumbira or *moto* is a disease provoking a cough and a high fever which appears when a woman or a man commits adultery. People think that the contagion takes place when the person at fault partakes of meals from the same plates as the rest of the family, cooks, puts wood on the fire, takes children in his hands, without taking any precautions. During an epidemic, it is the children who are stricken first. To remedy it the elderly people bring together the whole village in order to identify the source of the evil. After the confessions, the one to blame undergoes rites of purification. Afterwards he distributes the medicines which will heal the persons who have fallen ill through his fault. For several weeks he will have to take care of them. This is why many people do not commit adultery in order to avoid such scandals. In addition, before the colonial administration, adultery was punished by death, the culprits (men and women) being thrown into a great fire. Today the fine consists in paying a cow.

In analyzing the facts from close quarters, we can say that this taboo used to permit among other things protection against sexually transmitted diseases, these latter propagating rapidly if the society did not take control measures. The HIV/AIDS pandemic which is today causing havoc on the population would not be so endemic if the taboos would be kept.

We can say in conclusion that, from the economic point of view, migration contributed in its time to the prosperity of many people. But the situation proved dramatic when men found themselves obliged to travel abroad to search for a paying job. The women, not knowing what difficulties migration would entail, ran into heart-rending family problems. The women who remained in the village over years became the targets of general criticism.

Historical Events

Vimbuza acquires a historical dimension through its references to events of the past. The only inconvenience is the fact that everything is presented in a caricature manner thus rendering the process of decoding difficult; nevertheless the songs can serve as landmarks of important moments in the history of the Ngoni-Tumbuka.

Ngoni Invasions

The theme of the Ngoni wars has remained in the Vimbuza songs despite the fact that a whole century has passed since the arrival of the missionaries, at which time the Ngoni wars came to an end. No doubt these wars were a very hard blow for the Tumbuka and the other ethnic groups of the region. Talking about these same invasions, Pike and Rimmington paint a tragic situation:

> Zwangendaba's Ngoni entered Malawi earlier than Maseko's Ngoni. They encamped for a time on the Lilongwe Plain, depopulating the area by their destruction of Chewa villages, in which they killed the adult males and took away the women and children. They continued northwards along the Luangwa-Nyasa watershed to the headwaters of the Luangwa near the Southern Shores of lake Tanganyika. Some sections of this group were later to return to Malawi, where they settled in the Henga valley in 1851. Mombera's Ngoni, as this group became, carried out numerous raids on the Tumbuka, Tonga, Chewa and Nkonde tribes living in the area. The Tumbuka, who were more numerous than others, and who had been densely settled in the fertile Henga valley, suffered most of all. The result was that they fled to the Nyika and Rift valley escarpments.[50]

---

[50] J.G. Pike and G.T. Rimmington, *Malawi. A Geographical Study*, London: Oxford University Press, 1965, pp. 126-127.

One rediscovers the menace which the Ngoni warriors represented with their spears and shields, as is illustrated by song no 112 (*Nisebele na ba Ngoni*).

Sebele na ba Ngoni	I must play with the Ngoni
Ye	Ye
Na ba Ngoni	With the Ngoni
Wiza mukale	He has arrived, the angry one
Na ba Ngoni	With the Ngoni
Ye	Ye
Na ba Ngoni	With the Ngoni
Wiza mukale	He has arrived, the angry one
Na ba Ngoni	With the Ngoni
Niye	That I go
Na ba Ngoni	With the Ngoni

The song makes reference to genies who disguise themselves as Ngoni warriors.

The First World War

The events of the colonial epoch played an important role in the composition of Vimbuza songs. It is fitting to say that songs have come forth from each important event. People made out of them critical commentaries against, for example, the two world wars. What is inconvenient with this type of songs is that they disappear or are forgotten as soon as people stop talking about the event. As a consequence, it has been very difficult for us to find enough songs on colonization.[51]

One of the songs that we have collected dates back to the years after the war. It is about the First World War (1914 – 1918) when Nyasaland sent detachments of combatants to Tanganyika to fight against the Germans, given that these two countries share a common border over several hundred kilometres. This song is called *Ndimwe Anzathu* (no. 64).

---

[51] See Jan Vansina, *Oral Traditions*, London: Penguin, 1965 for the problem of the collection of oral literature as a source of history.

Ndimwe anzathu, welewele	You our fellows, welewele[52]
Welewele welewele	Welewele welewele
Mukatenge mutokoma	Go and take the load
Ndimwe anzathu welewele	It is you, those from home, welewele
Welewele welewele	Welewele welewele
Ndimwe anzathu welewele	It is you those from home, welewele

"Welewele" is an onomatopoeic term which indicates here the sound which one hears when one is clearing a path across the bush of the savannah, notably across high grass during the dry season. The noise is reported at the passage of Blacks recruited as carriers in transporting provisions of food and munitions. Apparently their recruitment was often done by force. By dint of carrying heavy loads over long distances while the roads were not well marked out and lions constituted a menace, the *tengatenga* (porters) led a perilous life. In fact many of them lost their lives on the route to the front. Thus those who remained in the villages composed songs such as this one to the memory of their lost comrades or relations.

The Eve of Independence

The years leading up to 1959 were marked by an intensification in the political war. The importance which the struggles for independence have assumed has given birth to songs turned to this previously unknown dimension. They played a significant role in this matter, as the song *Nyamkhulama* (no. 130) illustrates:

| Nyamkhulama mukawere | Nyamkhulama, go and come back |
| Nyamkhulama ukawere namacero | Nyamkhulama, you should come back tomorrow |

Chorus 1

| Bazungu (2x) | The Whites |
| Bakukana (2x) | They refuse |

---

[52] An ideophone depicting the movement of the carriers winding their way through the bush.

| Kuya kwabo namacero eh | To go home tomorrow |
| Enya Nyamkhulama | Yes Nyamkhulama |

Chorus 2

Bazungu (2x)	The Whites
Bakukana (2x)	They refuse
Kutema simbo	To be tatooed
Enya Nyamkhulama	Yes Nyamkhulama

According to our informants, Nyamkhulama was an indigenous woman who had married a white man. As the relations between the two worlds became tense, it was unthinkable that one of their own should marry a white man. That's why there is an appeal in the first couplet 'Nyamkhulama, you must return'. People explained to us that the message was not at all literal. The indigenous people did not have the intention of chasing the whites as individuals. But they were rather attacking the policy that had installed a new regime from 1953, the Federation of Rhodesia and Nyasaland.[53] With this Union the Blacks could not hope one day to achieve independence. They had noticed that their masters wanted to appropriate the country, while neglecting the culture of the indigenous people. "To be tattooed" means here to recognize and accept the culture of the population, which was not the case.[54]

Vimbuza as an Entertainment Dance

Vimbuza, although considered essentially as a therapeutic dance, includes characteristics peculiar to dances described as entertainment. This observation is confirmed when we evoke the entertainment side of the dance.

In the first place, Vimbuza can be considered as an entertainment dance at two levels. On the one hand, its performance is more or less seasonal. On the other, the villagers go to the dance specially to relax. The

---

[53] For a scholarly discussion of these events see: Kings M. Phiri, John McCracken, Wapulumuka O. Mulwafu (eds), *Malawi in Crisis. The 1959/60 Nyasaland State of Emergency and its Legacy*, Zomba: Kachere, 2012.

[54] Interview W.J. Tembo and W.K. Chirwa.

repeated séances take place during the long dry season from April to October, a period when one is not taken up with field work. Certainly, one cannot prevent the genies from attacking people when work is in progress, and such people, if they fall ill, are obliged to have recourse to the dance during the season of the rains from November to March. Nevertheless, the tendency is to despise such persons who seem to give the disease of possession as a pretext to avoid work in the fields. Therefore, there are few séances during the rainy season. Similarly, other types of entertainment dances like Malipenga, Mbotosya, Ingoma, Sendemule and quite a few others are also abandoned during the rainy season. . Therefore the dances take place almost all the days from the moment maize ripens (February - March), and also at night so that each one may attend without difficulty, that is, without neglecting daily chores. After a season of continuous work during which they were obliged to go to bed early and to wake up early, people want to amuse themselves before going to bed. As a spectacle Vimbuza generally attracts a lot of people. Moreover, we can say that certain séances of Vimbuza last the whole night, even several consecutive nights. It is fitting to recall that the audience participates actively throughout the séance. In this way those who like singing, do the you-you, beat drums, etc find there the opportunity to let themselves go.

The Vimbuza evening is propitious for meetings of entertainment. In fact, most of the people do not go to Vimbuza in order to enter the hut in which the performance takes place. Numerous are the men, women, boys and girls who remain outside playing the role of loungers around the house. They pass the time chatting. Alifeyo Chilivumbo even affirms that it's there that men meet their future spouses and vice versa. He summarizes the situation in this fashion:

> Vimbuza dance has another social function. It provides occasions for dancers to get lovers and even wives or husbands. In our research several people reported that they feigned suffering from Vimbuza in order to get a lover. Once this was achieved they stopped dancing Vimbuza. Information from our respondents says that this practice is most common among women whose husbands have gone away to work as migrant labourers. Such women may find in Vimbuza dance a means of getting new

husbands, presumably men Vimbuza dancers. Spectators, too, find in Vimbuza an occasion for flirting.[55]

According to Nyamsoli Chiumia, the situation which has just been described could also end up with sexual relations between participants in these meetings. This is what helps to explain the repression of Vimbuza in the 1930s by the colonial administration.

On another level, one can relate Vimbuza to other traditional dances. One aspect which seems evident is gestures. *Sacha* or *Kamchoma* was a dance where erotic songs and gestures were characteristic.

There are some male and female Vimbuza dancers who imitate such gestures. As to the songs in Vimbuza, one does not, strictly speaking, "dot the i's", for what relates to sexual activities is said by metaphors (see camouflage technique in next chapter). Although such dancers are tolerated there are all the same songs in which people accuse them of indecency. The following song (no. 39 *Wakwera lore*) gives evidence of such criticism:

> You have climbed a truck, you are riding a lorry
>
> You have climbed a truck, you are riding a hyena

Using metaphors, people compare the woman who is dancing to a person who finds herself on top of a lorry. This is an allusion to the bad state of roads at the time.[56] In fact, these road surfaces were like corrugated iron and when a vehicle was passing this provoked numerous jolts. The comparison extends also to the hyena which, it appears, serves as a means of transport to sorcerers. It would further seem that the rear legs of a hyena are shorter than the front ones. Its movements are thus very irregular. The lightness with which one executes the dance alludes to another motif.

Vimbuza dances have the tendency to attract the attention of the public. One of the reasons for these excesses is evoked by Brelsford and concerns a dance of the same category:

---

[55] A.B. Chilibvumbo, "Vimbuza of Kasungu" (1969), p. 4.

[56] Most of the great roads have been tarmacked since independence.

The woman dances in one spot wriggling buttocks and breasts with the obvious purpose of stimulating sexual excitement in the on-lookers.[57]

Such a dance is disapproved of as the following song witnesses:

People say the buttocks.
There is a woman whose buttocks move indecently.

Girl wriggling her bottom

It is important to underline the fact that Vimbuza offers, as an entertainment dance, a mechanism for self-criticism. Across the songs, one attempts to discourage turning this dance into an erotic dance.

Vimbuza as an educative instrument

Apart from the entertainment that the Vimbuza dance can offer, the analysis of the songs seems to indicate that the dance also extends to people's education.

At this level Vimbuza comes close to the folktale whose primary role is to instruct while entertaining. As is the case elsewhere, in situations already described; the messages go down better than if it was just a question of giving the lesson squarely to someone. The distance thus created by the anecdotal song means that the accused person doesn't feel that he is directly targetted. Nevertheless he takes note of the words that have been addressed to him.

---

[57] W.V. Brelsford, "African Dances of Northern Rhodesia", in Rhodes-Livingstone Museum Occasional Papers, no. 2 (1948), p. 11.

In inverse proportion to *Sacha*, where the allusive chants were of great vulgarity, we note a moderate tone in those of Vimbuza. In both cases the songs are carriers of lessons of various kinds. We give hereafter some examples which illustrate our point.

In the song that follows people denounce jealousy. On the day of the wedding there is a special ceremony where the elderly (men and women) give counsel to the young married couple on the conduct to follow to lead a happy married life. Each one in turn tells an anecdotal story: a veritable foretaste of marriage. According to our informants, Vimbuza borrows some elements of this ceremony. The following song (no. 73) takes up one of the lessons to learn; a man and his spouse ought to have mutual confidence.

Bawona awoli bawo biza	He has seen his wife coming
Baleka gule	He has stopped dancing
Bawona asweni bawo biza	She has seen her husband coming
Baleka gule	She has stopped dancing

In this couple neither wants to see the partner participating in the dance and it is for the reasons we evoked above (entertainment). In contrast, when he is all alone, the husband amuses himself, but as soon as he sees his wife, everything comes to an end. The woman reacts in the same manner. The lesson seems to be that jealousy can cause bad habits in either one or the other. The song thus forewarns the couple of this danger. Elsewhere people denounce jealousy from the fact that it goes beyond the family context. The dance is considered as a community patrimony in which everybody is expected to take part. To prevent somebody from taking part seems excessive.

Hygiene is a subject that is also broached in Vimbuza songs, as the following song testifies (no. 46 *Siyageza*):

One does not wash oneself
One does not wash oneself
At the place where one washes linen.

In the past, people used to bathe in the courses of rivers. But they also washed linen there. Thus the water was dirty. For a long time the situation has changed, also thanks to the modern school. People had the idea of constructing small structures without a roof close to houses in the guise of bathrooms (*bafa*). The women had to take hot water there in big jars. These have now been replaced by modern basins (*dichi*). A bath taken in this way is considered clean and decent. In the end, the song satirizes people who continue using river courses for their baths. In another version, the song actually says "*siyageza mazi ghamthombo*" (we wash with water from the wells).

Fashion and infatuation with modern clothes are part and parcel of the repertoire of Vimbuza songs. People seem to accord them importance as the following song underlines (no. 69 *Tamkumana ku Ghana*):

> I die of envy to have leather shoes
> Plastic shoes are for work in the fields
> Oyayiwe we are going to meet in Ghana
> Go buy me beautiful shoes from Bata
> To wear leather shoes from Bata, ah, that's my dream.

This song dates from 1963 when a delegation of Malawian politicians went to the Ghana of Kwame Nkrumah. Among the personalities in that delegation was Traditional Chief Mzukuzuku[58] who said a lot of good things about Ghana. He spoke notably of the way the people of Ghana were dressed: the robes, the costumes and the shoes; it was the "High Life." All those who had heard the life in this young independent nation recounted, wanted to go there in their turn. But to do that, it was necessary to dress oneself well, hence this song in which the woman asks her husband to buy her *Bata Maluwa* shoes which were in leather and presentable. She no longer wants to hear of *Bata Maliposa* shoes, good value for money but of a poor quality. Moreover, the *Bata Maliposa* were worn by 'rich' women while they were working in the fields. The moral of the story: "it is important to evolve in matters of clothing."

There are some songs which give lessons on sexual relations. Ordinarily this domain is full of taboos; we won't go into the details.

The following song (no. 72 *Nkhagonenku*) talks of a situation where a man cannot sleep with his wife because the baby is still little.

---

[58] His chiefdom is situated round Embangweni (now renamed Loudon) Mission in the south of Mzimba District. This was Mzukuzuku Tifaphi Jele.

Solo: "Where can I lie down, the child is in the middle"
Audience: "Stop your deadly behaviour"

The woman protects herself from her husband's advances by putting the child in between ("my child is in the middle").

People explain this taboo as a way of preventing the couple from having sex before weaning. In this way people avoid pregnancies while the child is still suckling.[59]

Another domain which is often evoked in the songs is that of diviner/healers. There is a story to the effect that a diviner caused the death of several people through insufficient knowledge of plants. It's this fraud which is emphasized in song no. 75 *Chirimbanyungu*:

Oyaye, oyaye, chirimbanyungu (2x)   Chirimbanyungu kills people

The false diviner was using *chirimbanyungu*, a plant which produces a poison. One can say that there are charlatans looking for a better economic situation. This is what, in fact, is denounced in the following song (no. 127 *Kasero Kane*):

My basket is unlucky today
It passes from hand to hand still light.

The *ng'anga* (diviner-healer) is a professional who lives off what he earns as diviner and healer. Usually he multiplies the occasions for getting a little more money. That's how he imposes a sum for the divination séance, another sum of money for his trip into the bush and the collection of his curative plants (*mboni ya mankhwala*), and a hefty sum of money if one is healed.

Our informants think that the *ng'anga* are particularly demanding when it comes to the payment of their honoraria. The song that we have presented above is sung by a *ng'anga* in the course of the divination ceremonies or the exorcism of sorcerers. If people do not put money in the basket which he exposes publicly, he can even withdraw his services. Finally there are still other forms of payment. One can also pay with a goat, with a sheep, some chickens and even sometimes with a cow.

---

[59] Weaning was normally done in those days after two years.

114

We can conclude by underlining that the Vimbuza dance is a privileged place where one can draw the rudiments of traditional wisdom.

Conclusion

The inventory of functions reveals that it is necessary to consider the Vimbuza songs as a manifestation of social facts. The status of an oral genre is conferred on Vimbuza as this possesses some literary characteristics which one can find in other oral genres such as the tale.

Social criticism seems to be the pole round which revolve the other functions. Speaking of the functions of oral literature in general, Betty Wang writes:

> One of the most important functions of folklore is its service as a vehicle of social protest. Whenever there is injustice and oppression, one can be sure that the victim will find some solace in folklore. Through jokes, songs and proverbs, the anger of the folk is vented upon the often frighteningly unassailable individual or institution.[60]

It is in fact in this perspective that Vimbuza songs seem to be composed. The principal procedure consists in caricaturing or satirizing some individuals or situations, which proves efficacious as a means of exerting pressure to ameliorate the situation.

We have drawn five functions in addition to the two others analyzed in Chapter 2: Therapeutic and exorcism of sorcerers. Here is what we can retain:

social criticism
resolution of social and family conflicts
transmission of information
Vimbuza as an entertainment dance
Vimbuza as an educative instrument

It seems that people recognize themselves in this dance, given the fact that the songs evoke situations as diverse as life and as real as possible.

---

[60] Betty Wang, "Folksongs as Regulators of Politics" in Alan Dundes (ed): *The Study of Folklore*, Englewood Cliffs: Prentice Hall, 1965, p. 308.

Chapter 4: Style in Vimbuza Songs

"Style is the utilization of the language of current communication in order to transmit a message responding to a 'literary' intention, that is to say supporting aesthetic preoccupations. Each literature uses for that processes determined by the language and the culture which has produced it, that's why the study of texts should not be conducted except through them."[1]

The analysis of Vimbuza songs appears, in this sense, incomplete from the moment when one does not force oneself to apprehend the manner in which the different texts are structured. As our study has a bearing on a relatively restricted sample (130 songs), we cannot attempt an exhaustive presentation of the totality of stylistic procedures which one can uncover through all the Vimbuza songs. Nevertheless, we should be able to formulate the primary foundations necessary for any new approach. The choice was made on the basis of the study of linguistic and prosodic structures, and this for two reasons:

firstly; these are the structures which are most frequently
encountered
secondly; they are verifiable in other genres of oral literatures

We have utilized all the material that we had at our disposal. It seemed to us necessary to start from the texts themselves in order to understand their mechanism. The characteristic aspects of Vimbuza songs are:

repetition
meaningless syllables
parallelism
digression
ideophones
onomatopoeia
synecdoche
borrowings from English
gestures

---

[1] Geneviève Calame-Griaule, "Pour une étude ethnolinguistic des literatures orales Africaines", *Languages*, no. 18, 1970, p. 40.

On another level, we have observed the existence of a technique which we have christened the "camouflage technique" or the hidden meaning. We are going to approach it in the first place; for it seems to us to serve as a superstructure in the majority of texts analyzed.

Preliminary Remarks

Melody in Vimbuza Songs

Conscious of the necessity of speaking of the musical aspect in the songs that we were studying,[2] we had these last analyzed by some musicologists, notably Madame Annick Préaubert.[3] Two observations come out of this analysis. On the one hand, the melody does not correspond to the Western mould, on the other, it is difficult to write this music; for there exist, in reality, several melodies in the same song. A song is presented in fact as a superposition of several rhythms marked by different percussions, drums, handclaps, bells and whistles while the voices criss-cross in order to provide the melodic base.

Finally, it is fitting to point out that the songs are grouped under three rhythmic categories, these last correspond to three types of possession. The six songs are distributed thus:

Vimbuza: Chiwayawaya (no. 33), Bulangeti (no. 38), Ine lero namtengwa (no. 40)
Virombo: Rondo (no. 76), Waziroya (no. 58)
Vyanusi: Uthwasile (no. 106)

Nevertheless, within each category the melody can vary.

The "Camouflage Technique" in Vimbuza Songs

The stylistic aspect which we call the "camouflage technique" is perhaps the most important in the songs we are examining. The procedure consists

---

2   Musicology is an area we are not familiar with.
3   Annick Préaubert, Teacher of music in the Ministry of Education, Paris.

in presenting the message in an enigmatic form, hiding the true sense of the song,[4] especially when they are allusive.

According to our own observation, this tendency not to reveal what one wants to say in reality is an ancient tradition. We have been able to observe its diffusion in other literary traditions of this region, especially in the tale and the proverb. Studies undertaken on Chewa poetry (songs of *Gule Wamkulu* for example) have shown that there, too, exists this particular technique. According to Sam Mchombo, the linguistic analysis of a song would not be coherent if one did not take into account the hidden sense of the text.[5] This technique would be close to linguistic procedures such as metaphor, metonymy, polysemy and synecdoche. Now, this procedure which he calls cryptic meaning refers to the entirety of the text one studies. Put otherwise, the analysis demands that one decodes the message carried in this type of songs.

To resort to the "hidden sense" seems to serve as self-censorship. There are a certain number of things that one would not mention in public, especially all that concerns sexual relations. This creates a special vocabulary. The Ngoni-Tumbuka have a very strict moral code. The special language is used especially when there are several age groups together. The elders can in this way communicate without the youngest ones being able to seize the meaning of the message. This practice is the rule for every day life and is reflected in the dances too. As for the songs, the final product is supposed not to be damaging to relations between the individuals mentioned in the song. That is why the real names of persons are replaced by generic pseudonyms. Finally the last point, not the least, is that this type of songs is inspired by events or situations drawn from lived experience. Polemic is therefore often associated with them.

We are going to study some songs chosen in order to illustrate our analysis. It will be a question of putting in evidence the "camouflage technique" and "self-censure."

---

[4] See Geneviève Calame-Griaule, "Essai Etude Stylistique d'un Texte Dogon" JWA, (1967) vol. 4,I, pp. 15–23.

[5] S. Mchombo, "Cryptic Meaning in Chichewa Poetry" in *Kalulu*, 1976, pp. 27–34.

Gripa Jele (song no. 1) is an *ingoma* song (war dance), salvaged by Vimbuza, which presents the "camouflage technique":

Line 1:   Do you know what happened to Gripa Jele
Line 2:   Gripa Jele was caught in the act
Line 5:   He spread some branches
Line 7:   On the road
Line 8:   Eh yes, Gripa Jele was caught in the act

The "camouflage technique" is used to avoid speaking openly about the sexual act. It is formally forbidden, in fact, to describe sexual relations in public. This flows from some traditional values which consider sex as a sacred act which assures the fertility and the survival of society. So numerous taboos have been formulated in order to sacralize sex. In order to accede to institutional love it is obligatory to pass through several stages, for example, to pay the bride price and get married. Outside this framework, one cannot have sexual relations without being pursued by traditional justice.

To begin with, the significance of this song appears altogether different. The facts reported are disconcertingly few. All that one is saying is that people found Gripa Jele in the process of spreading some branches on the road. Certainly, this is just a misdemeanor which runs the risk of causing accidents. But the real theme does not concern, properly speaking, such a crime! It is rather about adultery committed by Gripa Jele. The song thus has a polemical character; for Gripa Jele has brought blemish on the society.

Gripa Jele is a man whom someone has surprised in *flagrante delito* of adultery with a woman in the forest, infringing several rules. Firstly, the sexual act is not to be conducted during the day. Secondly, the sexual act cannot take place outside. Finally, the sexual act cannot take place but between married people. What remains is to analyze some lines:

Line 2: Gripa Jele has been caught in the act. Someone who was passing by saw this man with a woman. But that does not necessarily presuppose that something passed between them.

Line 5: He spread some branches. It is from this line that one begins to understand.

Line 7: On the road

The composer then begins to mix the story up by situating the scene on the road. In reality, nobody can risk to commit such a misdemeanor on a road used by a crowd of people. The aim of this technique is thus to "camouflage" the story. Gripa spread the branches in the forest, and as it would be too evident as an indication, the technique consists in suppressing the key element of the story. We have noted, elsewhere, the use of this technique concerning sexual relations in a poem by Senghor. There is a cut just at the moment that the act is produced.[6]

The advantage of the "camouflage technique" seems to reside in the fact that it avoids angering people targeted by the criticism. In this connection, we have already evoked situations where this type of criticism takes place without provoking quarrels of a social character (the Pathuli: Chapter 4). Elsewhere the oral tradition recounts in connection with this precise case that Gripa Jele took pleasure in participating in the *ingoma* dance where people sang the very song that he was the subject of, even the hero.[7]

To complete our study, we shall study three songs which present other elements of discussion. These last naturally go in the same direction.

Kaujo kamdambo (no. 2)

Kaujo kamdambo	Little grass at the stream
Nati m'pondepo	I wanted to step on it
Nawopa kuterera, ine, yayi!	I was afraid to slide, me, no!
Namwana wakhanda	I was like a little baby
Amuna akali mukuyenda	My husband is still abroad

The song carries very precise sexual allusions, sexual relations outside of her marriage, despite a great temptation to do it (line 2). She no doubt

---

[6] Léopold Sedar Senghor, *Poèmes*, Paris: Editions du Seuil, 1964, p. 12 "Nuit de Sine." The cut takes place between lines 14 and 15.

[7] He transgresses a taboo, which confers upon him a certain prestige. The fact that a member of the society is glorified for an act contrary to social morality reflects the phantasms of the collective unconscious!

fears *mapinga*[8] (line 3). According to the informants, this wife is already pregnant, thus she does not want to endanger her pregnancy by contracting this redoubtable disease, which would endanger not only her child but herself too. Her husband went to work in the mines or on the plantations (line 5).

Donald Fraser described the belief in this disease at the beginning of the 20th century. According to him, people believed that the problems of protracted labour were directly connected to *mapinga*. The following extract describes an incident which would have cost the life of a young woman and her baby, if they had not gone to the missionary hospital at Loudon.

> Now while he is far away, the time of her trial has come. The husband's relatives are there, and the house is full of women. Two days have passed, and the child has not been born. Vukeya is worn and frightened, and the kind looks about her have changed to black suspicion. Hour after hour two old women have been urging her to confess the names of her guilty lovers. No one doubts that she has been unfaithful, else why this trouble and delay? Pains and terror are over her, but no looks of sympathy greet her. "Confess", they cry "or you will die." But she protests her innocence, and begs for help. "Confess", is the only answer. Then someone, who is no friend of her husband, says, "It is he who has done this. Far away at the plantations he has sinned. Now his wife is suffering for his sin."[9]

It is important to point out in passing that this type of songs is understood only by the initiated, that is to say, those who are capable of decoding the hidden sense. This situation applies equally to the following song: *Munde mundete* (no. 3).

Line 4:   (syllables without meaning)
Line 5:   *Khalanga* woman! Where should I sleep?
Line 6:   The cobweb has covered my house

---

[8]   *Mapinga*: disease connected to the belief which explains the problem of protracted labour, attributed to the infidelity of one or the other of the couple during pregnancy.
[9]   Donald Fraser, *African Idylls,* London: Seeley Service, 1925, pp. 196-197.

The image which this song presents is one of a deserted house. Usually, it's there that cobwebs are to be found, but here we are talking about a house occupied by a childless couple lamenting their sterility. Knowing the attitude of the society with regard to sterility, the woman who interprets this song is overwhelmed by sadness and fear; for sterility gives rise to incessant conflicts in the bosom of the couple, one accusing the other. Fecundity is a determinant aspect of married life.[10] A couple without a child becomes sooner or later the laughing stock of the society. In fact, people treat a woman without a child as a celibate and a celibate as a child.[11]

Such is the interpretation of the above song. Elsewhere we observe that the success of this stylistic step depends on the images that one paints. These last come naturally from the society. Thus in order to understand the hidden sense, it is necessary to recognize these images.

The following song presents itself equally across the symbolism of images. The women who cannot say what is the matter with them have recourse to this technique. It is a matter of commenting on the demographic situation at a time when many men went to work abroad.

Kupula kubaba (no. 4)

Kupula kubaba ngati ungalyanga waka	To pound causes pain, I wish one could eat without effort
Uli nchembere!	You are a grown up woman!
Mwana wamunyako para wakulina	Someone's child, if he cries
mtole umubape	Put him on your back
Ulimbire wako wachizungu	Your insistence in these modern days
chino ukamutolenkhu?	To have your own child, where will you get that?

We simply underline the "loaded" lines of this song.

---

[10] A Tumbuka proverb says "Mwana ndi m'kusa wa nthengwa" (The child is the string which holds the marriage in place).

[11] Songs no. 63 (*Chilije mwana*) and no. 37 (*Bamuphala*).

The song presents a digression starting from line 6. It is in fact this digression which is of interest to us. According to our informants, here is its interpretation:

Line 6: If a married man (someone else's baby) makes advances (begins to cry), accept to have sexual relations with him (take him on to your back, woman).

Line 7: The situation of the marriage has changed (in this world of today), men make themselves scarce (where will you get that?)

The message is addressed to single women in general. People incite them to take lovers among married men. In the modern world, the women should not have illusions: it is difficult to find a husband in a nest as it were. The problem is that not only do men make themselves scarce,[12] but most of them no longer want to take a second or third wife.[13] The consequences of such a situation are baneful for the woman in particular, and for the society in general. One observes here a beginning devaluation of social and cultural values.

We shall say by way of a conclusion, that the songs ought always to be analyzed at several levels. We have shown that each signifier in this type of songs can take us back to several other signifiers. Elsewhere, it would be difficult to accord them a hidden meaning without having beforehand knowledge of the context in which they are created.

Repetition

Repetition is a linguistic procedure which is very widespread in Vimbuza songs. We encounter it as much in profane songs as in sacred ones. Given the importance of this procedure, we can consider that it is part of the style and affirm that repetition belongs to so many other genres.[14]

---

[12] A reference to the migrant workers who do not want to return home (*machona*). That produced a marked depopulation in certain villages.

[13] This is the influence of Christianity.

[14] Wamde Abimbola, *Ifa Divination Poetry*, New York, London, Lagos: Nok Publishers, 1977, p. 22. "Repetition is the most important stylistic feature found in Ifa divination poetry."

Repetition is presented under several forms; we shall limit our study to those seven types most frequently encountered in Vimbuza songs: lexical; substitutive; lineal; adjunctive; suppressive; through exte3nsion of lines and through alliteration or assonance.

Lexical Repetition

The procedure consists in taking up the word several times after its first utterance. The repetition of the word seems to indicate that this constitutes the principal theme of the song. Let's take an example:

Waya (no. 5):

Iyaya lero namtola waya	Iyaya, today I am going to get the wire
Ahe waya eh	Ahe wire eh
Nkhuya ku Jonizibeki	I am going to Johannesburg
Namtola waya	I am going to get the wire
Ahe waya eh	Ahe wire eh

In each one of the lines, it's the word *waya* (wire) which is utilized as the object of repetition, it thus assumes a certain preeminence. In reality this wire is a copper wire, another way of saying "money", as the pennies were made of copper.

Substitutive Repetition

Contrary to lexical repetition, where the same term is used several times, in substitutive repetition the composer resorts to a synonym. This procedure corresponds to a widespread technique which develops synonyms used in the current language or that of oral literature. Here we have been able to observe the use of a foreign word as a substitute for local terms, as this example from the song *Mphika wanyole* (no. 6) testifies:

124

Asungwana balero, korokoto[15]	The girls of today, korokoto
Pa mphika wankhuku abo	Love to scratch the chicken pot
Pa mphika wankhuku abo	Love to scratch the chicken pot

Nkhuku is the Tumbuka word for "chicken", and *nyole* is the Tonga word for "chicken."[16]

The tendency to use loan words in this type of repetition has been pointed out for Ipolowo poetry of Nigeria.[17]

Lineal or Structural Repetition

Structural repetition consists, not in taking up a term several times, but a whole line or a segment. That holds principally in a situation which requires that the audience and the soloist should respond to each other in a dialogue. The audience thus takes up what the soloist has thrown to it. In the song *Uyaya wanitayamo* (no. 7), we note the double structural repetition.

Line 1: Uyaya, eh, uyaya, eh	Desire, eh, desire, eh
Line 6: Uyaya, eh, uyaya, eh	Desire, eh, desire, eh
Line 2: Uyaya, wanitayamo, eh	Desire has put me into trouble
Line 3: Uyaya, wanitayamo, eh	Desire has put me into trouble

Speaking of the funeral songs *Ntandu*, Nsuka zi Kabwiku gives the following explanation which could well apply to Vimbuza songs:

> It would seem that this species of repetition is a test which allows even a non-prudent public to verify whether the singer is not giving way to fantasy. To repeat in fact a line which comes after a series of others and according to the same plan as they, requires certain personal performan-

---

[15] An ideophone which recalls the noise which one produces when one rubs the bottom of a pot.

[16] The Tonga language is situated to the East of that of the Tumbuka in Nkhata Bay District.

[17] N. Òsúndáre, N., "Poems for Sale: Stylistique Features of the Content, Form, and Performance of Yoruba Ipolowo Poetry", Sixth Ibadan African Literature Conference, Ibadan, 27.7.–1.8.1981, p. 8.

125

ces; it is a proof in any case that the text and its total structure are truly present in the spirit of the singer. And success for the singer consists in inserting the repeated text in its precise place.[18]

Adjunctive Repetition

There are many cases where the procedure adopted consists in making the original phrase a longer one by adding to it either a word or a syntagm. When the song is a dialogue between the soloist and the audience, it's the latter that practices this type of repetition. For the audience it is a question of avoiding monotony, but equally of playing an explicatory or interpretive role, even trying to give precise meanings. The song *Mwalowana mwabene* (no. 8) illustrates our point.--

Mwalowana mwabene	You have bewitched one another
Mwalowana mwabene	You have bewitched one another
Pa chibali, Mphanda	In the family, [it is] Mphanda [who says it][19]
Mwalowana pa nyumba yinu	You bewitched one another in your house
Pa chibali, Mphanda	In your family, [it is] Mphanda [who says it]

Firstly, we note that the audience adds new elements in the third line (*pa chibali, Mphanda*). Secondly, the soloist adds a syntagm to his first phrase (line 1) in order to form line 3. In line 4 and 5 the audience adds several more elements to their preceding line 3.

This procedure is very important for it permits the audience as well as the soloist an additional liberty of expression, but has as an inconvenience the modification of the initial text in the course of the years. In all the cases, the primary aim is to adjoin a new explanatory element to the lines.

---

[18] Nsuka zi Kabwiku, Chants de Deuil Ntandu. Présentation et Description, PhD, Université de Paris III et INALCO, Paris, 1976, p. 143.

[19] Mphanda is a spirit in the group of the *Virombo*. The *Mphanda* is speaking here.

Suppressive Repetition

This type of repetition is at the opposite pole of what we have just described. In fact, it is not a question of adding new elements to the lines, but of cutting them off. Let's take an example from song no. 9 (*Kakoŵa*):

Zanimuwone eh, (audience)	Come and see
Vinyanga a Kakoŵa eh (audience)	The horns of Kakoŵa
Zanimuwone (audience)	Come and see
Zanimuwone eh (soloist)	Come and see
Vinyanga a Kakoŵa eh (soloist)	The horns of Mr Kakoŵa, eh
Zanimuwone	Come and see

The repetition emphasizes the invitation to the spectacle. Kakowa (heron) is none other than the name given to the dancer because of his disguise. Properly speaking, the dancers do not wear "fetishes"; they are amulets which they wear on the chest. In this dance the spirit which possesses the individual, in the circumstances, the heron, can manifest itself through behaviour which recalls the bird.

Repetition through the Extension of Lines

We picked up several cases where the lines of a song share segments. The song *Awoli binu balero* (no. 10) will illustrate this case.

A Nyirongo 'mwe	Mr Nyirongo
Awoli binu balero bosina mwana	Your new wife pinches my child
Bosina mwana	She pinches my child
Bosina mwana chifukwa cha imwe	She pinches my child because of you
Chifukwa cha imwe	Because of you
Chifukwa cha imwe *mugona mwane*	Because of you *who passes the night in my house*

The song *Singo* (no. 11) presents a similar repetition. The repetition of segments seems to have as its aim to underline each point of information emitted. In the case above, the spouse insists on each one of the elements which points out the attitude of her co-spouse disapproved of by society. Usually, each woman has a right to a certain number of days during which the husband is at her disposal. To want to precipitate the return of the husband does not conform to the norms recognized by tradition.

Repetition in Vimbuza songs is a very important aspect in the literary language. Our affirmation rests on the fact that, in the first place, the songs seem to be monotonous. It's only when one analyses them that one realizes the diversity of their style. We think we have demonstrated that these repetitions are supported by precise rules which the audience seems to have internalized.[20]

Alliteration and Assonance

We have noticed a tendency to produce the same consonants and the same vowels in a given song. This form of repetition enriches the rhyme and the rhythm of the lines. The song *Wete walira mwana* (no. 12) illustrates our observation.

Walira wete wete	You are crying ,wete wete,
Walira wete wete	You are crying, wete wete,
Walya wekha mwana	You have eaten the child yourself [21]

Alliteration: On six segments or words, we count five times the semi vowel or glide [w]. The frequency of [w] is no doubt not accidental.

Assonance: In the same line we encounter two very privileged vowels:
anterior vowel (a): seven times
anterior vowel (e): five times

In the song *Chadoroka* (no. 13), we note the frequency of the vowel [i]. While line 7 counts nine times [i]; line 13 counts, for its part, ten times.

7: Tili babili eh yayawe tili babili	We are two, eh yayawe, we are two
13:Tili babili tili tili babili tili basga	We are two, we are two, we are slaves

Chadoroka is the name of a form of possession which makes the victim blind.

---

[20] G. Bernard, "Rédondance, répétition et récurrence," in B. Quémada, *Etudes de Linguistique Appliquée,* Didier, Paris, 1967, pp 23–82.

[21] The crying woman is accused of having herself killed the child she is crying over by witchcraft.

In the song *Muthengere muli minga* (no. 14), the consonant [m] is picked up in every line, including the refrain.

Line 1:   Muthengere muli minga (each word begins with [m])
           There are thorn-bushes in the bush
Line 4:   Mukaya muli viwawa (two out of three words begin with [m])
           There are quarrels in the village.

On the whole, we observe that alliteration and assonance are as much part and parcel of the style in Vimbuza songs as in any poetic genre.

Meaningless Syllables

Vimbuza songs (sacred or profane) attest to an important frequency of elements which we shall describe as "meaningless syllables"[22] that are empty of meaning. But their presence is desired, and they fill a number of roles. To understand their role, let's proceed to the analysis of different texts.

Utilization of "meaningless syllables" to fill a gap

During a song, it happens sometimes that the singer perceives that one or two syllables are missing. To fill this gap, he has recourse to meaningless syllables. An example of such a procedure we find in the song *Nkhwenda nkhule* (no. 15). It corresponds to the need to have an equal measure at the level of tempo.

Line 3/4: Chifukwa cha moba *we* nkhwenda nkhule = 11 syllables
Line 10: A wiske Timeyo *eh yahole he*   = 11 syllables
           Translation:
Line 3/4: Because of beer I move naked
Line 9: The father of Timeyo

The meaningless syllables are italicized.

Sometimes this technique of "filling up" is used abundantly. One has the impression that sometimes the singer does not want to say clearly what worries her, mostly in polemical songs. Such a song is *Zinyanga* (no. 16):

---

[22]   Our inquiry was completed thanks to the contributions of Messrs Despringle and Simha Arom on this subject, colloque, C.N.R.S., Paris, April 1982.

Line 1:	Ore yaya ore
Line 2:	Anh ore
Line 3:	Ore yaya *vinyanga* yayawe
Line 4:	Ore eya ore
Line 5:	Anh ore
Line 6:	Ore eya ore yaya ore
Line 7:	Orewe yayawe ore
Line 8:	Anh ore
Line 9:	Orewe yayawe *vinyanga mwa Tegha*

The meaningful words are italicized.

Very little is said in this text. Over the whole of nine lines, only two words have a meaning: *Vinyanga* (horns or charms) and *mwa Tegha* (at Tegha's). One can be surprised that only these two elements appear as if drowned in a crowd of sounds that signify nothing. One could perhaps see there a deliberate intention to jam the message. To accuse an individual of sorcery is not a light matter; the diviner, who uses this song, in the course of a séance of exorcism, refrains from revealing all he knows. It is, in fact, an indirect condemnation with the aim of minimizing the consequences in the bosom of the community.

Another form of utilization of meaningless syllables corresponds to the necessity for the singer to overcome a lack of inspiration; he may emit a large number of them until he rediscovers the thread of his ideas.

Utilization of "Meaningless Syllables" as Incipit

There are several procedures for preparing the audience for the type of songs which the dancer will intone. One of the procedures applies particularly to allusive songs. There is then an association between the "meaningless syllables" and such patronymic names as Nyirongo, Mkandawire and Mtonga. The following names are also used as stereotyped characters which the society employs to carry some messages: Nelesoni, Morotoni, Zerina. We have in this way noticed that for Nyirongo one has the incipit: *luluwe*.

Tambala kwa Mahekeya (no. 17)
Incipit: Luluwe, luluwe a Nyirongo, luluwe

130

Luluwe, luluwe, a Nyirongo luluwe
Ahe luluwe

At the end of this song one finds these meaningless syllables, but this time under a different order:

A Nyirongo luluwe, luluwe, luluwe
A Nyirongo luluwe, luluwe, luluwe
Ahe luluwe

One finds the same type of utilization for names like NyaMtonga in the song *NyaMtonga* (no. 18)

Incipit: Iyaya lero NyaMtonga (4x)

The same phenomenon we find in the song *A Nelesoni* (no. 19)

Incipit: A Nelesoni iyaya lero (4x)

Utilization of the "meaningless syllables" for rhyme

From their number and their repetition, we are in a position to affirm that the meaningless syllables contribute to rhyme. This impression is confirmed by the chorus of following song.

Mazgo ghane ni mungole (no. 20)

Ole
Herekuwe
Ole
Herekuwe
Yahore
Hereku yawa
Ole
Herekuwe
Hayiwe
Hereku yawa

One can observe the use of alliteration and assonance in these meaningless syllables.

131

Breadth of the Number of the "Meaningless Syllables"

The meaningless syllables assume, in certain texts, a greater importance than the words. In the song *Kuvina mutolerenge* (no. 21), of 55 syllables, 41 are meaningless syllables. Their importance is thus undeniable.

The Meaning

What remains for us to do is to give the significance of this use of seemingly meaningless syllables. Their use corresponds to different turnings; for example, their position in the song *Chamukarawula* (no. 22) indicates that people are subjecting to derision an excessive individual.

Caya kumuzi camukarawula hole	He is gone to the village to overdo it (finishing all the food)
Kumunda camukarawula	He is gone to the field to overdo it (to finish all the work)

This song constitutes a social critique notably towards people who have broken the rules recognized by the community. This person works and eats too much which gives him the manner of a schizophrenic.

The same procedure is encountered when the audience wants to avoid responding in concrete terms to the questions posed by the soloist. The song *KuJoni* (no. 23) corresponds to this dialogue of the deaf. In effect, the audience refuses to give answers or some commentaries, and to skirt the problem, it contents itself with emitting either a word which doesn't belong to the context or meaningless syllables:

Ninjani wanihale ine?	Who will replace my husband?
Amama eh he yayiwe	Aie, mother!
Watola NyapaGiro	You have married NyapaGiro!
Hamama	Aie, mother.

The responses are given are *amama* or *hamama* for "mother" and the meaningless syllables: *eh he yayiwe*.

After all that has been discovered so far, it is surely inappropriate to call these syllables "meaningless." In fact, people have recourse to this type of syllables for diverse functions among which are the following:
      rhythmic filling up at the level of syllables

formulae, at the beginning of songs
rhyme; a game which consists in juxtaposing sounds of the same
   nature: alliteration and assonance
dissimulation of true sentiments
means of dodging questions

Parallelism

Parallelism, as a morpho-syntactic figure, is widespread in Vimbuza songs. With the help of some examples, we shall try to give an idea of this figure which can be divided, roughly, into three parts: grammatical, rhythmic and synonymic.

Grammatical Parallelism

The analysis of the songs shows that there exist connections of similarity at the level of construction between certain lines of a song. These connections notably have a bearing on a segment (a word) or on several segments (a series or words) of a line.

At the level of the segment

An example is song no 24 (*Kurya baka ndiko*)

Kupula niliji kumanya	To pound maize I don't know
Kuphika nilije kumanya	To cook I don't know

One observes here a correspondence of the infinitive of one verb to the infinitive of another verb: To pound/to cook.

One finds the same situation in the song *Amamavyara* (no. 25):

Amamavyara bakuya ku maji	My mother in law, she goes to draw water
Bamujima ine	to talk evil about me
Amamavyara bakuya ku maji	My mother in law, she goes to the water
Bamusesa ine	To talk evil about me

It is a question here of verbal parallelism in the words *bamujima* and *bamusesa* (both meaning "she will slander me").

133

At the level of several segments:

Kurya baka ndiko (no. 24)

> Line 7: Apongozi munganituma *sinako mwana uyo*
> Line 9: Apongozi munganituma *bingako nkhuku izo*

Word for word translation

> Line 7: Mother-in-law / you-if-send me / pinch there / child / this
> Line 9: Mother-in-law / you-if-send me / chase there / chickens / those

We observe the following correspondences:

1. correspondence of two verbs in the imperative second person singular

2. correspondence of the suffixed locative I-ko (there) to suffixed locative I-ko (there) where is this

3. correspondence of two substantives ; *mwana* and *nkhuku*

4. correspondence of singular referential (*uyo*) to plural referential (*izo*): that/those

Grammatical parallelism is a stylistic aspect well exploited in Vimbuza songs.

Rhythmic Parallelism

Nsuka zi Kabwiku observes that this type of parallelism is based on the following conception:

> There are phrases which do not have necessarily the same meaning or the same construction but which attest to the existence of a certain parallelism from the point of view of the duration of the utterance. This parallelism is manifested through the duration of the syllables ... If there is the same number of syllables it's that these phrases rest on the same metric system.[23]

---

[23] Nsuka zi Kabwiku, Chants de Deuil Ntandu. Présentation et Description, PhD, Université de Paris III et INALCO, Paris, 1976, pp. 152 –153.

This principle can apply to Vimbuza songs, nevertheless it is fitting to formulate some reservations, as many other elements may intervene, which sometimes complicates the analysis. Our study has shown two tendencies;

in the first place, we shall be able to observe that the lines said by the soloist and those by the audience are of unequal length

in the second place, the soloist and the audience will be able to produce lines of the same length.

The illustration of our first argument can be verified in the song *Mwana mubapire weya* (no. 26).

The following lines are produced by the soloist:

Line 1: Mwana wachizungu chino ndiyo bapire weya   = 15 syllables
Line 3: Mupete bapire mwana ahe here wayawe   = 15 syllables
Line 4: Arere dyeko nyama mupete bapire mwana   = 15 syllables
Line 6: Ndiye mubapire weya ahe here wayawe   = 15 syllables

The lines of the audience are distinctly shorter than those of the soloist:

Line 2: Ahe yaya are ndyeko nyama   = 11 syllables
Line 5: Ahe eh mwana wachizungu chino   = 11 syllables

Our second argument that the soloist and the audience are able to produce lines of the same length is met in song no. 27 *Dyera*.

Line 3 (soloist): kuchipinda mwaonako   = 8 syllables
Line 4 (audience): Eh eh bakhalira dyera   = 8 syllables
Line 7 (soloist): kubanalumi babene   = 8 syllables
Line 8 (audience): kankhali kwetekwete   = 7 syllables
Line 1 (soloist): Banyake ndiwo yayi   = 7 syllables

Synonymic Parallelism

The procedure consists in expressing the same meaning in a song by using different words. It is a matter of either a segment, or several segments making up a line. In the following song, *Wangiloya* (no. 28), the word

135

wangiloya (he has bewitched me) is replaced in the subsequent lines by a synonym *wangithakata* (he has bewitched me).[24]

Uyo *wangiloya*	That one has bewitched me
Eyaye *wangiloya*	Eyaye, he has bewitched me
Eyaye *wangiloya*	Eyaye, he has bewitched me
Wakwela phezulu ng'endaba	He has climbed high up in the matter[25]
Eh *wangithakata*	Eh he ,has bewitched me
Eyaye	Eyaye
Yerere *wangithakata*	Alas, he has bewitched me
Eyaye	Eyaye
Yerere *wangithakata*	Alas, he has bewitched me
Wakwela phezulu ng'endaba	He has climbed above with the matter

By contrast in the song *Bamuzi uno nkhwerekwere* (no. 29), it is an ideophone which is used to replace the substantive. This use of the ideophone accentuates the effect of the meaning intended by the protagonists. The image is more striking than if an ordinary term were employed.

Line 2: Nkhwerekwere, nkhwerekwere[26]
Line 7: Bamuzi uno musinjilo
Translation
Line 2: You cannot escape slander
Line 7: In this village it's slander

Synonymic parallelism is a frequent feature. We think that it might come from the mixture of ethnic groups which was caused by the wars of the previous century, corollary to *Mfecane* in this case.

---

[24] The two syntagms are of Ngoni origin. If *wangiloya* had been kept under the form *wanilowa*, *wangithakata* would have disappeared. One finds the same root in the residue *mthakati* (sorcerer).

[25] He has become too strong for me.

[26] Ideophone where one can notice the repetition of consonants, a phenomenon characteristic of the formation of ideophones in the Tumbuka language. In English one could translate *nkhwerekwere* as "bla-bla-bla."

136

Digression in Vimbuza Songs

Digression is encountered principally in the profane Vimbuza songs. The technique of digression consists in employing two themes of which the correspondence is nil. The song thus consists of two stories between which there is no connection.

The dancers compete in this procedure, and it often happens that the song deviates from the norms. There are two influences at the origin of the appearance of digression:

> firstly, this technique is widely used in the tale. One is therefore entitled to think that its usage is nothing but an extension of this already well known procedure.

> secondly, the alternation, soloist/audience, which allows each one a liberty of expression, appears to us favourable to the production of digression.

We have defined digression as the procedure which consists in including two stories in the same song. But according to an informant digression would have as its aim a commentary of a current event, in some way a flashback on an event. One example will suffice to make the point clear. In the following song, *Kwithu ku Loudon* (no. 30), the audience profits by the situation to give itself over to digressions allowing it to evoke a matter being discussed at the *mphala* (men's council):

Yirenga Yirenga[27]	Yirenga, Yirenga
Yirenga eh yaya lero	Yirenga, eh yaya, today
Yirenga Yirenga	Yirenga, Yirenga
Yirenga eh yaya lero	Yirenga, eh yaya, today
Yirenga	Yirenga
Ayirenga kwithu ku Loudon	Yirenga, our home is Loudon[28]
Yirenga	Yirenga
Ayirenga ku mugodi wandarama	Yirenga, there is a mine of money
Yirenga aye yaya eh eh	Yirenga, aye yaya, eh eh

---

[27] First name of a young girl.

[28] Loudon is an important mission station established in 1902 in the South of Mzimba District, today often called Embangweni.

137

Chorus

<u>B</u>anyake bakukhaliramo	Certain people, they don't know a thing
<u>B</u>anyake bakukhaliramo	Certain people, they don't know a thing
<u>B</u>anyake bakukhaliramo	Certain people, they don't know a thing
Kuli makani eh ku mphala	There are matters at the mphala[29]

The song is divided into two parts. In the first place, one part relates to the attitude adopted by the people of Loudon with regard to any person not coming from Loudon Mission. For the population of Loudon these were "people of the bush" (*mapepenji*).

Yirenga is a young woman from another village who has married a man from Loudon. The song mocks her origins by depicting Loudon as a 'mine of money'. This last point is no doubt a reference to the economic superiority of the mission. If work was not lacking, each family had material goods in abundance such as clothes, bicycles and household utensils. This expansion profited the mission as much as nearby populations, thanks to commercial exchanges. Yirenga, with his prosperity is bitterly criticized by the population of Loudon because of her poverty.

A second part is about a matter as yet not divulged, which is being discussed at the council of men. As we have said elsewhere, Vimbuza séances represent a privileged place of communication for the community. It is during these séances that social critiques are formulated.

We have noted that the dancer or the audience can reciprocally launch the digression. Except in the function which has just been described, we observe that the procedure consists equally in varying the songs, which are often too monotonous. It is important to add to that the fact that the dancer changes style in the course of executing his steps. The dance in this way becomes more frenetic. The song can then be interrupted by the audience which whistles or shouts (the *nthungulu* of the women) in order to encourage the dancer. Occasionally, it is shouts of encouragement or praise which interrupt the song. Finally, the digression has no fixed place. One can find it at the beginning, in the middle or at the end of a song.

---

[29] *Mphala* was the place where the men congregated, and also the place to settle all sorts of issues.

Ideophones

Very few works deal with the ideophone in Bantu languages. We can cite notably the writings of C. Doke, one of the precursors in this domain,[30] G. Fortune who has worked on the Shona (Zimbabwe),[31] D. Kunene who has worked on southern Sotho[32] and P. Alexandre on the Bulu language in Cameroon.[33] Ideophones are a characteristic of Bantu languages, Tumbuka being no exception, where the current language attests to a great frequency and an extreme diversity in the utilization of ideophones. We are of the view that a profound research should be undertaken on this language so as to determine the nature of ideophones. We are not able to do this, but we hope to present the first rough sketches of such an enquiry.

Before analyzing the ideophones in Vimbuza songs, we wish to give a brief of the principal characteristics of ideophones in Tumbuka. This will take us a little away from the subject, but it seems to us reasonable to do it as there is no material upon which to lean.

Syntax

A certain number of statements have been drawn in books written on Tumbuka. We have noted the ideophones in them. The analysis reveals four tendencies of the origin of the ideophone. Nevertheless, we think that there are other conditions which favour the use of ideophones. Our enquiry was too restricted to give us a wider field of investigation.

(1) In numerous cases, the ideophone is preceded by a verb or a verbal predicate.

    (a) Chakurya bakasanga nchitayetaye

        Food/they found/it's throw throw

---

[30] C.M. Doke, *Bantu Linguistic Terminology*, London: Longmans Green, 1935.

[31] G. Fortune, "Ideophones in Shona," 1962.

[32] D.P. Kunene, *The Ideophone in Southern Sotho*, Berlin: Reimer, 1978.

[33] P. Alexandre, "Préliminaire à une présentation des idéophones Bulu," (Neue Afrikanistische Studien, ed. J. Lukas, Hamburg, 1966, pp 9–28), in *Langues et Langages en Afrique Noire*, Paris, 1967, p. 2.

They found a copious meal

(b) Yakusoza wakati fwelufwetu

Yakusoza/made/start
Yakusoza made a sudden start

(c) Mafuta ghali nunku-nunku

Oil/are/sweet smell
One smelt the odour of a perfume

(2) Mbwenu (then, after that) often involves the use of an ideophone.

(a) Sato mbwenu zunguruzunguru

Python/then/unrolls Unrolls
The python then started unrolling

(b) Iwo mbwenu buli

They/then/arrive suddenly
They then arrived suddenly

(3) Waka (simply)

(a) Banthu waka piringupiringu

People simply/swarm swarm
The people were swarming

(b) Wakakhala waka zwindi-i

He sat/simply/thinking
He was pensive.

(c) Bakawona maji ghali waka vunduvundu

They saw/water/are/simply/whirl
They saw water whirling

(4) The ideophones appear after a substantive:

(a) Chidongo katundu tolo-o-lo

Chidongo/load/enormous pile
Chidongo was carrying an enormous load

(b) Nyenyezi ku maso tu-u

> Stars/in the eyes/brilliant
> The stars shone in his eyes

(c) Banakazi mbwe-e-e

> Women/arrive in great numbers
> A lot of women arrived

In general the ideophone is found in the interior or at the end of a phrase.

Phonology

The study of phonology would necessitate an enquiry among Tumbuka speakers in order to determine the traits which characterize it. We wish to sketch hereafter some important traits.

Monosyllabic Ideophones

A certain number of ideophones are constituted of one syllable which alignes one sound to one image.

Ideophones with one syllable without relationship with a verb

> *gwi* (the fact of trapping rapidly, noose)
> *ndu* (the fact of being assembled, for example a pile of fish)
> *pha* (the fact of catching with the eyes)

To this list we can add monosyllabic ideophones with two syllables:

> *Pi –i* (the fact of taking or collecting at great speed)
> *Bi- i* (the fact of being anguished)

Disyllabic Ideophones

These form a very important group in Tumbuka

> *bewu* (arrive suddenly)
> *nyete* (water which spreads on the soil or the mattress)
> *bali* (flashes from the forge)

141

Trisyllabic Ideophones

These are often the result of the tripling of the monosyllabic ideophone with the aim of modifying this latter: repetition and continuity

zizizi (cold like ice)
khukhukhu (the fast beating of the heart)
yiyiyi (very calm; without news for a long time)

To this list we can add trisyllabic ideophones independent of monosyllabic ideophones

zunguru (the fact of unrolling: a python)
rapata (fall while stretching oneself, a serpent that falls from a tree)
lipiti (to be engulfed)

Quadrisyllabic Ideophones

These are often a duplication of disyllabic ideophones; with the idea of repetition and continuity

nyetenyete (a lot of water which spreads on the soil)
vunduvundu (the whirling of water)
phyorephyore (to cut into small pieces)
lipulipu (the heart beating faster than usual)

Ideophones with Five Syllables

These consist of a quadrisyllabic ideophone with an added prefix.

chikurukuru (very big)
chibalibali (flying object which flashes)

Ideophones with Six Syllables

These resulting from the duplication of trisyllabic ideophones.

zunguruzunguru (the fact of unrolling a long snake)
lipitilipiti (a crowd which is pressing to enter a church)
piringupiringu (a large crowd which is swarming)

Ideophone Accompanied by a Gesture

pye (collecting everything, the hand picks up everything at speed)
likiliki (shaking the head from left to right as in a moment of stupefaction)
tokatoka (to behave like a chicken that is preparing to lay eggs)

Accent in ideophones

1. Monosyllabic ideophones: the accent falls on the syllable

    'pi (the act of taking)

2. Disyllabic ideophones: the accent falls on the first syllable

    'lipu (the beating of the heart)

3. Trisyllabic ideophones: the accent falls on the three syllables.

    'zi, zi, zi' (cold like ice)

4. Quadrisyllabic ideophones: the accent falls on the first syllable of each part of the duplication

    'lipu 'lipu (accelerated beating of the heart)

5. Ideophones with five syllables: the accent falls on the second syllable of each part of the duplication:

    nchi 'taye 'taye (great quantity being thrown around).
    nchi 'kuru 'kuru (very big)

f) Ideophones with six syllables: the accent falls on the first and fourth syllables

    'tukuru 'tukuru (to struggle)

Morphology

a. *Derivation of ideophones from verbs. It's the most frequent:*

   (1)   Banthu bakakhara pa mzere *ndondondo*

         people/ remained / on queue/ one after the other
         The people formed an Indian file.

(2)   Cf. *kundonda* (verb): to put oneself in a file
       Banthu bakandonda pa mzere
       People placed themselves in a line

b. Derivation of ideophones from other ideophones:

>   *mujedu* (newly-born whose skin is very clean)
>   *mujedu-jedu* (tissue which scintillates)

c. Derivation of ideophones from animal cries:

>   *galu* (dog) *bwebwe* cf. Verb *kubwentha* (to bark)
>   *mbuzi* (goat) *meme* cf. verb *kumeta* (to bleat)
>   *ng'ombe* (cow) *bebe* cf. Verb *kubeta* (to low)
>   *nkhuku* (hen) *tetete* cf. Verb *kutetera* (to cackle)

d. The ideophone used to modify the sense of the original ideophone:

(1) repeated action

>   *myangu* (to lick once)
>   *myangumyangu* (to lick several times)
Derived from *chimyangu*: a disease of the lips which are often licked

(2) Speed (including the idea of repetition)

>   *pupurupupuru* (a small bird which beats wings at full speed to free itself
>   from a trap)

e) Phonic characteristics of ideophones:

Onomatopic aspect of ideophones
>   *popopo* (the noise water makes under a fall)
>   *thithi'thi* (the noise the feet make when one is running)
>   *didididididi* (the noise made by an elephant's feet)
>   *hu-u hu-u-u* (the noise of a steam train: the hooting)

In order to return to our subject, we wish to analyze some ideophones picked from Vimbuza songs. The influence of the current language is general enough in the ideophonic form.

144

a. Ideophone used to convey a complex impression

The ideophone *korokoto* in the song *Mphika wanyole* (Song no. 6) has been chosen, so it seems, to express two joint significations, something the use of a verb would not have been able to render.

Line 1: Selina korokoto pa mphika wa nkhuku
Line 2: Asungwana balero korokoto pa mphika wa nkhuku

Translation:
Line 1: Selina likes to go and taste chicken.
Line 2: Today's girls like to go and taste chicken

We observe that this ideophone, *korokoto*, is derived from the verb *kukorokota,* whose exact translation means ''to scour the bottom of cooking pots.'' On the literal plane, then, Selina would like to clean the bottom of pots. But one may ask oneself what pleasure she experiences in doing such a job. This leads us to the second meaning covered by the ideophone which corresponds to a criticism addressed to Selina in particular and to the young in general. This criticism has as its source the distortion by the young of a custom practised during the period of engagement.

The period of engagement is marked by the frequent visits which the future married couple must make to each other. On the occasion of these visits, the host family has to honour the daughter-in-law or the son-in-law, as during the meal a whole chicken is offered to the guest. According to custom it is only this type of meat which can be brought to the table. The young people of the new generation have the tendency to abuse this tradition; also the parents resent an impression of waste; for not only does the visit last on average three to four days; but the engaged couple rarely moves alone. Three or four persons accompany them and the host family is obliged to feed everybody.

Among the Ngoni-Tumbuka, chicken is considered at once as luxurious food and a noble dish reserved for grand occasions (reception of important people, sacrifices). The young in this way profit by the situation and eat chicken dishes with avidity before their marriage; for they know that, later on, they will have but few opportunities to taste such food. They even boast of this gluttony amongst themselves.

145

For their part, the adults understand this "little game" very well. The song cited in reference shows their displeasure and condemns this practice.

The exact semantic field of the ideophone *korokoto* thus covers at once a warning against the doings of the young towards a traditional custom which has lost a little of its significance over a period of thirty years; as well as confirmation that chicken is a rare dish. In fact. it's not a matter of eating chicken for the sake of eating chicken, but of considering it as a symbol for sealing a matrimonial union.

Apart from this use, chicken serve as basic food in the rites of passage. We are talking about boys who have attained maturity (between 14 and 18 years). An uncle or an elder brother is charged with the responsibility of looking after the young man. The rite consists in making him eat cooked chicken along with roots in a cooking pot. The young man eats this mixture with *sima* (the principal dish) over two or three days, depending on the size of the chicken. The significance of the rite concerns the young man's sexual life and the roots should assure his fertility. This practice is no longer in force except in the rural areas at the moment.

A white chicken is used for paying symbolic fines in conflicts between individuals. An example is that of a younger brother who marries before his elder. Usually, people consider this conduct as an offence, and, in order to appease the elder brother, it is necessary to give him this chicken which he must eat. People believe that this type of fine cleanses the offence. After this payment the climate of hostility subsides and the brothers reconcile.

We recall, finally, that the chicken, particularly the cock, serves as a sacrificial animal (*chilopa*) in the Vimbuza cult.

Ideophones used to vary the sense of verbs

This type of ideophone is formed from a verb to which it is linked and to which it confers the meaning of a repeated action. The ideophone itself takes the radical of the verb.

Example 1 verb: (to return)

> Ku – wel – a
> Class 1- root - Suffix

146

Ideophone composed of radical and suffix (duplicated)
        Wel – u Wel –
        Welu welu

In the song *Tiwonjele fumu* (no. 31) the function of the ideophone underlines the fact that the spirits, of which the person who is performing the dance is possessed, return for the nth time

Tiwonjele fumu zawela weluwelu	Let's greet the chiefs,[34] they have come (back)

We find the same type of situation in Song no. 32 (*Mazombwe*)

Nikwere uli nili Mazombwe	How will I climb I am Mazombwe,
Kwerukweru	Climbing, climbing
Nikwere uli?	How can I climb?

The ideophone, in this case, imitates the action of climbing which the subject is undertaking. This "imaginary" climbing must give the illusion of a long march of which the end appears distant and uncertain.

Ideophone as an expression of a situation

We are talking about ideophones which describe a movement, a state, an action. The idea is to lead the audience to perceive a visual or auditory representation of what is going to happen.

In the following song the ideophone expresses the state of a person who is in need. Having failed to find the appropriate verb, the composer took the opportunity to use the ideophone in Song no. 33 *Chiwayawaya*.

Chiwayawaya [ideophone]	Poverty
Basungwana bakulira gelu gelu gelu[35]	The girls cry to become nannies, girl, girl, girl
Chiwayawaya	Poverty

This ideophone cannot be understood without gestures. From these gestures, the audience understands that the girls seek jobs as maids; in fact

---

[34] Here the chiefs are the possessing spirits with their different names.

[35] From the English word *girl*.

147

the gestures in question evoke clothes in tatters. It seems that it was the movement of the woven material in rags that gave birth to this ideophone. About this type of ideophone, Daniel Kunene notes:

> The ideophone attempts to bring before the listener, for first hand perception, actions or states which took place or existed in the past, or will take place or exist in the future. It is an attempt to make the audience see for themselves what happened, or will happen.[36]

This type of ideophone is widespread in Vimbuza songs, see song no. 34 *Chitewe mwataya*.

We could multiply these examples, but we have restricted ourselves to this choice which we believe is representative of the whole of our corpus.

Onomatopoeia

We are tempted to relate onomatopoeia in Tumbuka to the group of ideophones as much through their function as through their formation. In his analysis of ideophones in Shona (Zimbabwe), Fortune also identifies some ideophones having onomatopoeic characteristics.[37] In a general fashion, the Ngoni-Tumbuka seem to have an ear particularly attentive to the sounds they perceive. In this way one will record a lot of onomatopoeia.

Our analysis shows that we can divide the onomatopoeia into three principal sub-categories. In the first place it is a matter of a category of ideophonic onomatopoeia. In the second place comes the category of substantives susceptible of producing onomatopoeia. It is necessary to point out, nonetheless, that certain onomatopoeia can come from the two different categories defined here.

(a) Ideophonic onomatopoeia

> *Hauhau* cf. Verb *kuhaula* (to shout in order to chase away lions).
> *Popopo-o* cf. Verb *kupopoma* (noise made by water in a fall)
> *Pu-u- pu-u* cf. Verb *kuputa* (to whisper: wind)

---

[36] D.P. Kunene, *The Ideophone in Southern Sotho*, Berlin: Reimer, 1978, pp. 34-35.

[37] G. Fortune, "Ideophones in Shona", 1962, p. 30.

(b) Imitation of sounds

Huhuhu	(the dog that barks)
Wawawawa	(the beating of hands)
Ng'ang'ang'a	(the crying of a baby)
Pyopyopyo	(the noise of a whistle)
Tililili-tililili	(the snore of a sleeper)
Gudugudu	(the noise of a drum) – *kuguguma* (the noise of a fuel tanker)
Ng'eng'eng'e	(the noise of leather soles on sandy soil)
Twe-e – twe-e	(the noise of the spoke of a bicycle on the move)
Pipi – i- i	(the hooter)

(c) Onomatopoeia coming from substantives

ngerengere; cf. *chingerengere* (wheel of a bicycle or a car, without tube and tyre or the noise of a wheel on soil)

thuthuthu cf. *mthuthuthu* (a motor bicycle, the noise of the motor of a large motor cycle at the beginning of the 20th century)

popopo cf. *chipopoma* (fall, precipitation)

Vimbuza songs present onomatopoeia of category (b), that is, imitations of noises. Here are four examples:

The sound of a cock is imitated in the song *Tambala walira kumsito* (no. 35):

Line 1: kokoriko	(kokoriko)
Line 3: kokoriko	(kokoriko)
Line 5: kokoriko	(kokoriko)
Line 6: Tambala walira kumsito	The cock has cried in the forest
kokoriko	kokoriko
Line 8: Tambala walira kumsito	The cock has cried in the forest
kokoriko hole	(kokoriko) oho

The morning cry of a bird is reproduced in song no. 36 *BaMng'ombwa*. This bird has as its name *Mng'ombwa*.

Line 1: Hete hete baMng'ombwa bakulira
   (onomatopoeia) the Mng'ombwa is singing
Line 2: Hete hete baMng'ombwa 'akulira kwacha
   (onomatopoeia) the Mng'ombwa is singing, its dawn.

149

(c) The noise produced by the rubbing of women who are scouring pans[38] is reproduced in Song no. 27 *Dyera*

Lines 8, 9 and 12:   Kankhali *kwetekwete*
The small casserole is rubbed
Er – er- er – er

We note that the noise of a rubbed pan is not perceived in the same way in Tumbuka as it is in French or English.

(d) The cries of men to chase away lions when these latter enter a village are found in song no. 85 *Maloto*.

Line 1: Hawuhawu maloto   (onomatopoeia) dreams
Line 6: Hawuhawu maloto   (onomatopoeia) dreams

In conclusion, it is necessary to point out that there are onomatopoeia, which are forbidden to the whole community. Any noise of which the auditory image would evoke the sexual act (the play of the tongue in the mouth), or those able to attract night animals and snakes (the act of whistling) are banned.

Synechdoche

Our corpus unfortunately does not have a sufficient number of songs which present a synechdoche coloration. However, we have often been able to observe their presence in other songs which we were not permitted to record. In other respects, constructions of this type abound in the other literary genres: the story (*vilapi*); the riddle (*ntharika*); the proverb (*vinthanguni*).

Nevertheless, we have to point out that the elements of distinction between synechdoche and metonymy seem to us to correspond more to a subjective state than to an objective one. For us, the two procedures have a similar significance, as Ntole Kazadi also observes:

The very difficulties connected with the definition itself of these figures oblige us to be more prudent. In fact the divergences on the point at which

---

[38] People are using earlier earthen pots less and less. The names of pots (*mphika* or *nkhali*) can be applied to pans.

to distinguish what is a synechdoche from what is metonymy are enormous. Sometimes these divergences even have a bearing on the point of determining whether such or such an expression is part of rhetoric or not. [39]

In the first song we analyze, the synechdoche is the mechanism which consists in taking one part for a whole. The usefulness of this technique rests on its satirical effect. Moreover, it attracts the attention of the audience, which, in order to understand the message, must decode the term used. This is the example which one encounters in song no. 26 *Mwana mubapire weya*.

Line 1: Mwana wachizungu chino ndipo bapire weya

Translation:
Line 1: In this modern world, can one carry one's child in a goat's skin?

The hairs (*weya* or *maweya*) replace the skin which mothers used long ago as a cloth for carrying a child on the back. The singer chose to use *weya* (hairs) instead of *chikumba* (skin) to disguise the whole thing.

The song is addressed particularly to those husbands who do not take much care of their spouses in matters relating to clothes as pointed out earlier. This is a frequent problem.

We equally meet the synechdoche in song no. 5 (*Waya*).

Line 3: Nkhuya ku Jonizibeki namtola waya

Translation
Line 3: I am going to Johannesburg in search of wire.

The man who migrates to Johannesburg is looking for the wire which he will take home. It is a matter of money. The correspondence between the image given by the song and the reality which it concretizes comes from the source utilized. In order to make the pieces, people melted down bars of copper, this in order to produce electric wires. In this regard, a certain precision is imposed: the pennies or pence which were current in the

---

[39] Ntole Kazadi, Essai d'Etude Ethnolinguistique des Chants du Butembo et des Mikendi (Chez les Bahemba et les Baluba du Zaire), PhD, Université de Paris III, 1982, p. 202.

colonial era had as a local name *kopala* (singular); *makopala* (plural) from the English word "copper." It is therefore evident that when the dancer is speaking of "wire", he is making reference to the money he would make in the great city of Johannesburg.

It is not perhaps superfluous to add that in a neighbouring area, Katanga, very widespread commercial exchanges before the colonial era used to take place on the basis of copper bars, which would signify that money could always be symbolically represented by bars or wires in the collective unconscious.

Anglicisms in the Vimbuza songs

Historically, the influence of the English language is profound, and one encounters numerous expressions whose origin is a borrowing from English. Their use seems to have nothing devaluing, to the contrary it corresponds to a "valorisation," an attempt at "culturation", in so far as the majority of the dancers are illiterate. Let's take two examples: The first is from song no. 37 (*Bamumphala*)

Line 1: Sore, sore	Sorry, sorry
Line 6: Nanga muvware jekete, sore	Even if you wear a jacket, sorry

Sore is the adaptation of the English word sorry (grieved), Jekete has as its source the English word jacket.

This song is a critique of single men. Even though they are rich (wearing jackets), they are not respected, while they are not married. Society considers single men as children who do not know anything in the world of adults. In other respects, it is parents who take care of them as much at the level of clothes as of food. The aim of the song is to push single men to take a wife.[40] The other example comes from song no. 33 (*Chiwaya-waya*).

Chiwayawaya	Poverty [ideophone]
Basungwana bakulira, gelu, gelu, gelu[41]	The girls cry to become nannies, girl, girl, girl

---

[40]   Interview Doreen Chirwa.

[41]   From the English word *girl*.

Anyamata bakulira boyi, boyi, boyi we   The boys cry to be house boys, boys,
                                           boys

Chiwayawaya   Poverty

This is an allusive song; the words *gelu* and *boyi* were current in the colonial era.[42] *Gelu* is the English word "girl" which defines a housekeeping woman employed by an Indian trader.[43] Only occasionally did girls seek to occupy this category of work, principally, so it seems, because of the conditions which appeared to them to be bad.

Boyi signifies "boy." There was a difference between the employment of a domestic servant by an Indian and by a White. The employment of a domestic servant was more lucrative among the Whites and these last appeared much more generous towards their domestic servants than were the Indians. Moreover, their conditions of work were satisfactory.[44] This employment was found principally in the administrative centres, at the missions and on the plantations.[45]

One finds in our corpus many of these borrowings characteristic of the westernization of the material culture. Some examples demonstrate our point:

thawulo (towel) in song no. 40
waya (wire) in song no. 5
phadiloku (padlock) in song no. 23
bulangeti (blanket) in song no. 38
lore (lorry) in song no. 39

---

[42] Today the tendency is to avoid these terms, which have become pejorative. In this place people increasingly use servant and nanny.

[43] Malawi had 5,682 Asians according to the Malawi Population Census of 1977.

[44] Interview Kwenda Phiri.

[45] The job of a boy is the object of a novel in Cameroon. F. Oyono, *Une Vie de Boy*, Paris: Julliard, 1956.

153

Gestures

Apart from the linguistic aspects which we have just studied, it is necessary to talk succinctly about gestures in Vimbuza songs. Thanks to the video film which we shot about two dancers, we have been able to pick out a certain number of significant gestures. Nevertheless we do not pretend to have been able to register everything given the fact that the gesture plays a very complex role in the dance. Moreover, it is important to note that one encounters the gesture as much in the sacred as in the profane.

The gesture

Vimbuza songs are sometimes accompanied by gestures. Outside the dance movements which one executes, it happens that the dancer wants to transmit a message. That's when one can distinguish clearly the dance properly speaking from the gesture. We have been able to establish that everything happens as in certain traditional dances in Malawi; we are thinking, in particular, of the dances which accompany initiation ceremonies. Here, apart from the verbal instructions which the instructors give to the initiates (*wali*), there is also instruction through demonstrations and gestures. In this connection, James Msosa describes the importance of gestures:

Where a visual aid is used, fewer words are needed to explain it.[46]

We can affirm in passing that the capacity of the Vimbuza dance to assimilate the gesture confirms our thesis that it is a very open oral genre carrying numerous procedures of expression.

As an artistic creation, the performance of Vimbuza would be boring if one did not use the gesture. Geneviève Calame-Griaule reports rightly that according to her informants, gestures confer taste upon the tale.[47] To that it would be necessary to add the point by István Sándor who attempts to explain:

---

[46] J. Msosa, "How Poetic are Nyau Songs?" *Kalulu* no. 2, 1977, p. 24.

[47] Geneviève Calame-Griaule, "Ce qui donne du goût au conte," (1982), pp. 45-46, 54-55.

Like any experience stimulating artistic creation, the experience of tale-telling keeps the whole being of the reciter moving, of course within the limits due to the particularities of peasant life and to the fact of reproduction. Speech is nothing more than the leading part, while the total effect is produced not only by the communicative function of speech but every means establishing contact between the reciter and his audience.[48]

In fact, the gesture proves itself very useful as a procedure of expression. It seems that the majority of songs would be incomprehensible if one did not take into account the gesture in their analysis.

In the pages that follow we attempt to give some examples where gestures are superimposed on the songs.

Specific gestures

A dancer can begin using gestures of despair recognized as such by the audience to transmit a message. That often happens in this way when the dancer seeks to rouse the sympathy of the audience. We have picked up this type of gesture in song no 41 (*Namulandane*).

Line 1: Namulandane, namulandane
Line 2: Nichali papano namulanda, nichali kulindilira namulanda

Translation:
Line 1: I am truly an orphan
Line 2: I am always there waiting for him

It is about a woman who describes her distressing situation. First of all, she complains because her husband migrated a long time ago to work in South Africa. She receives neither news nor financial assistance from him as he has become a *muchona*. Moreover, this woman finds that she cannot seek divorce; having lost all her relations in her village of birth, she is obliged to remain in her husband's village.

When one is evoking the state of an orphan, one keeps the arms crossed on the chest, the hands placed on the shoulders. The gesture for bereavement consists in putting the hands on the head (as is the case in

---

[48] István Sándor, "Dramaturgy of Tale-Telling," *Acta Ethnographica*, Tomus xvi, Fasciculi 3-4, Akadémia Kiadó, Budapest, 1967.

song no. 12 *Wete walira mwana).* These two examples tend to demonstrate a codification of gestures in Vimbuza; we owe it to ourselves to add that all the gestures are not strictly codified fitting a given situation and that a number of them are left to the appreciation of the dancer.

Gestures which replace ideophones

Numerous gestures are used where an ideophone normally would have been. The relation between ideophones and gestures has been pointed out by Lilian Sorin-Barreteau who notes:

> The gestures are linked to the strong moments of phrases: ideophones, negations ... interrogation ... But they are for the most part linked to ideophones. The same facts told with or without ideophones systematically entail the presence or absence of gestures.[49]

In song 24 *Kurya baka ndiko*, line 9 is accompanied by a gesture:

| Apongozi, | Mother in law, |
| munganituma b̲ingako nkhuku izo | You can send me to chase the chickens |

The usual ideophone for chasing chickens is *fyaa!* In the absence of this ideophone, the gesture consists in directing the right arm, the hand open, and in giving the impression of striking several times, in the direction of the chickens.

In another connection, we should point out, the presence of several types of gestures in the song to which we have just made reference. Each one of the lines we are going to cite has its own ideophone.

| Apongozi munganituma | Mother in law if you ask me |
| Zawumenyepo pano | To come and eat with you |

Here the dancer makes the gesture of taking a lump (of *sima*) when one is eating. The right arm projects towards a plate of *sima*[50] and rapidly breaks off a lump.

---

[49] L. Sorin-Barreteau, "Gestes narratifs et langage gestuel chez les Mofu (Nord Cameroun)," Cahiers de Littérature Orale, no. 11 Paris, INALCO, 1982, pp 36–93 [40].

[50] *Sima* is prepared from the flour of maize, millet or cassava.

| Kuphika nilije kumanya | To cook I don't know, |
| Pakulya ndipo | To eat I do |

The gesture consists in holding a fictitious cooking stick (*mthiko*) and in stirring.

| Apongozi | Mother in law |
| munganituma sinako mwana uyo | you can ask me to pinch that child |

The dancer several times joins the thumb and the index finger in the form of pinching.

| Kulima nilije | To hoe I don't know, |
| Kumanya pakurya ndipo | But to eat I do |

The two closed hands hold a fictitious handle, pull and push it.

We could multiply these examples in the totality of our corpus.

Gestures which accompany the ideophone

We have picked up situations where gestures go together with ideophones. A typical example is presented by song no. 42 *Dende palije*:

Line 1: Bakwabo	To her own [relatives]
Line 2: Mbwambwambwa	She trembles with joy welcoming them
Line 5: Bakuchanalume	To her husband's family
Line 6: Dende palije ehe dende palije	[she says in an angry tone] there is no relish

Bakwawo	Those from her home
Mbwambwambwa	"Welcome, welcome!" (Ideophone)
Bakwawo	Those from her home
Mbwambwambwa	"Welcome, welcome!" (Ideophone)
Bakuchanalume	Those from the husband's side
Dende palije ehe dende palije	"There is no relish, ehe, there is no relish." [in an angry tone]

Line 2 may lead to confusion for the ideophone also signifies the fact of trembling due to cold or fever. But in the song the ideophone is alluding to the warm welcome which a person reserves for his or her own people.

In a general fashion, the gesture *mbwambwambwa* signifies "to tremble with joy." The dancer exaggerates in making the body tremble and especially the hands as if he was suffering from fever. In this way, on the occasion of a visit by people from her home, this woman prepares a copious and appetizing meal. She is happy to receive them. But when people from the husband's family come to the house, she shows her unhappiness and refuses to prepare food under the pretext that she has no relish. This type of conduct on the part of a spouse is often the cause of conflicts which range the husband against the other members of his clan. These latter see themselves as being deprived of services due to them according to tradition.

Another situation in which the ideophone is accompanied by a gesture is found in song no. 33 (*Chiwayawaya*).

Chiwayawaya	Poverty [ideophone]
Basungwana bakulira gelu gelu gelu[51]	The girls cry to become nannies, girl, girl, girl

In order to make the ideophone *chiwayawaya* comprehensible the gesture consists in showing that one is wearing rags. One shakes the body violently (see our explanation of the context in which the song was composed).

Dramatization

In the course of our enquiry we observed gestures which tend to confer a theatrical element on the Vimbuza dance. It happens often that during the dance there are scenes which we would qualify as "sketches" or "playlets" of which the aim is to reproduce everyday life in the context of Vimbuza. We can affirm from them that Vimbuza becomes a veritable microcosm of Ngoni-Tumbuka society. These scenes last a short while. We are going to illustrate our point with the help of two examples.

---

[51] From the English word *girl*.

1. Presents

When the spirit wants to receive a present, often in the form of a chicken, eggs or money, the possessed person starts the song *Mwana wankhuku* (no. 43). At the moment, women who have children in their hands are on their guard; for the possessed person may grab their child. When he takes a baby, he throws it on his back and, without holding it with his hands, throws himself into a frenetic dance. People say on this point that the baby cannot fall for it is supported by the possessing spirit. According to the practice, the dancer keeps the child until the mother finds the ransom required. Sometimes she is obliged to borrow from others.

Now, the use of this song is familiar among the Ngoni-Tumbuka. It is used currently as a warning to chickens when an eagle flies above the village with the intention of trapping a chick. Usually everybody agitates the hands while shouting in order to chase the eagle (*luhera*) away. To this common song one can add the following line: "chibawi cho."

Here is the complete song:

Mwana wankhuku eh	Chick
Mwana wankhuku chenjera	Chick, be careful
Mwana wankhuku eh	Chick, eh
Chibawi 'cho	Here comes the rapacious bird!

This is how the scene passes, recalling the moment when the village defends chicks against the eagle or the hawk. The resemblance is all the more striking as one also hears cries among the women in the audience. The action of the possessed person sows fear and panic among the women, if only for a few moments.

2. Marriage

A little like in the preceding scene, the dancer invites a young woman (often a girl of nubile age) to join him in his circle. He holds her by the hand and places her beside him, and together they march in the manner of a young married couple at the moment of matrimonial ceremonies. Song no. 44 *Wamupala moto* is used on this occasion:

Wamupala moto lero wamupala	He is going to take fire today, he is going to take fire

159

We point out in passing that the Tumbuka expression *kupala moto*, outside its literal translation, means to get married. The woman is associated with the fire of the hearth.[52]

In conlusion we point out that gestures play indeed an important role in Vimbuza songs. Thanks to the gestures the understanding of the texts is facilitated. Given its symbolic dimension, it would be necessary to undertake, in further studies, a deep analysis of the gestures in Vimbuza.

The aesthetic regard manifest in Vimbuza songs compels us to say that these constitute an oral literary genre. In the first place, we establish the existence of stylistic procedures in the performance. The elements which we have brought out (ideophones, rhyme, repetition, synechdoche, parallelism) demonstrate our point. In the second place, Vimbuza songs prove to be an efficacious way of carrying messages. It is to be noted that the song is composed in such a way that the transmission of the message is effected in conditions conforming to traditions, that is, in the manner of tales or proverbs. In this regard, we recall what we said in Chapter 3. Vimbuza borrows songs, gestures and the way of dancing from other dances. In all this we do not pretend to have done an exhaustive analysis of the style as the repertoire of these songs is very vast and we have only a limited sample.

Conclusion

In the preceding study, it was part of our duty to attain the goal which we had set for ourselves, that is, to show that Vimbuza is an oral literary genre. To show this was the object of two chapters. On the one hand, we have compared Vimbuza to other genres. On the other, we have studied the stylistic procedures which one can disclose in the songs that accompany the dance. This step is all the more important as the spirits of Vimbuza don't seem to enjoy the dance and the music when their victim executes these in an artistic fashion. Steven Moyo describes this situation in the following manner:

---

[52] For a related meaning see the song no. 30 *Chikuni chakolera* in Rachel NyaGondwe Fiedler, *Coming of Age. A Christianized Initiation among Women in Southern Malawi,* Zomba: Kachere, 2005, p. 66.

It is claimed by some performers that the apostrophised, especially spirits, can only be placated through use of certain types of art: the musical. The spirits are in this case the listeners and *izingoma* as an auditory art. This aspect of *izingoma* is especially critical in situations involving *Vyanusi* spirit possession. There can be no exorcism without the heavy singing intended for the ears of the spirits, presumably embodied in the person of who is possessed.[53]

In the course of this study on Vimbuza, we have touched only on what we thought was essential. It would have been difficult to do otherwise in a domain so little explored in the geographical area considered.

It has seemed to us opportune to proceed in the following manner:

- A historical study imposed itself in order to be able to explain the reasons for which the colonial administration attacked Vimbuza dancers. The high points of the history of Vimbuza are the following:
- The penetration of Christianity which ran against religious practices described as animist. Here we have proven the fact that it was on the advice of the missionaries that the administration struggled against Vimbuza.
- The reasons for the rapid development of Vimbuza during the first quarter of the 20th century
- The draconian measures taken against Vimbuza which led the dancers to go into secrecy
- The official policy after independence: the revalorization and preservation of the Malawian socio-cultural patrimony.

On the ethnological plane, we have established that Vimbuza, of foreign origin, has integrated itself well into the Ngoni-Tumbuka culture. We have shown that the ease with which it has imposed itself is due to the fact that this possession cult fitted into the system of pre-existing beliefs. Elsewhere, we have taken account of the problem posed by the co-existence of two types of Vimbuza, the sacred and the profane. To better

---

[53] Steven Moyo, A Linguo-Aesthetic Study of Ngoni Poetry, PhD, University of Wisconsin, 1978, pp. 69–70. See also Ntole Kazadi, Essai d' Etude Ethnolinguistique des Chants du Butembo et des Mikendi (Chez les Bahemba et les Baluba du Zaire), PhD, Université de Paris III, 1982, p. 218.

understand each one of these types, we have proceeded to individual examinations by evoking the aspects which characterize them.

With "sacred" or ritual Vimbuza (cf Chapter 2), it has been necessary to study the possession cult in its three manifestations: Vimbuza (generic term), Virombo and Vyanusi. The analysis has been effected on three levels. In the first place, we have considered the cult in relation to the system of beliefs which surrounds it. Secondly, we have reported a series of rites which usually stretch over several weeks. Finally, we have shown how possession gives birth to diviner/healers whose task is to care for the sick and to fight the misdeeds of sorcery.

Without going into any details, the list below indicates the principal points which we have touched on:
- the vestiges of the indigenous religion
- the denomination of possession
- the diagnosis of the "disease"
- the phases of the unfolding of a séance
- esoterism: possession generates divination

As for "profane" Vimbuza, we have examined its role as a social fact. Man has known how to provoke exaltation by artificial means in order to surpass himself and to excel in the art of composing songs. In this connection, we have noted the utilization of a plant, *seketela* or *mphelele* as defence against aggression by spirits. The analysis has essentially been on the social functions presented by the songs. We devoted ourselves to the analysis of five social functions which we considered very important:
- social critique; we have considered the destruction of a traditional institution for the benefit of modernism
- resolution of social and family conflicts; we have examined the subjects of disagreements between co-wives and family relations
- transmission of information; the genre takes on an historical dimension, the themes concern migrant workers, Ngoni invasions, the First World War, political struggles.
- Vimbuza as an entertainment dance; the dance can be seasonal, and includes certain traits of profane dances
- Vimbuza as an educative instrument; to instruct while entertaining is one approach in other oral genres, in the circumstances, the tale.

Apart from the functions, we have established through the songs, that Vimbuza seems to identify itself with an oral genre. We have pointed out, in this regard, that it shares with other oral literary genres stylistic traditions and procedures. This takes us to Chapter 4 where these procedures have been studied in detail.

A certain number of rhetorical figures have been brought out. Moreover, we have noted the existence of a technique which the composers use in the songs which smacks of satire and caricature. We have christened this technique: "camouflage technique." It is characteristic of songs which reduce themselves to two or three lines and of which the literal sense is profoundly remote from the true sense.

We are conscious of the fact that our thesis is going to raise questions to which we would not have replied at the end of this work. We are thinking notably about an aspect which we have touched lightly in passing.[54] It is "African theatre" about which the debate is assuming more and more importance in African literary circles. People ask themselves whether African playwrights can draw their inspiration from oral genres such as Vimbuza. The following extracts speak volumes:

> The question that is a preoccupation on this week's column is the whole concept of the African theatre – whether indeed there is such a thing as African theatre in the first place.

> By definition, theatre is something that is dramatic and purposefully entertaining. Where this takes place depends on the culture - formal in the West, and informal on the African continent. Here stories, myths, as well as legends are dramatized either at the fire-side in the evenings, at break time in the gardens or at a beer party where some adults will do mimes as spontaneous entertainment. This is a theatre in that it is drama in a non-formal context. And when these informal presentations become formalized by writers who project them onto a formal stage for the convenience of modern society, out goes the spontaneity at the behest of technical production. Here is the uncomfortable part - transposing a cultural experience onto the stage...

> Trying to present drama by using various stage techniques to recreate the African theatre as an accepted way of life of the Africans, or is it an elitist

---

[54] See our discussion on dramatization in the Vimbuza dance in chapter 4.

exercise by the few who can afford to laugh at puns at the club plays in between their drinks? The same question looms as to who the African playwrights are writing for if their people do not relate to the formal stage life.[55]

These points demonstrate that it is not an easy thing to transpose oral genres into stage plays. Nevertheless that should not dissuade the researchers from digging more with the aim of better understanding these genres. The situation becomes much clearer with regard to Vimbuza. According to Isaac Chirwa, this would already have taken the aspect of a veritable theatre. This evolution would be due to the appearance of profane Vimbuza:

> The Vimbuza dance festival is more prophetic than entertaining. The dancer is possessed by his ancestral spirits to reveal through his singing spirits[56] their (spirit) disgusts, warning, praise or condemnation to the society or its individuals. Although this was meant to be objective there were cases where it was meant to be subjective for a Vimbuza dancer could claim that he was possessed and that it was not him but the spirit who said whatever he said through his singing. This then was a dramatization through music and dance of the message from the ancestral spirits. It had its creation, purpose and form. It expressed personal or impersonal feelings about the society and its individuals. It was a drama that spoke to the society and its peoples. It is a dance festival that need (sic) exploration and exploitation.[57]

Without going into details, we shall say that Vimbuza proves itself to be a multidisciplinary subject. Historians, anthropologists, sociologists and psychologists can draw a lot of lessons from it. We do not neglect, finally, the role which the diviner/healers can play in the knowledge of medicinal plants. Traditional medicine seems to be increasingly attracting the attention of Western researchers, as the following extracts would have us understand:

---

[55] Mike Kamwendo, "African Theatre. Is there such a Thing?" *Malawi News*, 2.9.1979.

[56] According to Isaac Chirwa it is the spirits who sing.

[57] Isaak Chirwa, "Malawian Drama Must Go Back Home", *Malawi News*, 4.2.1979, p. 18.

In the past few years more research has been done on African traditional medicine, and a strategy of cooperation has developed to enable the world understand that traditional healing can also play an important role in curing diseases.

Many international organisations are now inviting traditional healers to present their ideas for evaluations. Recently, there was a meeting of traditional healers from Africa, East Asia, the Middle East, Latin America and the United States who conferred with contemporary physicians and other health workers in Washington to draw up a strategy of co-operation among them as health services workers.[58]

Such is the nature of Vimbuza in the bosom of African oral literature. It is perhaps useful to add, finally, that much remains to be done in this domain as our work is nothing but a beginning of a vaster project on the oral literature of Malawi.

---

[58] Willie Zingani, "Traditional Medicine has a Part to Play in Nation's Health", *Malawi News*, 25.6.-1.7.1983, p. 5; (cf. "U.S. Conference for Traditional Healers" in *Daily Times*, 27.6.1983, p. 3).

Conclusion

Three decades after the initial full blown research into the Vimbuza healing dance, it appears that a generation has passed and the phenomenon has more or less evolved. During our attendance at a recent performance in honour of some visiting German friends, we noted a number of changes affecting the dance as it stands today. Our conclusion will therefore highlight a few of these changes which have taken place.

Our first research work in the field was in 1979 in Mzimba and Rumphi districts. If we consider 10 year old children who attended the dances at that time, today they are 43 years old. The people we interviewed were mostly above 50 years old and today they should be 83 years old and above. It is very unlikely that we can come across these people anymore especially to verify the information they gave us in the interviews we recorded. For the sake of future research on Vimbuza Healing Dance the following are the areas which can be said to have gone through the processs of change.

Abuse of the Sacredness of the Vimbuza Spirits

The audience seems no longer afraid of the presence of the spirits, beings which cannot be seen by the naked eye. One of the evidence of this trend is the unruly conduct of young men who are drunk. In the past it was not possible to see someone in a drunken state enter the arena of a dance session. The noise that these young men make disturbs the order in the room because the singers, the drummers and even the master of ceremonies (*musamu*) have to stop from time to time to impose silence. This is something that is difficult to manage. The possessed person seems absolutely helpless, since the spirits will vent their anger on her.

In the past the possessed person commanded a lot of respect and her instructions were supposed to be implemented all the time. If disobeyed, the dancer could throw fire on the culprits and could even chase them out of the house. There is need for safeguarding the management of the Vimbuza space.

Prayers during a Vimbuza Dance Session

It has now become fashionable that prayers are said before the dance can start. A woman or a man will stand up and lead in prayers. After the prayers, it is when the dance session starts. This new factor causes some confusion because prayers to God cannot be performed to leave ground there afterwards to Vimbuza spirits. This contradiction is probably not understood by the community. They think that the two can go together and this is probably the reason why there is now even use of the corss on the uniforms.

Use of Crosses

The vimbuza dancers have a uniform which was not there during the 1970's and which serves as a copy of the uniform which women's and men's guilds put on in churches. The cross is appended on the chest and back. It is said that in their dreams a request is made by the possessing spirit to make a uniform with a red or white cross. It is the spirits which want to use a cross. The uniform is officially handed over at a big dance ceremony but as expressed above, it is not clear what connection there is between the spirits possessing the patient and the latter's human faith in God. This phenomenon has spread to many areas and it is a must.

Kulamba

Related to the above practice is the practice of kulamba of foreign origin in which a patient or Vimbuza dancer prostrates in front of a dignitary or drummers if they beat so well or even to the audience if it sings well. It is a form of respect indicating appreciation for coming or performing well- We found this to be contradictory because the spirits are supposed to be above everyone else and that they are supposed to be the "guests of honour" and be treated as such. We think that the spirits are dishounouring themselves, or it is the dancers who are dishounouring the spirits.

Costume

One aspect which need immediate attention as far as the Vimbuza dance is concerned is the loss of proper costume to be worn by the dancers. Most lacking are skins made of a patchwork of stripes of goatskin which the dancer wears around the waist. When she is dancing, these radiate from the waist outwards. These skins are plentiful in the country. But the people who had skills to make this piece of costume, *madumbo*, are no longer there, hence their replacement by a simpler type of this apparel which is composed of a string holding a number of round shaped metals. This has completely changed the way the waist movements were coordinated with the bells (*mangenjeza* or *mangwanda*) worn on the ankles below. It is still possible to find people who can manufacture the *madumbo* and there should be someone who wants to promote and revitalize the manufacture of the original costume.

Language of Songs

Another point which we noted as having undergone change is the language of songs. For example in the past the Vyanusi songs were in SiNgoni and these songs were used during the dance of the same name. Most of these songs have either been forgotten or have been interpreted into ChiTumbuka. The same is true of the Virombo dance whose songs were originally in Chinyanja which are sung in ChiTumbuka. This realization of the language change requires that we revitalize the rich Vimbuza repertory of songs. There is need therefore to release the old songs on tape and give them back to the Vimbuza dancers. This can be done by playing the cassettes we recorded featuring original songs.

Vimbuza as Intangible Heritage

Realising that there is loss of a number of practices in the Vimbuza space, the dancers and diviners teamed up to form an organization for the promotion and safeguarding of their healing dance. This was done through the help of UNESCO which launched the "Vimbuza Healing Dance Safeguarding Project" between 2007 and 2009 which culminated in training the Vimbuza healers, dancers and chiefs on matters concerning intellectual property rights, appropriate health measures vis-à-vis HIV/AIDS prevention, mutual existence between Vimbuza healers and modern medical practitioners, gender and importance of education. This included the formation of the "Vimbuza Healers and Dancers Association of Malawi." A code of conduct was articulated for the members to present a positive image of the Vimbuza which had suffered poor publicity due to some unorthodox practices.

UNESCO also helped to develop an inventory of the Vimbuza Healing Dance which included an inventory of Vimbuza dancers existing as well as legends, giving their names, village and brief background information. Most important was the holding of Vimbuza Dance Festivals in Rumphi and in Mzuzu. The festivals provided an opportunity to the practitioners to gather together and share knowledge and skills in their profession. There were more than fifteen practitioners at each festival and this action boosted the moral among them. It was, in a way, a grand celebration of the existence of the healing dance which had suffered condemnation for so long. The dancers came from Rumphi, Mzimba and Nkhata Bay.

UNESCO further gave the opportunity to the practitioners to meet regularly for training workshops on current issues threatening the continuity of Vimbuza Healing. These meetings were attended by chiefs and officials from the Department of Culture. In addition, Mzuzu Museum mounted a permanent exhibition on the Vimbuza Healing Dance. The idea was to make it an evolving exhibition which could get updated as and when more artifacts are collected from the Vimbuza practitioners.

Finally, it is important to mention that the safeguarding project has gone as far as presenting radio and television panel discussions featuring practitioners, researchers and religious personalities. In a nutshell, this is the work that UNESCO has undertaken since it proclaimed the "Vimbuza Healing Dance" as a masterpiece of the oral and intangible cultural heritage of humanity in line with the 2003 UNESCO Convention of Intangible Cultural Heritage to which Malawi is a signatory.

Chapter 5: Vimbuza Songs

In this chapter we present the songs in their original version. It is proper to point out the preponderance of Vimbuza songs. These are all sung in Tumbuka, while those of *Virombo* and *Vyanusi* posed a problem of translation.[1]

Finally, each song is accompanied by the context in which it was composed and is summarized in several lines.

Song no. 1
Gripa Jele

Zina Gripa Jele	It is about Gripa Jele
Zina Gripa Jele, wamhlangabeza	It is about Gripa Jele, people surprised him
Zina Gripa Jele	It is about Gripa Jele
Zina Gripa Jele, wamhlangabeza	It is about Gripa Jele, people surprised him
Watandika mahamba	He spread leaves
Heyaye	Heyaye
Pakati pa msewu	In the middle of the road
Heyaye	Heyaye
Zina Gripa Jele wamhlangabeza	It is about Gripa Jele, people surprised him
Watandika mahamba	He spread leaves
Ho! Ho!	Ho! Ho!
Pakati pa msewu	In the middle of the road
Ho! Ho!	Ho! Ho!
Zina Gripa Jele	It is about Gripa Jele

---

[1] The majority of *Virombo* songs are in Chewa and the *Vyanusi* songs are in Ngoni.

| Zina Gripa Jele wamhlangabeza | It is about Gripa Jele, people surprised him |

This is an *Ingoma* dance song which recounts an amorous adventure.

Song no. 2
Kaujo Kandambo

Kaujo kandambo	Little grass at the stream
Nati m'pondepo	I wanted to step on it
Nawopa kuterera, ine, yayi	I was afraid to slide, me, no!
Namwana wakhanda	I was like a little baby
Amuna akali mukuyenda	My husband is still abroad

The temptation to infidelity of a woman whose husband went to work abroad.

Song no. 3
Munde mundete

Munde mundete, munde mundete	Munde mundete, munde mundete
Khalanga mayi nigone kuti nde?	Despair, woman! Where should I sleep?
Nde nyumba walanda chelekela	The spider has covered my house
Munde mundete munde mundete	Munde mundete, munde mundete
Khalanga mayi! Nigone kuti nde?	Despair, woman! Where should I sleep?
Nyumba walanda thandaude	The cobweb has covered my house
Munde mundete, munde mundete	Munde mundete, munde mundete
Khalanga mayi nigone kuti nde?	Despair, woman! Where should I sleep?
Nyumba walanda chilolera	The spider has covered my house

The family has been struck by a misfortune. There is no child. Everything goes on as if the house is uninhabited.

Song no. 4
Kupula kubaba

Kupula kubaba ngati ungalyanga waka	To pound causes pain, I wish one could eat without effort
Holiyaye	Holiyaye
Kupula kubaba ngati ungalyanga waka	To pound causes pain, I wish one could eat without effort
Uli nchembere!	You are a grown up woman!
Chema!	Call!
Mwana wamunyako, para wakulira	Someone's child, if he cries
mtole umubape	Put him on your back
Nchembere	Woman
Ulimbire wako wachizungu	Your insistence in these modern days
chino ukamutolenkhu?	To have your own child, where will you get that?
Nchembere we!	You woman!

This song has been borrowed from the *pathuli* pounding songs. It is a commentary on the demographic situation. The women experience difficulties in finding a husband as men are in short supply owing to migration.

Song no. 5
Waya

Eh waya[2] eh	Eh, wire, eh
Waya eh	Wire, eh
Waya eh	Wire, eh
Eh eh yaye waya eh	Eh eh yaye, wire, eh
Waya eh	Wire, eh
Ahe waya ehe waya eh	Ahe wire, ehe wire, eh
Ahe waya ehe waya eh	Ahe wire, ehe wire, eh

---

[2] Derived from the English word "wire"; *waya* alludes to the copper coins and the wire on which they were strung. Later *waya* came to mean money in general.

Iyaya lero namtola waya	Iyaya, today I am going to get the wire
Iyaya	Iyaya
Ahe waya eh	Ahe, wire, eh
Nkhuya ku Jonizibeki	I am going to Johannesburg
Namtola waya	To get the wire
Ahe waya eh	Ahe, wire, eh

Chorus

Waya eh	Wire, eh
Eh eh yeye ahe waya eh	Eh eh, yeye ahe, wire, eh
Waya eh	Wire, eh
Eh waya ahe waya eh	Eh wire ahe, wire, eh
Nkhuya ku Jonizibeki	I am going to Johannesburg
Namtola waya	I am going to get wire
Ahe waya eh	Ahe, wire, eh
Nkhuya ku Jonizibeki	I am going to Johannesburg
Namtola waya	I am going to take wire
Ahe waya eh	Ahe, wire, eh
Erere oh erere waya eh	Erere oh erere, wire, eh

The mines in neighbouring countries for a long time attracted Malawians to earn money (*waya*). It was the time of migrant labourers.

Song no. 6
Mphika wanyole

Selina korokoto pa mphika wankhuku	Selina is scratching in the pot of chicken
Asungwana balero, korokoto[3]	The girls of today, korokoto
Pa mphika wankhuku abo	Love to scratch the chicken pot

Chorus

Yale yale anke yale yale	Yale yale anke yale yale

---

[3]   An ideophone which recalls the noise which one produces when one rubs the bottom of a pot.

Korokoto pa mphika wankhuku	Scratching the chicken pot
Asungwana balero, korokoto	The girls of today, korokoto
Pa mphika wankhuku abo	Love to scratch the chicken pot
Sore, a Selina, korokoto	Sorry, Serina, korokoto
Pa mphika wanyole[4] abo	She scratches the chicken pot
Anyamata balero	The boys of today
Korokoto pa mphika wankhuku	Scratching the chicken pot
Anyamata balero	The boys of today
Korokoto pa mphika wankhuku	Scratching the chicken pot

If you go to visit and you are offered chicken, do not scratch the pot. The youth of today are fond of chicken.

Song no. 7
Uyaya Wanitayamo

Uyaya eh uyaya eh	Desire, eh, desire
Uyaya wanitayamo eh	Desire has put me into trouble
Uyaya wanitayamo eh	Desire has put me into trouble, eh
Lero wanitimba waka	Today you beat me up for nothing
Uyaya wanitayamo eh	Desire has put me into trouble, eh
Uyaya eh uyaya eh	Desire, eh, desire, eh
Uyaya wanitayamo eh	Desire has put me into trouble, eh
Muleke kunitimba	Stop beating me
Uyaya wanitayamo eh	Desire has put me into trouble, eh
Mwanitimba waka	You have beaten me for nothing
Uyaya wamitayamo eh	Desire has put me into trouble, eh

Uyaya is a term difficult enough to translate into English, the true sense is somewhere between sensual pleasure and the tendency towards infidelity. The song is about a woman who recognizes that she has compromised her marriage.

---

[4] Here a Tonga word for chicken is used.

Song no. 8
Mwalowana mwabene

Mwalowana mwabene	You have bewitched one another
Mwalowana mwabene	You have bewitched one another
Pa chibali, Mphanda	In the family, Mphanda[5]
Mwalowana mwabene	You have bewitched one another
Mwalowana	You have bewitched
Mwalowana	You have bewitched one another
Pa nyumba yinu	In your house
Pa chibali Mphanda	In your family, Mphanda
Malinga wakuchula[6]	Since you have been named.
Zomela tiwelenge,	Accept, so that we can go home.
Mwalowana mwabene	You have bewitched one another

A song in which one explains that the author of the crime is a close relative. In fact, people believe that sorcery only affects relatives.

Song no. 9
Kakoŵa

Bavwalira–vwalira akakoŵa	He is overdressed, Mr Kakoŵa
Eh zanimuwone	Eh, come and see
Bavwalira–vinyanga a Kakoŵa	He is dressed with horns,[7] Mr Kakoŵa
Eh zanimuwone	Eh, come and see
Bavwalira–vwalira a kakoŵa wehe	He is overdressed this Kakoŵa, wehe
Zanimuwone eh,	Come and see
Vinyanga a Kakoŵa eh	The horns of Kakoŵa
Zanimuwone	Come and see
Bavwalira jekete a Kakoŵa wehe	He is wearing a jacket, Kakoŵa, eh
Zanimuwone eh	Come and see

---

[5] Mphanda is a spirit in the *Virombo* group. The Mphanda is speaking here.

[6] This is a Chewa word *kutchula*, to name, to pronounce.

[7] Horns are typical witchcraft implements.

Vinyanga a Kakoŵa eh	The horns of Mr Kakoŵa, eh
Zanimuwone	Come and see
Bavwalira-vwalira a Kakoŵa	He is overdressed, Mr Kakoŵa
Eh zanimuwone	Eh, come and see
Bavwalira jekete a Kakoŵa	He is wearing a jacket, Kakoŵa
Eh zanimuwone	Eh, come and see

It's a matter of the objects which the possessed person wears on the chest, the head, the arms and the legs: the costume. Kakowa is a bird like the pelican. One compares the dancer to the bird on the basis of his clothes

Song no. 10
Anyirongo awoli binu balero

A Nyirongo 'mwe!	Mr Nyirongo,[8] you!
Awoli binu balero bosina mwana	Your new wife pinches my child
Bosina[9] mwana	She pinches the child
Bosina mwana chifukwa cha imwe	She pinches the child because of you.
Chifukwa cha imwe[10]	Because of you
Chifukwa cha imwe, mugona mwane	Because of you, who sleeps in my house

Chorus

Wayowoyenge wayowoyenge	Let her talk, let her talk
Wayowoyenge he sabata yindamane	Let her talk, the week it is not yet finished

Jealousy between co-wives often provokes conflicts which degenerate into drama.

---

[8] Nyirongo is a name that carries all the shortcomings of men in *vimbuza* songs.

[9] bo: third person plural used here as a mark of respect

[10] The woman uses the respectful form of 'you' for her husband while this latter uses the less respectful form to address her (*imwe* and *iwe*).

Song no. 11
Singo

Singo ah eh bavinila singo
Bavinila singo bavinila singo

Singo ah eh bavinila singo
Bavinila singo bavinila singo

Amayi, singo ni mwana ah eh
Bavinila singo bavinila singo

Bavinila singo bavinila singo

Neck, ah eh, they dance with the neck
They dance with the neck, they dance with the neck

Neck, ah eh, they dance with the neck
They dance with the neck, they dance with the neck

Mother, the neck is a child, ah eh
They dance with the neck, they dance with the neck

They dance with the neck, they dance with the neck

The song refers to a type of possession in which the dancer knocks the head on the ground with the neck all stiff.

Song no. 12
Wete walira Mwana

Wete walira Mwana
Walira wete wete[11]
Walira mwana
Walira eh
Walira wete wete
Walya wekha mwana
Walira wete wete
Walya wekha mwana
Walira eh

Wete, you are crying over the child
You are crying, wete wete
You are crying over the child
You are crying, eh
You are crying ,wete wete,
You have eaten the child yourself [12]
You have cried, wete wete
You have eaten the child yourself
You are crying, eh

---

[11] The sound which women make while weeping during the funeral ceremony.

[12] The crying woman is accused of having herself killed the child she is crying over by witchcraft.

The song is about the belief that witchcraft has no boundary and that the witch or wizard cries the most at the funeral.

Song no. 13
Chadoroka

Tili babili, tili bazga hela iwe	We are two, we are slaves, hela ,you
He iwe heyayiwe tili babili	He you, heyayiwe, we are two
Tili babili tili bazga	We are two, we are slaves
Chadoroka he tili babili	We are blind, both of us
Chadoroka he tili babili	We are blind, both of us
Munyane ni Chanda,[13] we	My friend, it is Chanda, we
Tili babili eh yayawe tili babili	We are two eh yayawe we are two
Tili babili tili bazga	We are two we are slaves
Chadoroka he tili babili	We are blind, both of us
Tili babili tili bazga	We are two, we are slaves
Munyane ni Chanda we	My friend it is Chanda we
Tili babili Chadoroka we	We are two, blind we are
Tili babili tili tili babili tili basga	We are two, we are two, we are slaves

Chadoroka is the name of a form of possession which makes the victim blind.

Song no. 14
Muthengere muli minga

Muthengere muli minga	In the forest there are thorns
Muthengere muli minga	In the forest there are thorns
Jimanyire wamwene	That you [should] know yourself
Mukaya muli viwawa	In the village there are noises (conflicts)
Mukaya muli viwawa	In the village there are noises
Jimanyire wamwene	That you know yourself

---

[13] Chanda: A *vimbuza* spirit of Bemba origin.

178

Chorus

Eh sunga muzimu[14]	Eh, keep the soul
Jimanyire wamwene	That you may know yourself
Eh sunga muzimu	Eh, keep the soul
Jimanyire wamwene	That you may know yourself

People compare the village quarrels to the thorn-bushes in the forest (opposition nature and culture).

Song no. 15
Nkhwenda nkhule

Nkhule we yahole ha	Naked, we yahole he
Chiwayawaya	(ideophone indicating the dangling of rags)
Chifukwa cha moba	Because of beer
We nkhwenda nkhule	I move naked
Chiwayawaya	(ideophone)
Basweni bane eh yahole	My husband, eh yahole
Chiwayawaya	(ideophone)
Nkhwenda nkhule eh yahole	I move naked, eh yahole
Chiwayawaya	(ideophone)
A wiske Timeyo eh yahole he	Father of Timeyo, eh yahole he
Chiwayawaya	(ideophone)

Alcoholism is sometimes the cause of misery in a home. The complaint of a wife whose husband passes the time drinking.

Song no. 16
Zinyanga

Ore yaya ore	Ore yaya ore
Anh[15] ore	Anh ore

---

[14] Usually *muzimu* is the ancestral spirit, but the word assumes here the Christian meaning "soul."

Ore yaya vinyanga yayawe ore	Ore yaya, horns, yayawe ore
Ore eya ore	Ore eya ore
Anh ore	Anh ore
Ore eya ore yaya ore	Ore eya ore yaya ore
Orewe yayawe ore	Orewe yayawe ore
Anh ore	Anh ore
Orewe yayawe	Orewe yayawe
Vinyanga mwa Tegha	The horns at Tegha's village
Holewe yayawe hole	Holewe yayawe hole
Ah hole	Ah hole
Holewe yayawe	Holewe yayawe
Vinyanga pa muzi uno hole	The horns in this village, hole
Hole eh yahole	Hole eh yahole
Inh hinh	Inh hinh
Hole yaya yaya hole	Hole yaya yaya hole

A song which the hired diviner uses during exorcism going round the houses in the village.

Song no. 17
Tambala kwa Mahekeya

Luluwe luluwe, a Nyirongo luluwe	Luluwe luluwe, Mr Nyirongo, luluwe
Luluwe luluwe, a Nyirongo luluwe	Luluwe luluwe, Nyirongo, luluwe
Ahe luluwe	Ahe luluwe

Chorus

Tambala wakanangachi kwa Mahekeya	What (wrong) did the cock do at Mahekeya's
Ahe luluwe	Ahe luluwe
Pakumudula mutu nangoda zake	To have his head cut off with the feathers[16]

---

[15] Anh indicates the nasal sound of the vowel a.

[16] This is an allusion to the dancer wearing the head of the cock fastened to his or her own head.

Ahe luluwe	Ahe luluwe
Tambala wakanangachi kwa Mahekeyi	The cock, what has he destroyed at Mahekeya's
Ahe luluwe	Ahe luluwe
Pakumudula mutu nangoda zake	To have his head cut off with the feathers
A Nyirong luluwe luluwe luluwe	Nyironga, luluwe luluwe luluwe
A Nyirong luluwe luluwe luluwe	Nyironga, luluwe luluwe luluwe
Ahe luluwe	Ahe luluwe

Usually *ngoda* means the running knots made from the hairs of a cow. By extension, *ngoda* can apply to the hairs and exceptionally here to the plumes (feathers). This is a song which people intone during the sacrifice of the cock (*chilopa*).

Song no. 18
NyaMtonga

Iyaya lero, NyaMtonga[17] eh!	Iyaya today, NyaMtonga eh
Iyaya lero, NyaMtonga eh!	Iyaya today, NyaMtonga eh
Iyaya lero, NyaMtonga eh!	Iyaya today, NyaMtonga eh
Iyaya lero ,NyaMtonga eh!	Iyaya today, NyaMtonga eh
Chijaro mwajara uli NyaMtonga eh?	How did you shut the door, NyaMtonga eh?
Iyaya lero Nyamtonga eh!	Iyaya today, NyaMtonga, eh
Chijaro mwajara uli, NyaMtonga eh?	How have you shut the door, Nyamtonga, eh?
Iyaya lero, Nyamtonga eh!	Iyaya today, NyaMtonga, eh
Mwanalume wafumamo, NyaMtonga eh!	A man has just come out (of the house), NyaMtonga, eh
Iyaya lero, NyaMtonga eh!	Iyaya today, NyaMtonga, eh
Mwanalume, wafumamo,	A man has just come out (of the house)
NyaMtonga eh!	NyaMtonga, eh

---

[17] Nya – a term of address reserved for women, prefixed to the name, for example, NyaMtonga or NyaGondwe.

Iyaya lero NyaMtonga eh!   Iyaya today, NyaMtonga, eh

People accuse a woman whose husband has gone to work abroad of committing adultery.

Song no. 19
A Nelesoni

Incipit

A Nelesoni iyaya lero	Nelson, iyaya, today
A Nelesoni iyaya lero	Nelson, iyaya, today
A Nelesoni iyaya lero	Nelson, iyaya, today
A Nelesoni iyaya lero	Nelson, iyaya, today
A Nelesoni iyaya lero	Nelson, iyaya, today
A Nelesoni njinga mumika munthowa	Mr Nelson, you put your bicycle on the path
He eh yayiwe tiyeni	Ha! Ha! not you, let's go
A Nelesoni mvine mkuwera bweka	Mr. Neleson, dance when you come back, no matter when
He eh yayiwe tiyeni	Ha! Ha! Not you, let's go

Chorus

Tiwerenge	That we may return
Heyaye eh yahore	Ha! Ha! Ha!
Heyaye tiyeni	Ha! Ha! Ha! Let's go
Kuli mwezi	There is moonlight
Heyaye eh yahore	Ha! Ha! Ha!
Heyaye tiyeni	Ha! Ha! Ha! Let's go

A woman accuses her husband of unfaithfulness.

Song no. 20
Mazgo ghane ni mungole

Mazgo ghane ni mungole	My voice is like
Ghakwimba mu wayilesi wole	The harmonica on the radio, wole.
Hereku yawa	Hereku yawa

Mazgo ghane ni mungole	My voice is like
Ghakwimba mu wayilesi wole	The harmonica on the radio, wole.
Hereku yawa	Hereku yawa

Chorus

Ole Herekuwe	Ole Herekuwe
Yahore	Yahore
Hereku yawa	Hereku yawa
Ole	Ole
Herekuwe Hayiwe	Herekuwe Hayiwe
Hereku yawa	Hereku yawa
Iyaya lero iyaya lero ole	Iyaya today iyaya today ole
Hereku yawa	Hereku yawa
Mazgo ghane ni mingole amama	My voice is like the harmonica, mother
Ghakwenda muwayilesi, olewe	Which they play on the radio, olewe
Hereku yawa	Hereku yawa

Appreciation of the quality of the voice. The regard for the aesthetic is undeniable in this song.

Song no. 21
Kuvina mutolerenge

Anh olewe he eh eh	Anh olewe, he eh eh
Oh olewe hayo oh	Oh olewe, hayo oh
Oh oh eh oh eh	Oh oh eh oh eh
Anh he eh eh he eh eh	Anh he eh eh, he eh eh
Mazgo mutolenge ghane	Take after (imitate) my voice
Amama eh yaye	Mother eh yaye

Chorus

Tiwerenge	Let's return
Eh yaye	Eh yaye
Kuli mwezi	There is moonlight
Eh eh eyaye	Eh eh eyaye
Tiwerenge	Let's return
Eh yaye	Eh yaye
Kula kwithuwe	(Over) there is our home

Eh eh eyaye	Eh eh eyaye
Mama eh yaye	Mother, eh yaye
He eyaye ehe	He, eyaye, ehe
Kuvina mutolerenge	Imitate [take after] my dancing
Amama eh yaye	Mother, eh yaye

One appreciates the quality of the voice of the singer. A song from the repertoire of profane Vimbuza where one can at times give oneself over to competitions.

Song no. 22
Chamukarawula

Caya kumuzi camukarawula hole	He is gone to the village to overdo it (finishing all the food)
Anh hole anh caya	Anh hole, anh caya
kumunda camukarawula	He is gone to the field to overdo it (to finish all the work)
Hayo oh	Hayo, oh
He eh eh he caya kumunda	He eh eh, he he is gone to the field
Camukarawula	He is going to clean it up
Hole eh	Hole, eh
Oh yayawe eh caya kumunda	Oh yayawe eh he is gone to the field
camukanawula	He is going to clean it up
Hayo	Hayo
Eh eh yaya hole caya kumuzi	Eh eh yaya hole, he is gone to the village
Camukarawula	He is going to eat a lot
Hayo	Hayo
Ye yaya haye caya kumuzi	Ye yaya haye, he is gone to the village
Camukarawula	He is going to eat a lot
Hine	Hine
Eh eh he eh caya kumunda	Eh eh he eh, he is gone to the field
Camukarawula	He is going to clean it up.

The caricature of an excessive person whom people deride.

Song no. 23
KuJoni

Imwe namkuti ku Joni uko	You, I am talking to you, there in Johannesburg (my husband)
Heeeeee	Yes
Ninjani wanihale ine?	Who must inherit me?
Amama eh he yayiwe	Mother, eh he yayiwe
Watola NyapaGiro	You have married NyapaGiro[18]
Hamama!	Mother!
Nyumba wazenga yangomi	You have built a rectangular [modern] house
Hamama!	Mother!
Chijaro chaphadiloku	It even has a door with a padlock
Hamama!	Mother!
Ninjani wanihale ine?	Who must inherit me?
Hamama ehe yayiwe	Mother, ehe yayiwe

A wife seeks remarriage. Her husband, who left a long time ago, has chosen to settle in Johannesburg where he lives with another woman.

Song no. 24
Kurya baka ndiko

Apongozi munganituma	Mother in law, if you ask me
Zawumenyepo pano	To come and eat with you
Kuphika nilije kumanya	To cook I don't know
Pakulya ndipo	To eat I do
Apongozi munganituma	Mother in law, you can ask me
Sinako mwana uyo	To pinch that child
Kuphika nilije kumanya pakulya ndipo	To cook, I don't know, to eat I do
Kupula niliji kumanya	To pound maize, I don't know
Kuphika nilije kumanya	To cook, I don't know
Apongozi munganituma	Mother in law, you can ask me

---

[18] The preferred, sometimes foreign woman, sometimes wealthy.

Sinako mwana uyo	To pinch that child
Kuphika nilije kumanya	To cook, I don't know,
Kurya bako ndiko	To eat only, yes
Apongozi munganituma	Mother in law, you can send me
bingako nkhuku izo	To chase those chickens
Kulima nilije kumanya pakurya ndipo	To hoe, I don't know, but to eat I do
Kulima nilije kumanya	To hoe, I don't know
Kuphika nilije kumanya	To cook, I don't know
Apongozi munganituma	Mother in law, you can send me
Sinako mwana uyo	To pinch that child
Kuphika nilije kumanya	To cook, I don't know,
Kulya baka ndiko	To eat is all I know

A lazy daughter-in-law who can perform neither domestic tasks nor the work of the fields.

Song no. 25
Amamavyara

Amamavyara	My mother in law,
Bakuya ku maji bamujima ine	She goes to the water to talk evil about me
Amamavyara	My mother in law,
Bakuya ku maji bamusesa ine	She goes to the water to talk evil about me

A daughter-in-law denounces her mother-in-law's slander against her.

Song no. 26
Mwana mubapire weya

Mwana wachizungu chino[19]	This child of the White people's world[20]

---

[19] Weya literally means "hair", and by implication the hairy skin of a goat which was used in the olden days to carry a baby.

186

Ndipo bapire weya!	How can I carry it in a skin?
Ahe yaya arere ndyeko nyama	Ahe yaya arere, I eat the meat
Mupete bapire mwana	Why go so far as to carry the child
Ahe here waya we	Ahe here, waya we
Arere dyeko nyama	I eat the meat
Mupete bapire mwana	And go as far as carrying the child [21]
Ahe eha mwana wachizungu chino!	Ah eh, child of the white people's world!
Ndiyo mubapire weya	It is he that you carry with hair,
Ahe here, waya we	Ahe here, waya we

Chorus

| Aherere waya aherere waya | Aherere waya, aherere waya |
| Aherere waya | Aherere waya |

A caricature of a husband who is not suitably concerned about his family in matters of dressing.

Song no. 27
Dyera

Banyake ndiwo yayi	Certain people are not much
Banyake ndiwo yayi	Certain people are not much
Kuchipinda mwawonako?	What have you seen in the bedroom?
Eh eh bakhalira dyela	Eh eh, they just stay there, coveting
Banyake ndiwo yayi	Certain people are not much
Banyake ndiwo yayi	Certain people are not much
Kubanalumi babene	The husbands of other women

Chorus

Oh oh bakhalira dyera	Oh oh they stay there coveting
Yebili dyera we	Yebili, coveting, we
Eh yayawe	Eh, yayawe

---

[20] *Bazungu* are the white people. Here the mother speaks of the modern times, which have been brought about by contact with the white people.

[21] These days the goat is for eating, not for carrying babies using the goat's skin.

Dyera ilo	Coveting that
Eh eh bakhalira dyera	Eh eh, they have remained there coveting

Kankhali kwetekwete[22]	Scratching the small pot, kwetekwete
Kankhali kwetekwete	Small pan, kwetekwete
Kubanalumi babene	Coveting other women's husbands
Yo oh bakhalira dyera	Yo oh, they have remained there coveting
Kankhali kwetekwete	Small pan, kwetekwete

A wife denigrates other women, accusing them of covetousness.

Song no. 28
Wangiloya

Uyo wangiloya	That one has bewitched me
Eyaye wangiloya	Eyaye, he has bewitched me
Eyaye wangiloya	Eyaye, he has bewitched me
Wakwela phezulu ng'endaba	He has climbed high up in the matter[23]
Eh wangithakata	Eh, he has bewitched me
Eyaye	Eyaye
Yerere wangithakata	Alas, he has bewitched me
Eyaye	Eyaye
Yerere wangithakata	Alas, he has bewitched me
Wakwela phezulu ng'endaba	He has climbed above with the matter

The spirit reveals to the victim the cause of the disease: witchcraft.

---

[22] Onomatopoeia.

[23] He has become too strong for me.

188

Song no. 29
Bamuzi uno nkhwerekwere

Bamuzi uno nanga unozge	Those of the village, even if you do a good thing
Nkhwerekwere nkhwerekwere	Slander, slander [ideophone]
Nanga unozge	Even if you do good
Nkhwerekwere nkhwerekwere	Slander, slander
Ine lero nanga unozge	Even if I do good today
Nkhwerekwere nkhwerekwere	Slander, slander
Bamuzi uno musinjilo	Those of the village, they despise me
Nkhwerekwere nkhwerekwere	Slander, slander

A daughter-in-law complains about mistreatment in her husband's village.

Song no. 30
Kwithu ku Loudon

Yirenga Yirenga[24]	Yirenga, Yirenga
Yirenga eh yaya lero	Yirenga, eh yaya, today
Yirenga Yirenga	Yirenga, Yirenga
Yirenga eh yaya lero	Yirenga, eh yaya, today
Yirenga	Yirenga
Ayirenga kwithu ku Loudon	Yirenga, our home is Loudon[25]
Yirenga	Yirenga
Ayirenga ku mugodi wandarama	Yirenga, there is a mine of money
Yirenga aye yaya eh eh	Yirenga, aye yaya, eh eh

Chorus

Banyake bakukhaliramo	Certain people don't know a thing
Banyake bakukhaliramo	Certain people don't know a thing

---

[24] First name of a young girl.

[25] Loudon is an important mission station established in 1902 in the South of Mzimba District, today often called Embangweni.

Banyake bakukhaliramo   Certain people don't know a thing
Kuli makani eh ku mphala   There are matters at the *mphala*[26]

Those who live around Loudon feel they are closer to Western civilization
than the others, hence they show a sort of scorn for the inhabitants of
the "bush."

Song no. 31
Tiwonjele Fumu

Tiwonjele fumu zawela weluwelu[27]   Let's greet the chiefs,[28] they have
                                       come (back)

Tiwonjele fumu zawela weluwelu   Let's greet the chiefs, they have come
                                       (back)

Tiwonjele fumu zawela weluwelu   Let's greet the chiefs, they have come
                                       (back)

A welcoming song during the "descent" of the spirits.

Song no. 32
Mazombwe

Kwerakwera   Climb, climb
Nikwere uli nili Mazombwe   How will I climb, I am Mazombwe,
Kwerukweru   Climbing, climbing
Nikwere uli?   How can I climb?
Nthenda yikunisuzga kwerukweru   The illness is troubling me, climbing,
                                     climbing.

Nikwere uli?   How can I climb?
Nili Mazombwe yayiwe   I am Mazombwe, yayiwe

---

[26] Mphala was the place where the men congregated, and also the place to settle
all sorts of issues.

[27] ideophone formed from the verb *kuwela*: to return.

[28] Here the chiefs are the possessing spirits with their different names.

Nikwere uli?	How can I climb?
Nikwere uli kuchanya kwerukweru?	How can I climb to heaven, climbing, climbing?
Nikwere uli?	How can I climb?
Kuli kunjira vibanda kwerukweru	There are spirits (in heaven), climbing, climbing
Nikwere uli?	How can I climb?
Nili Mazombwe eyi eyi	I am Mazombwe, eyi eyi
Nikwere uli Kum'dima ine?	How can I climb in the darkness?
Nili Mazombwe yayiwe	I am Mazombwe, yayiwe
Mwana wali kumsana amama	I have a child on my back, mother
Nili Mazombwe yayiwe	I am Mazombwe, yayiwe
Katundu wali pa mutu	A load is on my head
Nikwere uli nili Mazombwe yayiwe	How can I climb, I am Mazombwe, yayiwe
Manyi nikwere uli amama	I do not know how to climb, mother
Nili Mazombwe kwelawe	I am Mazombwe, now you climb

Imitation of an insect when the possessed, on all fours, moves after the manner of this insect *mazombwe*.

Song no. 33
Chiwayawaya

Chiwayawaya	Poverty [ideophone]
Basungwana bakulira	The girls cry to become nannies
Gelu gelu gelu[29]	Girl, girl, girl
Chiwayawaya	Poverty
Basungwana bakulira gelu	The girls cry to become nannies, girl
Chiwayawaya	Poverty
Basungwana bakulira	The girls cry to become nannies,
Gelu gelu gelu	Girl, girl, girl
Chiwayawaya	Poverty
Anyamata[30] bakulira boyi[31]	The boys cry to be house boys

---

[29] From the English word *girl*.

Chiwayawaya	Poverty
Anyamata bakulira boyi	The boys cry to be house boys,
Boyi boyi we	Boys, boys, we
Chiwayawaya	Poverty

Dire need pushes the girls and the boys to look for jobs as domestic workers.

Song no. 34
Chitewe mwataya

Chitewe mwataya	You have thrown the skin clothing
Tayataya mdambo taya	Have thrown it into the swamp
Chitewe mwataya	You have thrown the skin clothing
Tayataya mdambo taya	Have thrown it into the swamp

Chorus

| Chitewe mwataya | You have thrown the skin clothing |
| Ahe yaya lero ahe yay lero ahe yayawe | Ahe yaya, today, ahe yaya, today, ahe yayawe |

A song of Chitiviri (dance) which hunters used to sing when they had brought game. In this dance one sways the buttocks a lot at the risk of dropping the skin clothing. *Chitewe* is a Ngoni word.

Song no. 35
Tambala walira ku msito

Kokoriko	Kokoriko
Tambala walira ku msito[32] oho	The cock has crowed in the forest, oho
Kokoriko	Kokoriko

---

[30] Linguistic deviation, for usually people would say: _banyamata_ as is the case with _basungwana_ (girls).

[31] From the English word *boy*.

[32] From the Bemba *umushitu*: "high evergreen forests along rivers."

Tambala walira ku msito oho	The cock has crowed in the forest, oho
Kokoriko	Kokoriko
Tambala walira ku msito kokoriko	The cock has crowed in the forest, Kokoriko
Ole anha	Ole anha
Tambala walira ku msito kokoriko hole	The cock has crowed in the forest, Kokoriko hole
Tambala walira ku msito	The cock has crowed in the forest

An allusion to the cock which people use for the sacrifice of *chilopa*. People sing this song during the moments of the sacrifice.

Song no. 36
Baming'ombwa[33]

Hete hete baming'ombwa bakulira	Hete hete, the ming'ombwa is singing
Hete hete baming'ombwa akulira	Hete hete, the ming'ombwa is singing
Kwacha	It's dawn
Hete hete baming'ombwa bakulira	Hete hete, the ming'ombwa is singing
Hete hete baming'ombwa akulira	Hete hete, the ming'ombwa is singing,
Kwacha	It's dawn

The Mng'ombwa is a bird which one hears singing at dawn. It is possible that the Vimbuza spirits disguise themselves as birds in this case.

Song no. 37
Bamumphala

Sore sore sore	Sorry, sorry, sorry
Sore bamumphala eh	Sorry, those in the (bachelors') dormitory
Sore sore sore	Sorry, sorry, sorry
Sore bamumphala eh	Sorry, those in the dormitory
Sore	Sorry

---

[33] The name of a mountain bird.

Nanga muvwale jekete, sore	Even if you wear a jacket, sorry
Sore bamumphala eh	Sorry, those in the dormitory
Ine sore nanga muvwale jekete	Me, sorry, even if you wear a jacket
Ine sore sore bamumphala eh	I feel sorry for those who live in the dormitory

A song pointing out that if you are single, you are not recognized in society.

Song no. 38
Bulangeti

Zawona ine zawona ine	They [the problems] have seen me
Zawona ine zawona ine	They [the problems] have seen me
Bulangeti munyumba mulije	There is no blanket in the house
Nizgokere uku	If I turn this side
Kuli chibowo kuli chibowo	There is a hole, there is a hole
Chibowo chalutilira asweni bane	The hole continues [to grow], husband of mine
Nizgokere ukuso	If I turn to the other side
Kuli chibowo kuli chibowo	There is a hole there is hole
Chibowo chalutirira asweni bane	The hole continues [to grow] husband of mine
Bulangeti munyumba mulije	There is no blanket in the house

Without a child the couple cannot be happy.

Song no. 39
Wakwera lore

| Wakwera lore,[34] heyaye | You have climbed a lorry, heyaye |
| Wakwera lore wakwera pa chimbwe | You have climbed a lorry, you have climbed a hyena |

---

[34] From the English word "lorry."

Wakwera lore heyaye lero babe[35]	You have climbed a lorry, heyaye, today, sir
Wakwera lore heyayiwo	You have climbed a lorry, heyayiwo
Wakwera lore wakwera pa chimbwe	You have climbed a lorry, you have climbed a hyena
Wakwera lore heyaye	You have climbed a lorry heyaye

The song deplores the way a woman is dancing, alluding to her erotic movements.

Song no. 40
Ine lero namtengwa

A Nyirongo, lero naliwona ine	Mr. Nyirongo, today I have seen [the problem]
Fumbani mwana winu	Ask your son
Mwana wino wachona lero	Your son has stayed away too long
Ine lero namtengwa	Today I am getting married
Chihengo ncha kwadada	The winnowing basket comes from my father
Kalikhezo nkha kwadada	The spoon comes from my father
Thawulo nda kwadada	The towel comes from my father
Kalikose kumnyumba yane	Everything in my house (comes from my father)
Ine lero namtengwa	Today I am getting married
Sokola nja kwadada	The basket comes from my father
Kamusi nkha kwadada	The [pounding] pestle comes from my father
Kasefa nkha kwadada	The little sieve comes from my father
Kalikose kamnyumba yane	Everything in my house (comes from my father)
Ine lero namtengwa	Today I am getting married

The woman demands divorce as her husband does not return from South Africa, so that her father has to provide all her needs.

---

[35] Babe is a term of respect to address elder persons of male gender.

Song no. 41
Namulandane

Namulandane namulanda	I am an orphan, I am an orphan
Nichali papano namulanda	I am still here, the orphan
Nichali kulindirira namulanda	I am still waiting, me the orphan
Namulandane namulanda	I am an orphan, I am an orphan
Nichali papano namulanda	I am still here, the orphan
Nichali kulindirira namulanda	I am still waiting, me the orphan

Chorus

Adada	A father
Nilije	I don't have
Amama	A mother
Nilije	I don't have
Nichali kubalindirira namulanda	I am still waiting for him [the husband]

The song is about a woman whose husband went to work abroad a long time ago. She is obliged to wait for him and complains about her state.

Song no. 42
Dende palije

Bakwawo	Those from her home
Mbwambwambwa	"Welcome, welcome!" (Ideophone)
Bakwawo	Those from her home
Mbwambwambwa	"Welcome, welcome!" (Ideophone)
Bakuchanalume	Those from the husband's side
Dende[36] palije ehe dende palije	"There is no relish, ehe, there is no relish."
Bakuchanalume	Those from the husband's side
Dende palije ehe dende palije	"There is no relish, ehe, there is no relish"

---

[36] *Dende* refers to all relish: fish, chicken, vegetables.

It is wrong for a wife to welcome only people from her own family, she should be equally welcoming to the relatives from her husband's side.

Song no. 43
Mwana wa nkhuku

Mwana wa nkhuku eh	Child of a chicken, eh
Mwana wa nkhuku chenjera	Child of a chicken, beware
Mwana wa nombo	Child of a vulture
Mwana wa nkhuku chenjera	Child of a chicken, beware

This song is intoned by the dancer while he is preparing himself to claim gifts from the audience. He may pick a baby or a small child for whom ransom must be paid.

Song no. 44
Wamupala moto

Uyo mwana wane	That child of mine
Wamupala moto lero wamupala	He is going to take fire today, he is going to take fire
Uyo lero	There he is today
Wamupala moto lero wamupala	He is going to take fire today, he is going to take fire
Hoyo leye	Hoyo leye
Wamupala moto lero wamupala	He is going to take fire today, he is going to take fire
Uyo mwana wane	There he is, child of me
Wamupala moto lero wamupala	He is going to take fire today, he is going to take fire
Uyo Rosi	There she is, Rosi
Wamupala moto lero wamupala	She is going to take fire today, she is going to take fire

A song which talks of getting married, to start a new home.

197

Song no. 45
Kalulu nisebele nayo

Kalulu nisebele yayaya	I play with the rabbit, yayaya
Ziroya nisebele nayo yayaya	Ziroya, I play with her, yayaya

Chorus

Nane nisebele nisebele	And me, let me play, let me play
Pamuchenga panekha	On the sand, alone
Ahele yaye ahele yaye hanh	Ahele yaye, ahele yaye hanh
Ahele yaye ahele yaye hanh	Ahele yaye, ahele yaye hanh
Nane nisebele nisebele	And me, let me play, let me play
Pamuchenga panekha	On the sand, alone

Kalulu tilye tose yayaya	Rabbit, can we eat together, yayaya
Kalulu tilye tose	Rabbit, can we eat together
Kalulu tilye naye yayaya	Rabbit, can we eat together, yayaya

Kalulu and Ziroya are crafty personalities in oral tradition

Song no. 46
Siyageza

Siyageza	We do not bathe
Siyageza kumchapa saro, Ziroya	We do not bathe at the washing place,[37] Ziroya
Siyageza	We do not bathe
Siyageza kumchapa saro, Ziroya	We do not bathe at the washing place, Ziroya
Tiwerenge eh	Lets go back, eh
Anh hole hole we Ziroya	Anh hole, hole we, Ziroya
Anh hole hole we Ziroya	Anh hole, hole we, Ziroya
Kuli mwezi we	There is moonlight we

---

[37] The washing place is where clothes are washed. The Ngoni phrase "siyageza" is not complete, it should read "asigeza" to convey the meaning intended.

Anh hole hole eh Ziroya
Anh hole hole eh ziroya

Anh hole, hole we, Ziroya
Anh hole, hole we, Ziroya

A lesson in hygiene and good behaviour, not to bath where drinking water is drawn.

Song no. 47
Kayuni Karyarya

Kayuni karyarya	The little cunning bird
Kawila mulomo kawila	It has been caught by the beak, it has been caught
Kayuni karyarya	Little bird cunning
Kawila mulomo kawila	It has been caught by the beak, it has been caught
Tuyuni turyarya	Little birds cunning
Twawila mulomo twawila	They have been caught by the beak, they have been caught
Tuyuni turyarya	Little birds cunning
Twawila mulomo twawila	They have been caught by the beak; they have been caught
Twawila	They have been caught
Twawila mulomo twawila	They have been caught by the beak. they have been caught

Originally an *Ulumba* (cult of hunting) song, it was taken later by *Vimbuza* to serve as a caricature in the description of crafty and wicked individuals.

Song no. 48
Ku Joni bakopakochi?

Ku Joni mukopakochi?	What do you fear in Johannesburg?
Banalume bamuzi uno?	The menfolk of this village?
Ku Joni bakopakochi?	What do you fear in Johannesburg?
Bali komako mu Zungu?	Have they killed a White man there?

199

The song incites the men to leave and look for work in the mines of the South.

Song no. 49
Mphapo yamala a Nyirongo

A Nyirongo[38] lero	Mr Nyirongo, today
A Nyirongo ehe luluwe	Mr Nyirongo, ehe luluwe
A Nyirongo lero	Mr Nyirongo, today
A Nyirongo we ah eh eh	Mr Nyirongo, we ah eh eh

Chorus

Balitola gozoli[39] a Nyirongo luluwe	He has caught syphilis, Mr Nyirongo, luluwe
Gozoli wamala mphapo	The syphilis has finished his seed
A Nyirongo luluwe	Mr. Nyirongo, luluwe
Luluwe luluwe luluwe luluwe	Luluwe luluwe, luluwe luluwe
Balitola gozoli a Nyirongo luluwe	He has caught syphilis, Mr Nyirongo, luluwe
Gozoli wamala mphapo	The syphilis has finished his seed
A Nyirongo luluwe	Mr. Nyirongo, luluwe

Migrant labour leads to the contraction of sexually transmitted diseases that lead to sterility.

Song no. 50
Apongozi mbaheni

Apongozi mbaheni	My Mother in law, she is bad
Banibisa karata 'ne henya	She has hidden from me the letter, true!

---

[38] Nyirongo is the name that carries all the shortcomings of men.

[39] A strange term which appeared when this disease became known, imported probably by migrant workers returing to the country,

200

Apongozi mbaheni	My Mother in law, she is bad
Banibisa karata 'ne henya	She has hidden from me the letter, true!
Apongozi mbaheni	My Mother in law, she is bad
Banibisa karata 'ne henya	She has hidden from me the letter, true!

Chorus

Hayiwe	Hayiwe
Diyere wera eh	My Dear come back, eh
Hayiwe	Hayiwe
Diyere wera eh hayiwe	My Dear come back, eh hayiwe
Hayiwe	Hayiwe
Diyere wera eh	My Dear come back, eh
Hayiwe	Hayiwe
Diyere wera eh hayo	My Dear come back, eh hayo
Mbaya mu Joni wane hayo	[I plead with you,] my dear, return from Johannesburg

The mother in-law prevents her daughter-in-law from having news of her husband who works in Johannesburg.

Song no. 51
Imwe mkuya ku Joni mwe

Imwe mkuya ku Joni imwe	You who go to Johonnesburg, you
Mukabanenerengeko	[If you meet him], tell him
Ine nkhule anyinamwe nkhule	That I am naked and your mother as well
Mukabanenerengeko	[If you meet him], tell him
Ine nkhule anyinamwe nkhule	That I am naked and your mother as well
Ine nkhule	I am naked
Ahole	Ahole
Anyinamwe nkhule	Your mother is naked

| Mwana wakwenda mumanja | I carry the child in my hands[40] |
| Ine nkhule anyinamwe nkhule | I am naked and your mother as well |

The song portrays the problem of migrant labourers who spend a very long time abroad (*machona*) and whose family at home lacks material support.

Song no. 52
Kumitala

Kumitala kuli moto iwe yayi we	Polygamy is fire, you, no, you
Dyela lane iwe	My desires, you
Yayiwe	Yayiwe
Dyela lane iwe	My desires, you
Dyela lane yayi oh	My desires, no, no
Ati nakhalira dyela para namnyinu'we	They say I stay because of my desires, my friends
Dyela lane iwe	My desires, you
Yayiwe	Yayiwe
Dyela lane iwe	My desires, you
Yayiwe	Yayiwe
Dyela lane lamitala	My desires in polygamy

Despite its painful aspects, polygamy proves to be a refuge for certain women.

Song no. 53
Tamala wabenge mwanalume

Mwana wane Tamala	Tamala, my child,
Wabenge mwanalume	If only she had been a boy
Eh yayi lero	Eh, no, today [It's not the case]
Mwana wane Zifa	Zifa, my child,
Wabenge mwanalume	If only she had been a boy

---

[40] I have no cloth to carry my child on my back.

| Eh yayi lero | Eh, no, today |

Chorus

Yawa	Yawa
Yawa eh yawe	Yawa, eh yawe
Yawa	Yawa
Yawa eh yawe	Yawa, eh yawe
Yawa	Yawa
Yawa eh yawa yawa yawa	Yawa, eh yawa, yawa yawa

The woman regrets not having a boy child who would help in her everyday tasks, as her husband has abandonned her.

Song no. 54
Tamala

Mwana wane Tamala	My child Tamala
Nkhanyeze[41] hanh woya woya	She is a little star, hanh woya woya
Nkhanyeze	She is a little star

The song appreciates the beauty of a girl child.

Song no. 55
Jesinala

Baba wako baba wako Jesinala	Bear your own [child], bear your own, Jesinala
Anhe he he he	Anhe he he he
Baba wako eh hole baba wako eh	Bear yours, eh hole, bear yours, eh
Ziwelelane Jesinala ha ah eh yaye	Return the complement, Jesinala, ah eh he yaye
Eh he Jesinala baba wako eh	Eh he, Jesinala, bear yours, eh
Baba wako nilelepo ahe he he eh	Bear your own [child] so that I can cradle it, ahe he he eh

---

[41] Name derived from the Ngoni word *inkanyezi* (star).

Baba wako Jesinala baba wako eh he	Bear yours, Jesinala, bear yours, eh he
Ziwelelane Jesinala ha ah eh he yaye	Return the complement, Jesinala, ah eh he yaye
Here yere Jesinala baba wako eh	Here yere Jesinala, bear yours, eh
Nilerepo Jesinala anhe he hehe	That I dandle it, Jesinala, anhe he hehe
Baba wako nilelepo ha	Bear yours that I dandle it, Jesinala, ha
Nilerepo Jesinala ah ha hehe yaye	That I dandle it, Jesinala, ah ha hehe yaye

The song is about a sterile woman who beats up the children of her co-wives. She is accused of not understanding maternal sentiments.

Song no. 56
Sanje

Nawe mphambede wako	You, it is your bed
Nane mphambede wane	Me, it is my bed
Zina awoli babo sanje	It is his wife who is jealous
Awoli ba Nyirenda	The wife of Mr Nyirenda
Zina awoli babo sanje	It is his wife who is jealous
Awoli ba Nyirenda	The wife of Mr Nyirenda
Zina awoli babo sanje	It is his wife who is jealous

This song expresses the jealousy between co-wives.

Song no. 57
Baba wako

Ati baba wako	People say, bear your own [child], bear yours
Eya eya eya	Eya eya eya
Baba wako lero	Bear your own today
Eya eya eya	Eya eya eya
Ngati ndine lero	As it is with me
Eya eya eya	Eya eya eya
Ujiwonere lero	See for yourself today
Eya eya eya	Eya eya eya

Baba wako le	Bear yours today
Eya amama eya amama eya	Eya mother, eya mother, eya
Baba wako le	Bear yours today
Eya amama eya amama eya	Eya mother, eya mother, eya
Baba ndiye eh	Bear it, it is you
Eya amama eya amama eya	Eya mother, eya mother, eya
Baba wako eh	Bear yours eh
Eya amama eya amama eya	Eya mother, eya mother, eya
Baba wako tikuwone	Bear your own, so that we see
Eya eya eya	Eya eya eya
Baba wako ndiyo	Bear your own indeed
Eya eya eya	Eya eya eya
Ujiwonere eh	That you see for yourself, eh

The song is about a jealous wife who has the habit of beating or pinching the children of her co-wives, having no child herself.

Song no. 58
Waziroya

Waziroya[42] hole	Waziroya hole
Amama	Mother
Waziroya we yahole	Waziroya, you, yahole
Amama	Mother
Amame ine	Mother, me
Zeru zamnyumba iyi	The wisdoms of this house[43]
Amama aye eh	Mother, aye eh
Zikunitola mtima	They [the wisdoms] take my heart from me
Amama eh Waziroya	Mother, eh, Waziroya
Nkhulekera dara kuyowoya	I have stopped talking about it, deliberately
Yayawe yayawe ya	Yayawe, yayawe, ya

---

[42]   A Zulu name.

[43]   Implied is the co-wife's house.

Waziroya   Waziroya
This song expresses the pain of broken family relations.

Song no. 59
Mwanituka waka

Tuke tuke[44]	To insult, to insult
Mwanituka waka lero eh	You have insulted me for nothing today, eh
Ine nkuwela eh naulanda wane he ine	I return home, he, with my misery, he, me!
Tuke tuke	To insult, to insult
Wanituka waka eya we	You have insulted me for nothing, eya, you
Ine nkuwela eh naulanda wane lero'ne	Me, I return home, eh, with my misery, today

Chorus

Badada	My father
Bali kumuwongo	He will support me
Bamama	My mother
Bali kumuwongo lero mwe	She too will support me today

A woman complains about the ill treatment she endures from her husband.

Song no. 60
Mandaba

Mandaba hiye lero mandaba	This court case, hiye, this court case
Hiye lero	Hiye, today
Mandaba kubenge kwithu mandaba	If my case would be heard at my village

---

[44] Ideophone derived from the verb *kutuka*, to insult.

Hiye lero mandaba	Hiye, today in the assembly
Mandaba ngichochozela mandaba[45]	That court case, I would whistle about it
Hoya hoya mandaba	Hoya hoya, that court case
Mandaba hiye lero mandaba	Assembly hiye, today assembly
Hiye lero	Hiye today
Mandaba ngivumeleni mandaba	You counsellors, accept me, you counsellors
Mandaba kubenge kwithu mandaba	If the case would be heard in my village, you counsellors
Hiye lero	Hiye, today [there would be no problem]

The text is in Ngoni and Tumbuka

In a divorce case, a woman thinks that she won't win her case because the tribunal can only be partial with regard to a stranger in the community (in a patriarchal and virilocal system).

Song no. 61
Bana pa mulomo

A Mkandawire	Mr Mkandawire
Anh oh oh hole	Anh oh oh hole
Lekani bayowoyenge bana pa mulomo	Let him to talk and talk, with his big mouth
Nabo eh ah hole	Him, eh, ah, hole
A Mkandawire	Mr Mkandawire
Anh eh he he hole	Anh eh he he hole
Bana pa mulomo	His has a big mouth
Anh hole anh hoyi	Anh hole anh hoyi
Lekani bayawoyenge mba Mkandawire	Let him to talk and talk, this is Mr Mkandawire
Anha ya eh nha he heyi	Anha ye eh nha he heyi

---

[45] She would whistle because in her village she would win the case.

Lekani bayawoyenge mba Mkandawire	Let him to talk and talk, this is Mr Mkandawire
Anh heya yahoyi	Anh haye yahoyi
Hoyayiwe	Hoyayiwe
Bana pa mulomo	He has a big mouth

The song criticizes people who are gossips

Song no. 62
Gulozela lachona

Gulozela[46] lachona muye	Gulozela, he has stayed away a long time, muye
Iye ehe	He ehe
Muye	Muye
Iye ah eh yaye	He ah, eh yaye
Gulozela lachona muye	Gulozela, he has stayed a long time muye
Iye ehe	He ehe
Muye	Muye
Iye ehe Gulozela lachona muyeni wane	That Gulozela, he has stayed a long time, that husband of mine
Aye nikhale niyeni muyeni wane aye	Aye, I am crying for my husband, aye
NyaBanda wajikoma muye	NyaBanda, she has killed herself, muye
Iye eh	He eh
Muye	Muye
Iye anh eh	He anh eh
NyaBanda wajikoma muye	NyaBanda, she has killed herself, muye
Iye ah eh NyaBanda wajikoma	He ah eh NyaBanda, she has killed herself
Wajikoma muyeni wane	She has killed herself, husband of mine

---

[46] Gulozela or Golovela is a fictional and pejorative name which evokes a dishonest person. Today one hears a third version: Guluvya.

The prolonged stay of migrant labourers can lead the women left in the village to divorce. This is a *vyanusi* divination song, performed by a man, playing the role of a woman.

Song no. 63
Chilijemwana nimbeta

Chilijemwana[47] yayawe	She has no child, yayawe
Chilijemwana	She has no child
Kunkhuni bawela waka hole	Collecting firewood, she comes back with nothing, hole
Chilijemwana	She has no child

Chorus

Chilijemwana	She has no child
Chilijemwana	She has no child
Chilijemwana nimbeta	She who has no child is a celibate
Hanh eh ya eh yayawe	Hanh eh ya eh yayawe
Chilijemwana	She who has no child
Kudambo bawelo waka hole	Drawing water, she comes back with nothing
Walije mwana nimbeta	Those without a child are just spinsters.

The song downgrades the social status of the married woman who has no child.

Song no. 64
Ndimwe anzathu

Ndimwe anzathu welewele	You, our fellows, welewele[48]

---

[47] This is a name based on the root -*lije* (to be without), referring to a co-wife who has no child.

[48] An ideophone depicting the movement of the carriers winding their way through the bush.

Welewele welewele	Welewele, welewele
Mukatenge mutokoma	Go and take the load
Ndimwe anzathu welewele	It is you, those from home, welewele
Welewele welewele	Welewele, welewele
Ndimwe anzathu welewele	It is you, those from home, welewele

During the First World War, local men were recruited to transport provisions and munitions to the front, supporting the British troops fighting the Germans. The Ngoni chief Chimtunga, king of Mombera Kingdom, refused the recruitement of his men and was detained in Nsanje for ten years.

Song no. 65
Mwana kumunena yayi

Eh, mwana kumutuka yayi	Eh, don't insult the child
Wamwe maji ghaye munthumbo	Let her drink water for her stomach[49]
Odi, amulamu mwana kumunena yayi	Excuse me, my brother in law, don't talk bad to the child
Wamwe maji ghaye munthumbo	Let her drink water for her stomach

Chorus

Oli, oli, hihihi, hihihi	Oli, oli, hihihi, hihihi
Oli, oli, hihihi, hihihi	Oli, oli, hihihi, hihihi
Niwele uli nkhakana yayi	How shall I go [home]? I didn't say no [to get married to you].
Odi, asebele, mwana kumunena yayi	Excuse me, *asebele*[50] do not talk bad to the child
Wamwe mayi ghaye munthumbo	Let her drink water for her stomach
Odi, athenga, mwana kumunena yayi	Excuse me, my go between, do not talk bad to the child
Wamwe maji ghaye munthumbo	Let her drink water for her stomach

---

[49] Proverbial expression which people use to say "to live in peace."

[50] Term of address between fellow parents in-law ("the ones I can play with").

Chorus

Oli, oli, hihihi, hihihi
Oli, oli, hihihi, hihihi
Nkhakananga, eh

Oli, oli, hihihi, hihihi
Oli, oli, hihihi, hihihi
I did refuse, eh

A woman is encountering difficulties in her marriage. Her parents intervene with the husband's family.

Song no. 66
Mukatore ng'ombe zinu

Odi athenga adada bakumuchemani	Excuse, my go-between, my father calls you
Mukatore ng'ombe zinu	Go and collect your cows
Odi atatavyara athenga bakumuchemani	Excuse me, father–in–law, the go-between is calling you
Mukatore ng'ombe zinu	Go and collect your cows
Ati nkuyimanya yayi	People say, I don't know it [marriage]
Nkuyimanya yayi nthengwa iyi lero	I do not know this marriage any more, even if that finishes the marriage

A daughter in-law demands a divorce

Song no. 67
Ntchito nkukagozga

Banyumba iyi baya kwabo	The people of this house have gone to their place
Banyumba iyi baya kwabo	The people of this house have gone to their place
Banyumba iyi baya kwabo	The people of this house have gone to their place
Para baya kwabo ntchito nkugozga	When they go to their place, they do nothing but gossiping
Nihambe munyumba iyi	If I go to that house

Namuti jiso go bali kuya, baya kwabo	If I go, I find that they have gone to their place
Nihambe munyumba iyi	If I go to that house
Para namkuti go baliya, baya kwabo	When I go, I find that they have gone to their place
Baya kwabo baya kwabo	They have gone to their home, they have gone to their home
Para baya kwabo ntchito nkugozga	When they go to their place, they do nothing but gossiping

A mother in-law reproaches her daughters in-law for their behaviour.

Song no. 68
Bakukana ubali

Abo na abo	Those over there and those over there
Baukana ubali	They have refused the kinship
Abo na abo	Those over there and those over there
Baukana ubali	They have refused the kinship
A Khuni na abo	Mr Khuni and those over there
Baukana ubali	They have refused the kinship
Ibo bakuti	They say
Ndamzenga pa ndekha	I am going to build alone [at my own place]
Ine a Khuni abo	Me, Mr Khuni, and those over there

Chorus

| Bakuti ndamzenga pa ndekha | They say that I am going to build alone |

Social conflicts often lead to the break up of a village.

Song no. 69
Tamkumana ku Ghana

| Nalira Bata Maluwa | I cry for the Bata Maluwa shoes |
| Maliposa nga kumunda | The Bata Maliposa shoes are for working in the garden |

212

Oyayiwe	Oyayiwe
Oyayiwe, tamkumana ku Ghana	Oyayiwe, we are going to meet in Ghana
Mukanigulire Bata	Buy Bata [Maluwa] for me
Maliposa nga kumunda	[Bata] Maliposa are just for the garden
Oyayiwe	Oyayiwe
Oyayiwe tamkumana ku Ghana	Oyayiwe, we are going to meet in Ghana

Chorus

Oyayiwe	Oyayiwe
Oyayiwe	Oyayiwe
Oyayiwe	Oyayiwe
Oyayiwe tamkumana ku Ghana	Oyayiwe, we are going to meet in Ghana
Oyayiwe	Oyayiwe
Oyayiwe	Oyayiwe
Oyayiwe	Oyayiwe
Oyayiwe	Oyayiwe
Oyayiwe tamkumana ku Ghana	Oyayiwe we are going to meet in Ghana
Salu ya Bata Maluwa we[51]	[Buy for me] Bata Maluwa cloth, we
Maliposa nga kumunda	Maliposa are just for the garden
Oyayiwe	Oyayiwe
Nalira Bata Maluwa we	I cry for Bata Maluwa, we

The song is a critique of men who are not concerned about what their spouses wear. The song goes back to 1963 when Inkosi Mzukuzuku of Embangweni went to Ghana and reported that he had seen the high life there. Ghana as the first independent African country (1957) had became the symbol for the advanced lifestyle in the minds of the villagers in Mzimba.

---

[51] *We* is an expression of insistence.

Song no. 70
Nichali mwana mchoko

Aheyaye aheyaye aheyaye	Aheyaye, aheyaye, aheyaye
Ndadabwa ndadabwa	I am surprised, I am surprised
Yoyoyoyo	Yoyoyoyo
Soka ilo	Bad luck is this
Yoyoyoyo	Yoyoyoyo
Soka ilo	Bad luck is this
Nichali mwana mdoko	I am still a small child, Sir,
Ambuye nadabwa	I am surprised
Yoyoyoyo	Yoyoyoyo
Soka ilo	Bad luck is this
Nichali mwana mdoko	I am still a small child, Sir,
Ambuye nadabwa	I am surprised

A young married woman dreads her husband's sexual activity. Possibly this marriage was concluded by eloping the girl.

Song no. 71
Mwana watowela nkhaza

Mwana wamucigololo kutowela nkhaza	The child of adultery is just too beautiful
Wajilenga	She has made herself like that
Mwana wamucigololo kutowela nkhaza	The child of adultery is just too beautiful
Wajilenga	She has made herself like that

Chorus

Ayiwe	Ayiwe
Oyayiwe	Oyayiwe
Ayiwe	Ayiwe
Oh holewe	Oh holewe
Ayiwe	Ayiwe
Oh yayiwe	Oh yayiwe
Ayiwe	Ayiwe

214

Oyayiwe	Oyayiwe
Wajilenga	She has made herself like that
Mwana wamucigololo kutowela thamo	The child of adultery is just too much
Wajilenga	She has made herself like that
Mwana wamucigololo kutowela thamo	The child of adultery is just too much
Wajilenga	She has made herself like that

Although an illegitimate child may have good qualities, that is often not respected.

Song no. 72
Nkhagonenkhu?

Nkhagonenkhu?	Where can I sleep?
Pakati pali mwana wane he eh	In the middle is the child.
Lekani zeru zakufwa nazo eh yaya	Stop your deadly behaviour [wisdom]!
Eti pakati pali mwana wane he eh yaya	Is there not the child in the middle?
Lekani zeru zakufwa nazo eh yaya	Stop your deadly behaviour [wisdom]!

Traditionally the couple had to abstain from sexual relations for at least two years to avoid births being too close to each other (*nthumbirwa*).

Song no.73
Bawona awoli bawo biza

Bawona awoli bawo biza	He has seen his wife coming
Baleka gule	He has stopped dancing
Bawona asweni bawo biza	She has seen her husband coming
Baleka gule	She has stopped dancing

People object to the hypocrisy which is found in jealous couples.

Song no. 74
Lumbiri Laruta

Bakwenda yumoyumo, lumbiri laruta — They have gone one after the other, the story has spread

M'nyumba yakwamama bana bamara — In the house of my mother the children are finished

Bakwenda yumoyumo, lumbiri laruta — They have gone one after the other, the story has spread

Chorus

Chiwawa[52] — Be qiet!

Enya — Yes

Chiwawa — Be qiet!

Enya — Yes

Chiwawa — Be qiet!

Nilekenge chara kwimba chibanda wuka — I will not stop singing; spirit get up!

M'nyumba yakwamama bana bamara — In the house of my mother the children are finished

Bakwenda yumoyumo lumbiri laruta — They have gone one after the other, the story has spread

M'nyumba yakwamama bana bamara — In the house of my mother the children are finished

Bakwenda yumoyumo lumbiri laruta — They have gone one after the other, the story has spread

This is a household in which the children are dying one after the other and the story has spread.

Song no. 75
Chirimbanyungu

Oyaye oyaye, chirimbanyungu[53] — Oyaye oyaye, chirimbanyungu

---

[52] Chiwawa is used to impose silence.

[53] Chirimbanyungu is the name of a plant used for a poison ordeal.

Oyaye oyaye, chirimbanyungu	Oyaye oyaye, chirimbanyungu
Chirimbanyungu chamara <u>b</u>antu	Chirimbanyungu has finished people
Oyaye chamara <u>b</u>anto	Oyaye it has finished people
Chirimbanyungu chamara <u>b</u>antu	Chirimbanyungu it has finished people
Oyaye chamara <u>b</u>anto	Oyaye it has finished people

Someone has used the plant of *chirimbanyungu* to kill a lot of people. The existence of this plant is held secret for fear of causing more deaths.

Song no. 76
Rondo

Rondo aye Rondo[54]	Rondo, aye Rondo
Anh eh he Rondo ahe Rondo	Anh eh eh Rondo, ahe Rondo
Wiza mpanda wanga Rondo	He is going to sow poison, Rondo
Anyina uhambe	Mother of Uhambe[55]
Anh eh he Rondo ahe Rondo	Anh eh eh Rondo, ahe Rondo
Wiza mpanda wanga Rondo	He is going to sow poison, Rondo
Pena pa mzere	Somewhere in the ridges
Anh eh he Rondo ahe Rondo	Anh eh eh Rondo, ahe Rondo
Wiza mpanda wanga Rondo	He is going to sow poison, Rondo

Rondo is a Virombo spirit. These spirits are of Chewa origin, where they are called *zirombo*.

Song no. 77
Adada mukabakomera dala

Adada bakanangachi pakubakomela dala	My father, what wrong did he do to kill him deliberately?
Ayiwe yaye mwatondeka	Ayiwe yaye you have failed
Adada bakanangachi pakubakomela dala	My father, what wrong did he do to kill him deliberately?

---

[54] Rondo is a spirit of Chewa origin.

[55] The translation of this name is "You must go."

Olewe yaye mwatondeka	Olewe yaye, you have failed
Mwatondeka ndimwe yaye	It is you who has failed, yaye
Mwatondeka ndimwe yaye mwatondeka	You have failed, it is you, yaye, you have failed

A man is accused to have caused someone's death by sorcery.

Song no. 78
Hedemani

Hedemani eyaye	Headman, eyaye
Hedemani eyaye	Headman, eyaye
Zani pano mutangalire pano	Come here, stand with your legs apart
Achikanga eyaye	Chikanga,[56] eyaye
Bakuchema eyaye	He is calling, eyaye
Zani pano mutangalire pano	Come here, stand with your legs apart

The song was used during exorcisms at Chikanga's place, being intoned precisely at the moment that Pilatu 'shaved' (*kumeta*) the witches.

Song no. 79
Perekani kwa Chikanga

Perekani perekani	Hand over, hand over
Perekani para muli nazo Perekani	Hand over, what you have with you, hand it over
Perekani kwa Chikanga	Hand it over to Chikanga
Perekani para muli nazo Perekani	Hand over, what you have with you, hand it over
Eh eh yayawe	Eh eh yayawe
Perekani para muli nazo Perekani	Hand over, what you have with you, hand it over
Eh eh yayawe	Eh eh yayawe

---

[56] For more about the Nchimi Chikanga see: Boston Soko, *Nchimi Chikanga. The Battle against Witchcraft in Malawi*, Blantyre: CLAIM-Kachere, 2002.

Perekani para muli nazo Perekani	Hand over, what you have with you, hand it over
Mukaninenanga	You called me names
Perekani para muli nazo Perekani	Hand over, what you have with you, hand it over
Para mwakoma mwananga	If you have killed, you are wrong
Perekani para muli nazo Perekani	Hand over what you have with you, hand it over
Amdala mukulowa	Old man, you are a wizard
Perekani para muli nazo Perekani	Hand over, what you have with you, hand it over
Mwabira pa chande[57]	What you have done is obvious
Perekani para muli nazo Perekani	Hand over, what you have with you, hand it over
Musana padera	It can all be seen
Mukukoma basukulu	You kill school children
Perekani para muli nazo perekani	Hand over, what you have with you, hand it over
Vinyanga ukazuzi	The [witchcraft] horns are vicious
Perekani para muli nazo Perekani	Hand over, what you have with you, hand it over
Mwana wakulera wekha	The child you have raised yourself
Perekani para muli nazo Perekani	Hand over, what you have with you, hand it over
Pamanyuma ukukoma	After that you kill him
Perekani para muli nazo Perekani	Hand over, what you have with you, hand it over
Chinyanga chinonono	The horn is hard
Perekani para muli nazo Perekani	Hand over, what you have with you, hand it over
Para mwakoma mwananga	If you have killed, you are wrong
Perekani para muli nazo Perekani	Hand over, what you have with you, hand it over

---

[57] Proverb which explains that one is aware of what is happening in secret (Mwabira pa chande, musana padera).

A *makwaya* song used during divination at Chikanga's.

Song no. 80
Bangeya ku Mtenthe

Tamtora Bangeya ku Mtenthe eh	We are going to bring Bangeya from Mthente,[58] eh
Eh eh nilinde eh nilinde nilinde nilinde	Eh eh, wait for me, eh eh, wait for me
Galimoto[59] yawela niwelengewe	The motor car has come, let me go home
Nilinde eh eh nilinde nilinde nilinde	Wait for me, eh eh, wait for me, wait for me, wait for me
Nilinde galimoto yawela niwele uli?	Motorcar, wait for me, how can I get home?
Nilinde eh eh nilinde nilinde nilinde	Wait for me, eh eh, wait for me, wait for me, wait for me

Bangeya NyaLongwe was a great lady diviner and healer of the 1930s and 1940s. Her village was situated along the river Mtenthe at Mphongo on the West of Mzimba town.

Song no. 81
Wanga

Wanijimira chiphurusi[60]	You have dug up for me the *chiphurusi* root
Wayesa nga nimunkhwara	Do you believe that this is medicine?
Ati yaye yare–yare–yare, ati yaye–yaye	Ati yaye yare–yare–yare, ati yaye–yaye Is it not spread, spread, spread[61]

---

[58] In some areas Chimbwazi is substituted for Mthente.

[59] In Swahili *gari* means any kind of cart, and if that cart is propelled by fire (*moto*), it becomes a motor car (*garimoto*).

[60] A root without medicinal value.

[61] This refers to the herbalist spreading her or his medicinal roots for sale.

Eh wanga umene	Eh, nothing but poison
Wanijimira chiphurusi	You have dug up for me the *chiphurusi* root,
Wanijinira chiphurusi	You have dug up for me the *chiphurusi* root,
Mwayesa nga nimunkhwara	Did you believe that it was medicine?
Ahe yaye yere yare[62]	Ahe yaye yere yare
Ahi yaye yare – yare yare yare	Ahe yaye, spread it you did, spread it, spread it, spread it
Eh wanga umene	Eh, poison in fact

An accusation against false healers.

Song no. 82
A Jele Bafipa

A Jele <u>B</u>afipa bala 'kwiza para	Jele, the Black one, here he comes
Ti<u>b</u>apokerere	Let's welcome him
Ti<u>b</u>amange	Let's arrest him
A Jele <u>B</u>afipa bala 'kwiza para	Jele, the Black one, here he comes
Ti<u>b</u>apokerere	Let's welcome him
Ti<u>b</u>amange	Let's arrest him

Chorus

Heza eh heza eh	Heza eh heza eh
Heza eh	Heza eh
Tibamange	Let's arrest them
Heza eh	Heza eh
Tibamange	Let's arrest him
Tibamange	Let's arrest him
Tibamange	Let's arrest him
Tiyeni tibamange tiyeni tiwonge inde	Let's arrest him, let's thank him, yes
Tiyeni tiwonge	Let's thank him
Tibamange	Let's arrest him

---

[62] Ideophone which signifies that one spreads something (in a repeating way).

The Jele line is the one from which have come the Ngoni Chiefs in the area of Mzimba. Originally from Zululand this clan has a clear skin. In the song people express their surprise on meeting a Jele who has black skin, but the song does not speak of a living Jele but of a Jele spirit. The man alluded to was from Baleni Village, T.A. Mzukuzuku, Embangweni, Mzimba.

Song no. 83
Matete

Matete ghakulakata mudambo	The reeds are losing their leaves down at the swamp
Zamuwone he eh	Come and see, he eh
Matete ghakulakata mudambo	The reeds are losing their leaves down at the swamp
Zamuwone he eh zamuwone he eh	Come and see, he eh, come and see, he eh
Zamuwone matete ghakulakata mudambo	Come and see the reeds are losing their leaves down at the swamp
Zamuwone he eh zamuwone	Come and see, he eh, come and see
Matete ghakulakata	The reeds they are losing their leaves

The song is about a strange thing that occurred in a village. Usually reeds do not lose leaves; something unheard of has happened.[63]

Song no. 84
Katantha

Wiza katantha mulupiri wiza na vula	Katantha has come to the mountains, he has come with rain
Wiza katantha mulupiri wiza na vula	Katantha has come to the mountains, he has come with rain
Eh yilokwenge	Eh, it is going to rain

---

[63] There may be a reference to spirit possession here.

222

Yirokwenge vula yirokwenge	It is going to rain, it is going to rain
Yirokwenge vula yirokwenge	It is going to rain, it is going to rain
Eh yilokwenge	Eh, it is going to rain

Katantha is the spirit which leads the dancers to climb on posts, the wall and the ceiling of the house where the session takes place.

Song no. 85
Maloto

Hawuhawu,[64] maloto	Hawuhawu, dreams
Eyaye	Eyaye
Ho – we	Ho – we
Eyaye eh nalota chigololo	Eyaye eh, I have dreamt of adultery
Nalota nyifwa yane	I have dreamt of my death
Hawuhawu maloto	Hawuhawu, dreams
Eyaye	Eyaye
Ho – we	Ho – we
Eyaye eh nalota Chigololo	Eyaye eh, I have dreamt of adultery
Nalota nyifwa yane	I have dreamt of my death

A warning to those who commit adultery. In the past this crime was punishable by death for both men and women.

Song no. 86
Chiyekeza

Chiyekeza	Chiyekeza
Zamuwone Chiyekeza, dade	Come to see Chiyekeza, father
Chiyekeza	Chiyekeza
Zamuwone chiyekeza dade	Come to see Chiyekeza, father
Chiyekeza	Chiyekeza
Zamuwone chiyekeza dade	Come to see Chiyekeza, father

---

[64] Hawuhawu is a cry which people use to chase the lion when it is in the village.

223

The song is about an expert dancer, no doubt of the "profane" vimbuza type.

Song no. 87
Kukoma Munthu

Wamukoma munthu kuleka njati	You have killed a person instead of a buffalo
Yamnofu ukulu	Which has much flesh
Chiwombele wombele[65]	You are shooting randomly
Namukoma munthu kuleka njati	I am killing a buffalo instead of a person
Yamnofu ukulu	Which has much flesh
Hoho yaye hoho yaya	Hoho yaye, hoho yaya
Chiwombele wombele	You are shooting randomly
Namukoma njati namuleka muntu	I am killing a person instead of a buffalo
Chiwombele wombele	You are shooting randomly
Wamunofu wukhomi wamnofu wukhomi	Of flesh, thick of flesh, thick
Chiwombele wombele	You are shooting randomly

The song denounces sorcery.

Song no. 88
Kalizga ng'oma

Kalizga ng'oma mbiri yaya	Beater of drums, his fame has gone far
Kalizga ng'oma mbiri yaya	Beater of drums, his fame has gone far
Ha mbiri yaya kalizga ng'oma	Ha, the fame has gone far of the beater of the drums

---

[65] Usage of class 7 indicating the "manner of being or of acting" with repetition of the verbo nominal theme to indicate that an action is executed no matter how and several times.

Ha mbiri yaya kalizga ng'oma

Ha, the fame has gone far of the beater of the drums

Song of encouragement to the drummer so that he may beat more loudly.

Song no. 89
Msekeleleni

Uyo wawela	That one, he has returned
Sekelelani wawela sekelelani	Cheer him, he has returned, cheer him
Uyo waphuma	That one has come back[66]
Sekelelani wawela sekelelani	Cheer him, he has returned, cheer him
Uyo waphuma	That one has come back
Sekelelani wawela sekelelani	Cheer him, he has returned, cheer him

This is a song used during a vimbuza session to greet a returning spirit.

Song no. 90
Tiwonane

Tiwonane eh eh	Let us see, eh eh
Para ndizenecho[67] pera	If they are the real ones [the spirits]
Para ndiwe m'biza, m'bemba wonane	If you are Bisa or Bemba, let's see
Mwe eh eh ziwonane zekha	You, eh eh, let them show themselves
'Wonane mwe	Show yourselves
Munyinu uyo papo	Your friend [the possessed person] is there

The spirits fight to take their places during the dance session. That explains why the dancer sometimes changes the dance suddenly, passing from Vimbuza to Vyanusi, for example.

---

[66] The first stanza expresses the spirit's return in Tumbuka, the third in Ngoni.

[67] Understood as referring to *nthenda* (diseases or their spirits) – class 10.

Song no. 91
Muliro

Kozga muliro anh mvibanda	Light the fire that I see the spirits, anh are, spirits
Kozga muliro anh mvibanda	Light the fire that I see the spirits, anh are, spirits

Reference to Vimbuza spirits which are coming to possess a person

Song no. 92
Phuma Mngoma

Phuma Mngoma,[68] anyoko palije	Get out, Mngoma, your mother is not here
Phuma Mngoma anyoko palije	Get out, Mngoma, your mother is not here
Olewe yaye yaye anyoko palije	Olewe yaye yaye, your mother is not here
Yaye yaye anyoko palije	Yaye yaye, your mother is not here
Phuma mngoma anyoko palije	Get out, Mngoma, your mother is not here
Phuma mngoma anyoko palije	Get out, Mngoma, your mother is not here
Yaye yaye anyoko palije	Yaye yaye, your mother is not here
Yaye yaye anyoko palije	Yaye yaye, your mother is not here

An appeal to the spirits of Mngoma (Vyanusi), so that they may leave the place to make room for another category of spirits.

---

[68] Mngoma is a Vyanusi spirit.

226

Song no. 93
Kayisasule

Wayiwona kayisasule	You have seen it, eat it raw
Tiyeni sasula para uli na nkhongono	Let's go, eat it raw if you are strong enough
Sasula we	Eat it raw you
Tiwone para ungasasula	Let's see if you can eat it raw
Ndiwe pera sasula	It is you alone, you must eat it raw
Nkhongono zako nzenecho?	Are you really strong?
Tiyeni tiwone	Let's see

It is about an animal designated as a sacrifice, be it a rooster, be it a goat. People intone this song at the moment when the sick person is going to drink some blood (rite of *chilopa*).

Song no. 94
Kawuswe

Sebeza Kawuswe[69] walala	Do your work, Kawuswe is (still) sleeping
Munizomelere waka	Accept me as I am
Sebeza wole	Work, wole
Sebeza walala	Work, he is sleeping
Nili mwana wam'nyinu	I am the child of your friend
Sebeza wole	Work, wole
Sebeza kawuswe walala	Work, Kawuswe is (still) sleeping

Kawuswe or Luwuswe is a Vimbuza spirit that is invoked here to wake up.

---

[69] Kawuswe is an individual spirit of Bemba origin.

Song no. 95
Mngoma

Tola iwe	You take it!
Tola tola Mngoma	Take, take, Mngoma
Tola iwe	You take it!
Tola iwe	You take it!
Tola tola mngoma	Take, take, Mngoma

"Tola iwe" is a kind of encouragement which the audience shouts at the dancer so that he may redouble his frenzy. Mngoma are spirits of the Vyanusi family.

Song no. 96
Sebele nayane

Sebele nayane	With whom should I play?
Hoiye ah eh yaye	Hoiye ah eh yaye
Sebele na baRungwana	I will play with the Arabs[70]
Sebele na baRungwana	I will play with the Arabs
Eh eh eh eh eh eh	Eh eh eh eh eh eh
Sebele na baRungwana	I will play with the Arabs

Allusion to the spirits of the Swahili slave traders who have brought spirits from that region. BaRungwana are sometimes referred to as BaNdongondo in the SinNgoni languge.

Song no. 97
Baleza

Baleza bali ng'ang'a	The lightning! How it is flashing! They are flashes

---

[70] This is a reference to spirits from East Africa.

228

Tichite uli apa baleza aba	What should we do with such a lightening?
Mwe baleza bali ng'ang'a	You see the lighting, it is flashing
Tichite uli apa?	What should we do now?
We tizingirire nawe nku?	You, where should we take you?
Para ndiwe M'biza, M'Bemba	If you are a Bisa or a Bemba
Panji Makhabango	Or Makhabango

The spirits have disguised themselves as flashes, and people don't know which spirit is which. Bisa and Bemba are *vimbuza* spirits from Zambia, Makhabango are spirts from East Africa, and strong ones for that.

Song no. 98
Nkhalamu

Nkhalamu yalira jaraniko	The lion has roared, shut there (the door)
Nkhalamu yalira jaraniko	The lion has roared, shut there (the door)
Jaraniko mwe nkhalamu yalira	Shut the door, please, the lion has roared.
Ndatenge ndi nkhalamu	I thought it was a lion
Kweni ndi Vimbuza	But it is Vimbuza
Mwe penjani munkhwara	You, look for medicine
Ndi nkhalamu yayi	It is not a lion
Penjani penjani mwe	Look, look, please

The spirit which possesses the person has disguised itself as a lion.

Song no. 99
Chitimukulu

| Chitimukulu[71] wawela eh | Chitimukulu has returned, eh |
| Wawela hoye he | He has returned, hoye he |

---

[71] Chitimukulu is a big chief who fought the Ngoni of Mpezeni in Zambia.

Chitimukulu wawela	Chitimukulu has returned
Munivwarike mangerengeza	Put the dancing bells on me
Chitimukulu wawela eh	Chitimukulu has returned, eh
Wawela hoye he	He has returned, hoye he
Chitimukulu wawela	Chitimukulu has returned
Munivwarike mangerengeza	Put the dancing bells on me

Chitimukulu is the paramount chief of the Bemba in Zambia. But here we are talking about a spirit which people attribute to his dynasty. It is a song of initiation or welcome at the beginning of a session

Song no. 100
Muhalule

Amuhalule[72]	Muhalule
Amuhalule akurya nyama ya ng'ombe	Muhalule is eating the meat of a cow
Amuhalule	Muhalule
Amuhalule akurya nyama ya ng'ombe	Muhalule is eating the meat of a cow

The song is intoned during the moments when the possessed person swallows pieces of raw meat, which people don't usually eat.

Song no. 101
Saru yamaluwa

Saru yamaluŵa nkhayivwara karede	The cloth with flowers, I wore it a long time ago
Saru yamaluŵa nkhayivwara kare	The cloth with flowers, I wore it a long time ago
Nkhayivwarira palwande	I had worn it on the side
Saru yamaluŵa nindayivware karede	The cloth with flowers, I haven't worn it for a long time

---

[72] Muhalule was the father of Inkosi Mzukuzuku. He was rich in cattle, and owned more than even Inkosi ya Makosi M'mbelwa. Mhalule spirits are found even in Nkhatabay and Rumphi and are of the Vyanusi type..

Saru yamaluŵa nindayivware kare	The cloth with flowers, I haven't worn it a long time
Ndayivŵarila pali kanthude	I wear it because there is something
Muza tambala wanga opanda bweyade	My cock has come without his hair (feathers)
Wayivŵarila pali kanthu eh	She wears it, because there is something, eh
Saru yamaluwa nindayivware kare	The cloth with flowers, I haven't worn it for a long time
Saru yamaluwa nindayivware kare	The cloth with flowers, I haven't worn it for a long time
Wayivŵarila pali kanthu eh	She wears it because there is something, eh

It's about the costume the victim is wearing during the dance. One is called to wear it only when one is afflicted by the Vimbuza "disease." The cock refers to the *chilopa* ceremony, where the dancer will drink its blood.

Song no. 102
Kajibambe

Wafika Kajibambe	Kajibambe has arrived
Wabwera Kajibambe	Kajibambe has come

It is about a type of possession which makes the dancer to walk on live charcoal without hurting himself or to pick up burning coal with his hands.

Song no. 103
Basenga

Kwenda mukwata mukwata	Walk like trotting

| Basenga basenga | The Senga, the Senga[73] |
| Kwenda mukwata mukwata | They trot, they trot |

The Senga are Virombo spirits The song describes how one dances possessed by a Senga spirit.

Song no. 104
Chimbwi wakulira

Nhunhu[74] uwele uwele oh yaye	Nhunhu, come back, come back, oh yaye
Para chimbwi wakulira	When the hyena is crying
Chimbwe wamala bantho	The hyena has finished people
Nhunhu uwele yanh eh eh yanh eh	Nhunhu, come back, yanh eh eh, yanh eh
Para chimbwi wakulira	When the hyena is crying
Chimbwe wamala bantho	The hyena has finished people
Anh he uwele yanh eh oh yawe	Anh he, that you return, yanh eh oh yawe
Wakulira para kwacha	She cries when the day is dawning
Chimbwe wamala bantho	The hyena has finished people
Anh eh uwela anh eh yayawe	Anh eh, that you return, anh eh yayawe
Wanitolera para kwacha	She has grabbed me at the beginning of the day

The hyena in this song stands for spirits which attack people even in daylight, like a hyena that has caught rabies begins to attack people.

Song no. 105
Mwana wane wakula

| Mwana wane wakula lero | My child, today she has grown up |

---

[73] The Senga are a tribe in Eastern Zambia which influencd the *vimbuza* dance a lot.

[74] Onomatopoeia, the cries of hyena.

Timulange ninchembere	Let's instruct her in womanhood
Mwana wane wakula lero	My child, today she has grown up
Anh he anhe anhe he he	Anh he anhe, anhe he he
Timulange ninchembere	Let's instruct her in womanhood
Mwana wane wakula lero	My child, today she has grown up
Ha ho eh hi eh ya eh	Ha ho eh hi eh ya eh
Timulange ninchembere	Let's instruct her in womanhood

One of the songs presented immediately after initiation.

Song no. 106
Uthwasile

Uthwasile eh yanh hoyi hoya	He is being born
Wathwasanga	He has just been born
Uthwasile eh yanh hoyi hoya	He is being born
Wathwasanga	He has just been born
Eh uthwasile ha uthwasile ha	Eh, he is being born
Wathwasanga[75]	He has just been born

The song marks the beginning of Vyanusi possession in an individual. This individual has the possibility of becoming a diviner healer.

Song no. 107
Jikamalalo

Jikamalalo[76] eh	Jikamalalo, eh
Eh eh Jikamalalo	Eh eh, Jikamalalo
Bayesa jikama eh	They should kneel down
Jikamalalo eh	Jikamalalo, eh
Eh eh eh Jikamalalo	Eh eh eh, Jikamalalo

---

[75] *Kuthwasa* refers to the appearance of the new moon, hence the possible translation: to be born. Here the spirit that has come causes the new birth.

[76] Jikamalo is a spirit that makes a person bend his or her legs to dance on their knees.

Bayesa jikama eh	They should kneel down

A momentary manifestation of possession during which the victim dances by knocking the knees against the ground.

Song no. 108
Chota Muliro

Chota Muliro	Chota Muliro
Chota Muliro, eh mvibanda	Chota Muliro, eh these are spririts
Chota Muliro	Chota Muliro
Chota Muliro, eh mvibanda	Chota Muliro, eh these are spririts

The dancer reveals to the audience the name of the spirit which possesses him: Chota Muliro. (*Muliro* means fire.)

Song no. 109
BaMnjiri

Bamnjiri	You, Mnjiri[77]
Jimani bamnjiri jimani	Dig, Mnjiri, dig
Bamnjiri	You, Mnjiri
Oh oh le jimani ba Mnjiri jimani	Oh oh le dig Mnjiri, dig
Bamnjiri	You, Mnjiri
Jimani bamnjiri jimani	Dig, Mnjiri, dig
Eh awe	Eh, awe
Jimani bamnjiri jimani[78]	Dig, Mnjiri, dig

These spirits are like moles.

---

[77] Mnjiri is a type of mole.

[78] While singing this song the dancer makes movements with a little implement imitating the digging of a mole.

234

Song no. 110
Gwaza Lu Bemba

Gwaza lu Bemba eh
Wathyola mkondo wane nakwiya eh

Gwaza lu Bemba eh
Wathyola mkondo wane nakwiya eh

Gwaza lu Bemba eh
Wathyola mkondo wane nakwiya eh

Gwaza lu Bemba eh
Wathyola mkondo wane nakwiya eh

Gwaza the Bemba eh
Gwaza the Bemba, you have broken
my spear, I am angry, eh
Gwaza the Bemba, eh
Gwaza the Bemba you have broken my
spear, I am angry, eh
Gwaza the Bemba, eh
Gwaza the Bemba, you have broken
my spear, I am angry, eh
Gwaza the Bemba, eh
Gwaza the Bemba, you have broken
my spear, I am angry, eh

One of the songs which people intone on going out, at the end of the sssion. Usually the dancer holds a spear in the right hand while jumping, his back facing the door. Gwazu Lu Bemba is a legendary figure in the Limpopo Province of South Africa.

Song no. 111
Chikurukuru chiri kumtima

Asebele[79]
Asebele, para m'kuya kudambo
Muniwuzge tumabo
Nchikurukuru chiri kwa Bemba

Nchikurukuru chiri kumtima nchibanda

Asebele
Asebele

Sebele
Asebele, when you go to the river
tell me a word
It is big, a very big thing, it is with the
Bemba
It is big, a very big thing in my heart,
there is a ghost
Sebele
Sebele

---

[79] Term of address used between parents in law of both sides

235

Asebele, para m'kuya kumphasa	Asebele, when you go to fetch reeds for making mats
Muniwuzge tumabo	Tell me a word
Nchikurukuru chiri kwa Bemba	It is big, a very big thing, it is with the Bemba
Nchikurukuru chiri kumtima nchibanda	It is big, a very big thing in my heart, there is a ghost

Chorus

Aliyere vikwimba	Aliyere, they sing
Anh eh vikwimba eh	Anh eh, they [the spirits] sing, eh
Zanitola mabo leza wawa	They have stolen my voice, lighting has fallen
Vibanda wuka leza eh	Spirits wake up, there is lightning, eh

Allusion to a "descent" of the spirits disguised as lightning.---

Song no. 112
Nisebele na baNgoni

Sebele na ba Ngoni	I must play with the Ngoni
Ye	Ye
Na ba Ngoni	With the Ngoni
Wiza mukale	He has arrived, the angry one
Na ba Ngoni	With the Ngoni
Ye	Ye
Na ba Ngoni	With the Ngoni
Wiza mukale	He has arrived, the angry one
Na ba Ngoni	With the Ngoni
Niye	That I go
Na ba Ngoni	With the Ngoni

The spirits disguise themselves as Ngoni warriors.

Song no. 113
Nkhanga

Jopilo[80] kuli nkhanga zikupala

Jopilo kuli nkhanga zikupala

Kasi nthenda iyi yitimare?

Apa nkhanga zikupara!

Jopilo jopilo jopilo

Nkhanga izi mwe zananga

Jopilo kuli nkhanga zikupala

Jopilo, there are guinea fowls scratching

Jopilo, there are guinea fowls scratching

Will this disease finish us?

The guinea fowls are scratching!

Jopilo Jopilo jopilo

These guinea fowls are destructive

Jopilo, there are guinea fowls scratching

The spirits disguise themselves as guinea fowls.

Song no. 114
Chakupa Leza

Tikawone Mazabamba chakupa Leza

Tikawone Mazabamba

Chakupa Leza

Ah tikawone Mazabamba

Chakupa Leza iwe

Ahe he eh yayiwe, eh

Tikawone Mazabamba

Chakupa Leza naleka

Ahe he eh yayiwe eh yayiwe

Tikawone Mazabamba

Let's go to see Mazabamba the gift of God[81]

Let's go to see Mazabamba

Gift of God

Ah, let's go to see Mazabamba

You the gift of God

Ahe he he yayiwe eh

Let's go to see Mazabamba

The gift of God, I can't help it

Ahe he he yayiwe eh yayiwe

Let's go to see Mazabamba

It is believed that the Vimbuza disease is God given.

---

[80] Ideophone which expresses the jumps of the guinea fowl

[81] The expression "gift of God" refers to a lame person, and we accept that God has made him such.

Song no. 115
Nthenda ya vyanusi

Bamulengerera mwana wane	They have cast a spell on my child
He ya he	He ya he
Bamulengerera mwana wane	They have cast a spell on my child
He ya he	He ya he
Nthenda ya Vyanusi yikulima yayi[82]	Being possessed by Vyamusi, one does not cultivate
Eh ya he	Eh ya he
Nthenda ya Vyanusi yikulima yayi	Being possessed by Vyamusi, one does not cultivate
Eh ya he	Eh ya he
Bamulengerera yula mwana	They have cast a spell on that child
Ho ya he	Ho ya he
Bamulengerera yula mwana	They have cast a spell on that child
Ho ya he	Ho ya he

People believe that the *Vimbuza* disease is willed by God.

Song no. 116
Wawela lu Bemba

Uyo uyo, wawelo LuBemba eh	That one, that one, the Bemba has come back, eh
Uyo uyo, wawelo LuBemba eh	That one, that one, the Bemba has come back, eh
Wawela LuBemba kwa mazi gha mtambo	The Bemba has returned with the water from the clouds
Uyo uyo, wawela LuBemba eh	That one, that one, the Bemba has come back, eh
Uyo uyo, wawelo LuBemba eh	That one, that one, the Bemba has come back eh

---

[82] A person struck by this 'disease' suffers for a long time and is incapable of working well.

Wawela LuBemba kwa mazi gha mtambo The Bemba has returned with the water
from the clouds

The song evokes the "descent" of the spirits, here like a rain storm. Many
spirits come from Bembaland in Zambia.

Song no. 117
Uteka

Nkhendanga iwe eh eh yaya zeza	You, I was walking , wondering with my mouth agape
Nkhendanga iwe eh eh yaya zeza	You, I was walking , wondering with my mouth agape
Nkhendanga iwe eh eh yaya zeza	You, I was walking , wondering with my mouth agape
Nkhendanga iwe eh eh yaya zeza	You, I was walking , wondering with my mouth agape
Nkhizanga ine eh eh yaya we	I was coming, eh eh, yaye we
Nkhizanga ine eh eh yaya we	I was coming, eh eh, yaye we
Nkhasanga uteka ukwewuka zeza	I found the grass being blown away, my mouth agape
Nkhasanga uteka ukwewuka zeza	I found the grass being blown away, my mouth agape

The song refers to witchcraft, which makes things happen without
human involvement.

Song no. 118
Mazabamba

Kazambara wawela	Kazambara, he has returned
Ahe yaya ahe he yayawe	Ahe yaya, ahe he, yayawe
Tikawone Mazabamba	That we may go to see Mazabamba
Kazambara wawela	Kazambara, he has returned
Ahe yaya eh he eh yaya	Ahe yaya, eh he, eh yaya
Kazambara wawela	Kazambara, he has returned

Kazambara wawela tikaone Kazambara	Kazambara has returned, let's go and see Kazambara
Kazambara iwe	You, Kazambara, you
He eh yayawe	He eh, yayawe
He eh yayawe tikaone Kazambara	He eh, yayawe let's go see Kazambara[83]

This is one of the songs to welcome the spirits at the beginning of a session.

Song no. 119
Nthenda ni makorakora

Iyaya ya lero yawa eh	Iyaya ya , today [the spirt] has come ["fallen"]
Iyaya ya lero yawa eh	Iyaya ya , today [the spirt] has come ["fallen"]
Elele yawa ere iya elele yawa eh	Alas it has come ["fallen"]
Elele ndivyo mwanichemeranga	Alas is that why you have called me?
Elele yawa, eh?	Elele yawa, eh?
Mwanichenera wanuzi yawa eh	You have called me, the wanuzi [spirit], it has come ["fallen"]
Nthenda ni makorakora	The illness can catch anyone
Elele yawa eh elele yawa	Alas! she has fallen, eh alas! she has fallen
Yikukora na balanda	It catches even the orphans
Elele yawa eh elele yawa	Alas! she has fallen, eh alas! she has fallen
Zingilila tikumane[84]	Go around and let's meet
Eh yawa eh elele yawa	Eh, she has fallen, eh alas! she has fallen

The Vimbuza illness can strike no matter whom. It is a warning to those who mock Vimbuza adepts.

---

[83] Kazambara and Mazabamba are spirits of Bemba or Bisa origin.

[84] A riddle to which the response is 'a belt'.

Song no. 120
Chikunibenda

Chikunibenda chikunibenda yeyeye	It is stalking me, it is stalking me,
Chikunibenda we chikunibenda	Stalking me, stalking me
Chikunibenda chikunibenda yeyeye	It is stalking me, it is stalking me,
Chikunibenda we chikunibenda	Stalking me, stalking me
A Mwiza[85] na Chite yeyeye	Mwiza and Chite, yeyeye
A Muliro na Ng'ona yeyeye	Muliro and Ng'ona, yeyeye
ehe he ayowe	ehe he, ayowe
Bwana[86] Chibesa eh	Bwana Chibesa, eh
Bwana Chibesa yeyeye	Bwana Chibesa yeyeye
Bwana Chibesa eh	Bwana Chibesa, eh
Bwana Chibesa yeyeye	Bwana Chibesa yeyeye
Bwana Chibesa eh	Bwana Chibesa,eh
Ahe bwana Chibesa eh	Ahe Bwana Chibesa eh
Nam'nyinu chikunibenda ye eh he he eh	Me, your friend, I am being stalked
Chikunibenda yeye eh he he ayowe	It is stalking me, yeye eh, he he ayowe
Chikunibenda ye	It is stalking me

Reference to the Vimbuza illness. While *ntehnda* means illness,
Chinthenda means a big illness, in this case spirit possession.

Song no. 121
Iyo Mphanda

Iyo Mphanda[87] mwayiyangana	There is Mphanda, you have seen them

---

[85] Mwiza and the names following are names of spirits.

[86] Bwana is a borrowing from Swahili. The word was used during the colonial
era as a term of address to Whites. The commandants of district (D.C.) were
called Bwana Mdogo; the governor of the territory was called Bwana Mkubwa.
Today the term is used increasingly as a term of address to the indigenous people:
superiors, cadres, senior functionaries, etc.

[87] Mphanda or Mamphanda designates agroup of spirits of the *Virombo* type.

Mwayiwona yikujuma mukutenthema	You have seen them roaring, and you tremble
Mwayiiwona Mphanda	You have seen Mphanda
Mwayiwona mwayiwona eh	You have seen them, you have seen them
Mwayiwona mwayiwona eh	You have seen them, you have seen them
Mwayiwona Mphanda	You have seen Mphanda
Deledele,[88] zikulira	Deledele, they roar
Mwayiwona zikulira mupatuke	You have seen them roaring, give way to them
Mwayiwona Mphanda	You have seen Mphanda
Mwayiwona Mwayiwona eh	You have seen them, you have seen them, eh
Mwayiwona Mwayiwona eh	You have seen them, you have seen them, eh
Mwayiwona Mwayiwona	You have seen them, you have seen them

The spirit appears as a lion roaring.

Song no. 122
Nthenda ukali

Nthenda ukali he ho ehe eh	It's a strong illness, he ho, ehe eh
Nthenda ukali he howe ehe eh eh	It's a strong illness, he howe, ehe eh eh
Nthenda amama hehe hole hehe hehe	The illness, mother, hehe hole, hehe hehe
Nkhawone amama ah hole yehe hehe	I should go and see my mother, ah hole, hehe hehe
Nthenda ukali howe ehe eh eh	It's a strong illness, he ho, ehe eh
Nthenda ukale hehe hole hehe	It's a strong illness, hehe, hole, hehe
Nkhawone baBiza kuLuBemba	That I go and see the Biza in Bembaland

---

[88] Onomatopoeic for movement.

Ole ehe hehe	Ole, ehe hehe
Nthenda ukali hehe hole hehe eh	It's a strong illness, he ho, ehe, eh
Nkhawone b̠adada kuLuBemba	That I may go and see my fathers in Bembaland[89]
Ole ehe hole	Ole, ehe, hole
Nkhawone b̠aChota kuLuBemba	That I may go and see Chota in Bembaland

The spirits afflicting the Vimbuza dancers are often perceived as originating from and dwelling in Bembaland in Zambia,

Song no. 123
Nkhalamu zalira

Eyaya eh he he	Eyaya, eh he he
Ah eh yaya eh	An eh, yaya eh
Nkhalamu zalira ku Msoro[90]	Lions have been roaring at the Msoro tree.[91]
Para zikujuma muniwuske ine	When they are roaring, wake me up
Anh eh yaye he he	Anh eh, yaye he he
Ahe yayawe nkhalamu zalira ku Msoro	Ahe yayawe, lions have cried at the Msoro tree
Ku Msoro nkhawoneko	I should go and check there at the Msoro tree
Anh eh yaye eh he he	Anh eh, yaye eh, he he
Ah eh yaya eh nkhalamu zalira ku Msoro	Ah eh, yaya eh, lions have been roaring at the Msoro tree
Nkhawoneko nkhawoneko	That I may go see there, that I may go see there
Ah eh yaya eh nikwele uli?	How shall I climb there?

---

[89] The Biza are spirits who originate from Bembaland. Chota is a particular spirit of the Biza category.

[90] Pseudolachnostylis maprouneifolia Pax (Euphorb).

[91] The Msoro tree is in several cultures a place of sacrifice and prayer. The Tumbuka used to build a little shrine (*kavub̠a*) under it.

Ah eh yaya eh nkhalamu zalira ku Msoro | Ah eh, yaya eh, lions have been roaring at the Msoro tree
Para zikujuma nkhalingeko | When they roar, let me go to check
Ah eh yaya eh yayawe | Ah eh, yaya eh, yayawe
Ah eh yayawe nkhalamu zalira ku Msoro | Ah eh yayawe, lions have been roaring at the Msoro tree

Some spirits appear as lions and are found under the Msoro tree.

Song no. 124
Kazembe

Akazembe[92] balikuya we[93] | Kazembe, he is gone.
Waya[94] eh waya eh | He is gone, eh he, is gone, eh
Eh waya we | Eh he, has gone, we
Waya Kazembe walikuya | He has gone, Kazembe has departed
Walikuya ku Malambo[95] we | He went to Malambo,[96] we
Waya eh waya eh | He has gone, eh he, has gone, eh
Waya Kazembe walikuya | He has gone, Kazembe has departed

People believe that there are comings and goings of spirits. When a victim of the *Vimbuza* disease suffers that signifies that the spirits are there. When she has a period of respite, that means the spirits have returned to their country. Kazembe is the name of a Lunda dynasty in Zambia.

---

[92] Kazembe is a Bemba chief's spirit.

[93] The (we) of emphasis

[94] Waya is Bemba for going.

[95] Malambo is the area to the East of Zambia from which the possession dance came.

[96] Malambo is in the eastern region of Zambia close to the border of Malawi and is often used as aterm for the whole country.

Song no. 125
Kasaru kafuma kwa dada

Yayi nakana	No, I refuse
Kasaru kafuma kwa dada	The little cloth, it comes from my father
Oh ving'unu pera	Oh, such impundence
Nidikiskeko NyaLongwe	Cover me, NyaLongwe
Yayi nakana kasaru	No, I refuse the little cloth
kafuma kwa dada ako	It comes from my father
Oh ving'unu pera	Nothing but impudence
Analumi imwe, mwakhutapo moba	You man (husband), you are drunk with beer
Chinthumbo babarara kwa ine, he	The big belly shakes towards me, he
Mwaluwa naku Joni	You have forgotten even (going to) Johannesburg
Oh ving'unu pera	Oh, such impundence

A man who does not manage to assure the upkeep of his wife.

Song no. 126
Sima

Sima[97] niphikire uku niphikire uku	I cook *sima* for this side and for that side
Mama	Mother
Dende nigabire uku nigabire uku	Relish I must share this side and that side
Mama	Mother
Ine ziyendere	Must I go
Ziyendere uku ziyendere uku mama	Must I go here and there, mother?
Ine ziyendere	Must I go
Ziyendere uku ziyendere uku mama	Go here and there mother
Ine navwara mayinga yinga mayinga	I am just running around, this way and

---

[97] Main dish in this district.

245

yinga[98]	that way
Nimayingayinga haye	I am just running about, haye
Navwrmayula – yula[99] nikayula – yula	I am despised, dispised I am,
Mama	Mother

A woman, who is still involved in the traditional system of communal meals, complains that there is no longer reciprocity among the young.

Song no. 127
Kasero kane

Kasero kane kana wenje lero	The little basket of mine has hairs today.
Eyaye kasero kane kana wenje lero	Eyaye, the little basket of mine has hairs today.
Kakwenda museya – museya[100]	It is so light, just light[101]
Kana wenje kana wenje, iwe	It has hairs, it has hairs, you
Eyaye kasero kane kana wenje eh	Eyaye, the little basket of mine has hairs, eh
Kayenda museya – museya	It is so light, just light
Kasero kane ku madimba ine	The little basket of mine, in the garden at the stream
Eyaye kasero kane kana wenje lero	Eyaye, the little basket of mine has hairs today.
Kayenda museya – museya	It is so light, just light

This song is sung by a diviner healer during the ceremony of divination or exorcism of sorcerers. If people do not put enough money in the basket, he threatens to no longer offer his services.

---

98 Ideophone.

99 Ideophone.

100 Indeophone.

101 Here a diviner is speaking who feels unsufficiently rewarded for his services.

Song no. 128
Madando

Anyakasaru	Nyakasaru
Zuba ilo na madando ah eh	The whole day nothing but complaints
Ine nifwenge na madando	Me, I will die complaining.

Chorus

Swaya[102] mwana wane	Say it all, my child
Namwe adada	I told you, father
Ng'ombe zabene ziwele	Return the (bride wealth) cows to where they came from
Ziwelele kwa Mulefu	Return them to Mulefu
Na madando ahe	With complaints, ahe
Ine nifwenge na madando	I will die complaining
Namwe adumbu	And you, my brother, as well
Ine nkhamuphalirani	I told you
Ng'ombe zabene ziwele	Return the (bride wealth) cows to where they came from
Ziwelele m'chikaya chabo	They should return to their village
Nyumba yane kwa Mulefu	My house at Mulefu's
Ine kuno naliwona eh	Me, here, I am in trouble, eh
Na madando ah eh	Me, nothing but complaints, ah eh
Ine nifwenge na madando	I will die complaining

The wife can no longer stomach married life. She demands divorce and the restitution of the bride price.

Song no. 129
Njekulala

Walala walala	He sleeps, he sleeps
Eh yayiwe eh yayiwe	Eh yayiwe, eh yayiwe
Walizga ng'oma Njekulala	He has beaten the drum, Njekulala

---

[102] Onomatopoeira: the noise made by dead leaves.

Walala walala	He sleeps, he sleeps
Eh yayiwe he yayiwe	Eh yayiwe, he yayiwe
Walizga ng'oma Njekulala	He has beaten the drum, Njekulala
Chota[103] wane Njekulala	Chota of me, Njekulala
Eh yayiwe he yayiwe	Eh yayiwe, he yayiwe
Walizga ng'oma Njekulala	He has beaten the drum, Njekulala

Allusion to the fact that the spirit is capable of offering momentarily the gift of beating the drum like a specialist.

Song no. 130
Nyamkhulama

| Nyamkhulama mukawere | Nyamkhulama, go and come back |
| Nyamkhulama ukawere namacero | Nyamkhulama, you should come back tomorrow |

Chorus 1

Bazungu (2x)	The Whites
Bakukana (2x)	They refuse
Kuya kwabo namacero eh	To go home tomorrow
Enya Nyamkhulama	Yes, Nyamkhulama

Chorus 2

Bazungu (2x)	The Whites
Bakukana (2x)	They refuse
Kutema simbo	To be tatooed
Enya Nyamkhulama	Yes, Nyamkhulama

A song with a political dimension.

---

[103] Term of address for unspecified spirits.

Song no. 131
Malayilano

Malayilano	Good bye
Malayilano	Good bye
Malayilano	Good bye
Malayilano, sono tikuwela	Good bye, now we are going
Malayilano, malayilano	Good bye, good bye
Malayilano, sono tikuwela	Good bye, now we are going

The dancer is bidding good bye.

Bibliography

List of Recognised Practitioners Past and Present

Bangeya Longwe	Mtenthe, Zubayumo, Mzimba
Chazondeka Manda	Njuyu, Mzimba
Cheruzgo Chawinga	Katumbi, Rumphi
Chikanje Msowoya	Bwengu, Mzimba
Chimlondolondo Ziba	Mthetho Hara, Enukweni, Mzimba
Chizgoka Mpapomba	Chisimuka, Rumphi
Dr M.T. Chipeta	Sazu Home Mission, Manyamula, Mzimba
Filipu Munthali	Chisimuka, Rumphi
Gwaza Muwera	Nkhorongo, Mzuzu
Gwede Mhoni	Elangeni, Mzimba
Jeyeka Mbale	Rumphi Boma, Rumphi
Kazuba Mkandawire	Chikwawa, Rumphi
Kennedy Mvula	Mawumba Ndoro, Embangweni, Mzimba
Kezi Mphande	Emoyeni, Enukweni, Mzimba
Kwenda Phiri	Kaseka, Mzikubola, Mzimba
M`busa Mateyu	Mwachibanda, Hewe, Rumphi
Mariya Banda	Emoyeni, Enukweni, Mzimba
Matupi	Rumkhwara, Bolero, Rumphi
Mpaparika Zimba	Bowe, Mpherembe, Mzimba
Muganga	Chembe, Rumphi
Muwanga	Muteweti, Rumphi
Mwachibanda Munthali	Hewe, Rumphi
Nchimi Mlawula	Vhongo, Mzimba
Nchimi Tembo	Edlaleni, Milala, Mzimba
Nthangwnika Shela	Mdolo, Mzimba
Siyayo Mkandawire	Mtuzuzu, Embangweni, Mzimba
Tiwonge	Chisimuka, Rumphii
Visuzgo	Mwachibanda, Hewe, Rumphi
Zimba	Champira Turn off, Mzimba
Zondani Chirwa	Chindewe, Bwengu, Mzimba

Published

Abimbola, Wamde, *Ifa Divination Poetry*, New York, London, Lagos: Nok Publishers, 1977.

Alexandre, P., "Langues Bantu," Ch. 1, in *Les Langues dans le Monde Ancien et Moderne*, Paris: Editions du CNRS, 1981.

Alexandre, P., "Préliminaire à une présentation des ideophones Bulu", (Neue Afrikanistische Studien, ed. J. Lukas, Hamburg, 1966, pp. 9–28), in *Langues et Langages en Afrique Noire*, Paris, 1967.

Babalola, S.A., "La poésie Yoruba", no. 47 (Nouvelle Série), *Présence Africaine*, Paris, 1963, pp. 211-217.

Babalola, S.A., "The Characteristic Features of Outer Form of Yoruba Ijala Chant", I (1) (New Series), *Odu*, 1964, pp. 33–44; I (2), 1965 pp. 47–77.

Babalola, S.A., *The Content and the Form of Yoruba Ijala*, Oxford: Clarendon, London: Oxford University Press, 1966.

Bakary, Traore, *The Black African Theatre and its Social Functions*, Ibadan University Press, 1972.

Bamunoba, Y.K. and B. Adoukonou, *La Mort dans la Vie Africaine*, Paris: Présence Africaine – UNESCO, 1979.

Bassani, E., "A Kongo Drum Stand" in *African Arts*, UCLA, vol xi, no. 1 (Oct 1977).

Belinga, E.S.M., *Comprendre la Littérature Orale Africaine*, Issy–les–Moulineaux: Les Classiques Africains, 1978.

Beeman, William O., "Religion and Ritual Performance", *Interkulturelle Theologie*, vol. 39, 4/2013, pp. 320-341.

Bernard, G., "Rédondance, répétition et récurrence," *Etudes de Linguistique Appliquée*, Paris: Didier, 1967, pp. 23–82.

Mongo, Beti, *Le Pauvre Christ de Bomba*, Paris: Robert Lafont, 1956. (Editions Présence Africaine, 1976).

Boeder, R.B., "The Effects of Labor Emigration on Rural Life in Malawi", in *Land and Labor in Rural Malawi*, Part I (Spring 1973), Michigan State University

Bouquiaux, Luc, "L'arbre *ngbé* et les relations amoureuses chez les Ngbaka", in *Langages et Cultures Africaines*, Etudes réunies et présentées par Geneviève Calame-Griaule, Paris: Maspéro, 1977.

Brelsford, W.V., "African Dances of Northern Rhodesia", in Rhodes-Livingstone Museum Occasional Papers, no. 2 (1948).

Calame-Griaule, Geneviève, "Ce qui donne du gout aux contes," in *Littérature*, no. 45, Paris: Les Contes, Larousse, 1982.

Calame-Griaule, Geneviève, "De l'huile au miel", in *Recherche, Pédagogie et Culture*, no. 29 30, Paris 1977, pp. 9–13.

Calame-Griaule, Geneviève, "Essai Etude Stylistique d'un Texte Dogon" J.W.A., (1967) vol. 4, I pp. 15–23.

Calame-Griaule, Geneviève, "Pour une étude ethnolinguistique des littératures orales africaines", in *Langage* no. 18, Paris: Didier/Larousse, 1970.

Calame-Griaule, Geneviève, *Ethnologie et Langage: La Parole chez les Dogons*, Paris: Gallimard, 1965.

Calame-Griaule, Geneviève, *Le Théme de l'Arbre dans les Contes Africains*, Bibliothèque de la SELAF, Paris: Klincksieck, 1969–1974, 3 vls.

Chakanza, J.C., "Provisional Annotated Chronological List of Witch-finding Movements in Malawi 1850-1980," *Journal of Religion in Africa,* Vol. 15/3 (1985), pp. 227-243.

Chilivumbo, Alifeyo, "Vimbuza or Mashawe. A Mystic Therapy," *African Music Society Journal*, vol II, Roodepoort, 1972.

Chilivumbo, Alifeyo, "Malawi's Culture in the National Integration", *Présence Africaine*, no. 98, 1976.

Chirambo, G.R., *Kugomezgeka* [To be responsible], Lusaka and Blantyre: University of London Press in association with The Publications Bureau, 1956.

Chirwa, Isaak, "Malawian Drama Must Go Back Home", *Malawi News*, 4.2.1979, p. 18.

Chiwale, J.C., "Royal Praises and Praise Names of the Lunda-Kazembe", *Rhodes-Livingstone Museum Communications*, no. 25, 1962.

Cohen, M., *Matériaux pour une Sociologie du Langage*, vol. II, Paris: Maspéro, 1971.

Cook, D. J., "The Influence of the Livingstonia Mission upon the Formation of Welfare Associations in Zambia 1912 – 1931," in Terence Ranger and Jan Weller (eds): *Themes in the Christian History of Central Africa*, London, 1975.

Dadie, B., *Climbié*, London: Heinemann, (Version originale: Eds. Seghers, Paris, 1966).

Doke, C.M., *Bantu Linguistic Terminology*, London: Longmans Green, 1935.

Douglas, M., "Witch Beliefs in Central Africa", *Africa*, Journal of the International African Institute, vol xxxvii, no. 1.

Fiedler, Rachel NyaGondwe, *Coming of Age. A Christianized Initiation among Women in Southern Malawi*, Zomba: Kachere, 2005.

Finnegan, Ruth, *Oral Poetry. Its Nature, Significance and Social Context*, London: Cambridge University Press, 1977.

Fortune, G., "Ideophones in Shona", *Africa*, vol 33/2, 1963.

Fraser, Donald, *African Idylls*, London: Seeley Service, 1925.

Fraser, Donald, *Winning a Primitive People*, London: Seeley Service, 1914.

Gibbal, J.M., *Tambours d'eau*, Paris: Le Sycomore, 1982.

Greschat, H.J., "Legend? Fraud? Reality? Alice Lenshina's Prophetic Experience." *Africana Marburgensia*, I (1) 1968, pp. 8-13.

Hanna, J.L., "The Status of African Dance Studies", *Africa*, vol xxxvi, no. 3, 1966, London: Oxford University Press.

Harris, M., "Labour Emigration among the Mocambique Thonga", *Africa*, vol xxx no. 2, 1960, London: Oxford University Press.

Hazlewood, A. and P.D. Henderson, *Nyasaland. The Economics of Federation*, Oxford: Basil Blackwood, 1960

Houis, M., *Anthropologie Linguistique de l'Afrique Noire* Paris: Collection SUP, PUF, 1971.

Hurbon, Laennec, *Dieu dans Le Vaudou Haïtien*, Préface de G. Calame-Griaule, Paris: Payot, 1972.

Jeune Afrique, "Culture et Vie. L' Afrique des Sectes", no. 938/939 (27.12.1978), Paris.

Jeune Afrique: no. 791 (5.3.1976): "Lu pour vous."

Jeune Afrique: no. 940 (10.1.1976).

Johnston, T.F., "Conflict Resolution in Tsonga. Co-Wifely Jealousy Songs," *Africana Marburgensia*, vol. xi, no. 2. 1978, p. 23.

Johnston, T.F., "The Social Meaning of Tsonga Wedding Songs", *Africana Marburgensia*, VIII (2), Marburg, 1975, pp. 19–28.

Kabwiku, Nsuka zi, Chants de Deuil Ntandu. Présentation et Description, PhD, Université de Paris III et INALCO, Paris, 1976, pp. 152 –153.

Kalipeni, E., "Traditional African Healing of Mental Illness as Compares with Western Psychiatry (Clinical Psychology)", in *Dansk Psykolog Nyt*, 33, 1979.

Kamwendo, Mike, "African Theatre. Is there such a Thing?" *Malawi News*, 2.9.1979.

Kana, T.I., *Kasi mitala njiwemi?* Blantyre: CLAIM, 1972.

Khunga. C., "Too Strange not to be True", in David Cook (ed), *Origin East Africa. A Makerere Anthology*, Kampala, 1965, pp. 38–44.

Kotchy-N'guessan, B., "Le conte dans la société africaine" in *Annales de l'Université d'Abidjan*, Série D., Lettres, Tome 5, 1972, Littérature.

Kunene, D.P., *The Ideophone in Southern Sotho*, Berlin: Reimer, 1978.

Kurath, G.P., Remarks at the 1954 and 1964 Annual meetings of the Society of the Ethnomusicology, in J.L. Hanna, *The Status of African Dance Studies*.

Leiris, M., "La croyance aux génies 'zar' en Ethiopie du Nord", *Journal de Psychologie Normale et Pathologique*, Paris: Librairie Félix Alcan, 1938.

Lewis, I.M., *Ecstatic Religion. An Anthropological Study of Spirit Possession and Shamanism*, Harmondsworth: Penguin, 1971.

Linden, Ian and Jane, *Catholics, Peasants and Chewa Resistance in Nyasaland, 1889–1939*, London: Heinemann, 1974.

Lumwamu, F., "Le sens de la tradition", no. 29 30, *Recherche, Pédagogie et Culture*, Paris, 1977, pp. 3-5.

Malawi Government National Statistical Office, "Malawi Population Census 1977 Final Report", vol. I, 1980, Zomba.

MANA, "Herbalists Hold Seminar", *Daily Times*, 27.4.1981.

MANA, *Daily Times*, 27.4.1981.

MANA, *Daily Times*, 1980.

Martino, Ernesto de, *La Terre du Remords*, Paris: Gallimard, 1966.

McCracken, John, *Politics and Christianity in Malawi 1875-1940. The Impact of the Livingstonia Mission in the Northern Province*, Zomba: Kachere, [2]2000.

Mchombo, S., "Cryptic Meaning in Chichewa Poetry" in *Kalulu*, 1976, pp. 27–34.

Mchombo, Sam, "Cryptic Meaning in Chichewa Poetry", *Kalulu*, Bulletin of Malawian Oral Literature and Cultural Studies, University of Malawi, 1976.

Melland, Frank, *In Witch–Bound Africa. An Account of the Primitive Kaonde Tribe and their Beliefs*, London: Frank Cass, 1967.

Merriam, A.P., "The Music of Africa", in *Africa Report*, vol. vii (6), 1962, pp. 15–17 and 23.

Midauko na Makani gha Wangoni [Migrations and History of the Ngoni], Blantyre: Hetherwick Press, 1961.

Mkandawire, A.H.C., *Mahara gha Bana* [The Wisdom for the Children], Lusaka and Blantyre: Publications Bureau, 1975.

Mkandawire, A.H.C., *Wene-na-wene* [Brotherhood], Limbe: Malawi Publications and Literature Bureau, 1965.

Mongo, Beti, *Le Pauvre Christ de Bomba*, Paris: Robert Lafont, 1956. (Eds Présence Africaine, 1976).

Msosa, J., "How Poetic are Nyau Songs?" *Kalulu*, no. 2, 1977.

Nazombe, Anthony, "Spirit Possession Songs and Social Tension: A Comparative Study of Vimbuza and Nantongwe" Conference on Literature in Society in Southern Africa, University of York, 8–11.9.1981.

Ngoie-Ngalla, D., "Les Banganga", *La Semaine Africaine*, (14-20.2. 1980), Brazzaville.

Omoyajowo, J.A., *Witches. A Study of Belief in Witchcraft and of its Future in Modern African Society*, University of Ibadan, 1965.

Òsúndáre, N., "Poems for Sale: Stylistique Features of the Content, Form, and Performance of Yoruba Ipolowo Poetry", Sixth Ibadan African Literature Conference, Ibadan, 27.7.–1.8.1981.

Oyono, F., *Le Vieux Négre et la Médaille*, Paris: Union Générale d' Edition, 1972.

Oyono, F., *Une Vie de Boy*, Paris: Julliard, 1956.

Paulme, D., "Littérature Orale et Comportements Sociaux en Afrique Noire" *L'Homme*, I (1) Paris, 1961, pp. 37–49.

Paulme, D., *Femmes d'Afrique Noire*, La Haye: Mouton, 1960.

Paulme, Denise and Monique Gessau (eds), *Femmes d'Afrique Noir*, Paris: Mouton, 1960.

Phiri, D.D., *Malawians to Remember. Charles Chidongo Chinula* Lilongwe: Longmans, 1975.

Pike, J.G. and G.T. Rimmington, *Malawi. A Geographical Study*, London: Oxford University Press, 1965.

Report of the Ministry of Labour, Malawi, 1963–1967 "The Effects of Labor Emigration on Rural Life in Malawi", in *Land and Labor in Rural Malawi*, Part I (Spring 1973), Michigan State University.

Risdon, A. V., K.N. Banda & B.L. Kaunda, *Mulive Unenesko mu Ufwiti* [There is no truth in witchcraft] Blantyre: Hetherwick Press, 1967.

Ross, Andrew C, *From Colonialism to Cabinet Crisis,* Zomba: Kachere, 2009.

Rouch, Jean, *Religion et la Magie Songhay,* Paris: Press Universitaires de France, 1960, pp. 147-148.

Rouget, G., *La Musique et la Transe,* Préface de Michel Leiris, Paris: Gallimard, 1980.

Sándor, István, "Dramaturgy of Tale-Telling" *Acta Ethnographica,* vol. xvi, fasc. 3-4, Akadémia Kiadó, Budapest, 1967.

Schoffeleers, Matthew, "The Nyau Societies: Our Present Understanding", *The Society of Malawi Journal,* 1975, Blantyre.

Senghor, Léopold Sedar, *Poémes,* Paris: Editions du Seuil, 1964.

Seydou, C., "La devise dans la culture Peule: évocation et invocation de la personne", *Langage et Culture,* Essai d'Ethnolinguistique réunis et présentés par G. Calame-Griaule, Maspéro, Paris, 1977, pp. 187–263.

Shirokogoff, S.M., *Psychomental Complex of the Tungus,* London: Kegan Paul, Trench, Trubner, 1935, p. 256.

Soko, Boston J., *Nchimi Chikanga. The Battle against Witchcraft in Malawi,* Zomba: Kachere, 2002.

Soko, Boston J., *Stylistique et Messages dans le Vimbuza,* Paris: Musée de l'Homme, 1984 (microfiche).

Sorin-Barreteau, L., "Gestes narratifs et langage gestuel chez les Mofu (Nord Cameroun), in Cahiers de Littérature Orale, no. 11 INALCO Paris, 1982, pp. 36–93.

Tasie, G.O.M., "Africans and the Religious Dimension: An Appraisal," in *Africana Marburgensia,* vol xi (1), 1976.

Thompson, Jack, *Ngoni, Xhosa and Scot,* Zomba: Kachere, 2007.

Thompson, T. Jack, "Xhosa Missionaries in Late Nineteenth Century Malawi: Strangers or Fellow Countrymen?" *Religion in Malawi* 1998, pp. 8-16.P

Timpunza-Mvula, E.S., The Pounding Song as a Vehicle of Social Consciousness", Conference on Literature in Society in Southern Africa, University of York, 8–11.9.1981.

Turner, V.W., *Lunda Rites and Ceremonies*, Rhodes–Livingstone Museum Occasional Papers no. 10, 1953.

U.C.L.A., *Africa Arts*, vol XI., no. i, p. 35: "A Kongo Drum Stand."

Vansina, Jan, *Oral Traditions*, London: Penguin, 1965.

Vyaro na Vyaro, Makani gha Kukaya na Kutali (Published by Livingstonia Mission)
"Utesi uwo ukazgora wantu kukhara makora kwa myezi yakuweranga," vol I no. 14 (Nov. 1931).
"Ng'anga za utesi mcharo nzinandi" vol. 2 no. 4 (January 1933).
"Makani na Vyanusi: wawukwi", vol. 2, no. 7 (July 1933).
"The Belief in Witchcraft", vol. 4, no. 2 (Sept. 1935).
"Muchona wakulemba nauchona umo uliri", vol. 6, no. 1 (July 1973).
"Kasi nthenda ya Vimbuza wazungu nawo wali nayo", vol. 6, no. 1 (July 1937).
"Uchenjezi wa zgoro la Machona", vol. 6, no. 5, March 1938.
"Vimbuza", vol. 6, no. 5 (March 1938).

Wang, Betty, "Folksongs as Regulators of Politics" in Alan Dundes (ed): *The Study of Folklore*, Englewood Cliffs: Prentice Hall, 1965.

White, C.M.N., *Elements in Luvale Beliefs and Rituals*. The Rhodes-Livingstone Occasional Papers no. 32, Manchester University Press, 1961.

Williamson, J., *Useful Plants of Malawi*, Zomba: University of Malawi, 1975.

Wilson, P.J., "Status Ambiguity and Spirit Possession," *Man*, 1967, pp. 366–378 [375].

Zempleni, A., "La Dimension Thérapeutique du Culte des Rab." *Rites de Possessions chez les Lebon et les Wolof,* 1966.

Zingani, Willie, "Traditional Medicine has a Part to Play in Nation's Health", *Malawi News*, 25.6.-1.7.1983.

Zingani, Willie, "Traditional Medicine has a Part to Play in Nation's Health", *Malawi News*, 25.7.1983.

Zingani, Willie, "U.S. Conference for Traditional Healers" in *Daily Times*, 27.6.1983.

Unpublished

Adewoye, S.A., "Oral Literature as Moral Science among the Yoruba", Sixth Ibadan Annual African Literature Conference, Ibadan, 27.7.-1.8.1981.

Anyidoho, Kofi, "Realism in Oral Narrative Performance", Sixth Ibadan Annual African Literature Conference, Ibadan, 27.7.-1.8.1981.

Broderick, Modupe, S., "Time and Structure in Four Sierra Leonean Oral Narrative–The Child, the Home and the Community", Sixth Ibadan Annual African Literature Conference, Ibadan, 27.7.-1.8.1981.

Chavula, Serman, "The History of Loudon Mission: 1902–1973", History Seminar Paper, University of Malawi, 1974, p. 18.

Chilibvumbo, Alifeyo, "Some Traditional Malawi Dances, Preliminary Account", 1969.

Chilibvumbo, Alifeyo, "Vimbuza of Kasungu" (1969).

Chilivumbo, A.B., "Some Traditional Malawi Dances: A Preliminary Account", Occasional Paper, University of Malawi, (cyclostyled), July 1969.

Clamettes, Jean-Loup, The Lumpa Sect. Rural Reconstruction and Conflict, MScE, University College of Wales, Aberystwyble, 1978.

Dauphin–Tinturier, A., Piège pour un lion, Etude Ethnolinguistique de Conte Bemba–Zambie, 2 vls, PhD, Université de Paris V, 1983.

Ebeogu, Afamefuna, "The Igbo Kola Nut Ritual: Anthropological and Literary Dimension", Sixth Ibadan Annual African Literature Conference, Ibadan, 27.7.-1.8.1981.

Group Enquéte Frinfriger Jalve, "Achewa, Angoni, Yao", Archives of the White Fathers, Rome. (Enquéte effectuée au Malawi entre 1951 et 1958 par des missionnaires catholiques au Malawi).

Ifwanga–wa–Pindi, Les "Bardes" et leur production littéraire chez les Yaka du Zaire, Aspects Thématique et Linguistique d'un Genre Littéraire Oral, 2 vls., PhD, Université de Paris III, 1982.

Innes, Gordon, "Formulae in Mandinka Epic: Their Affective Function", Sixth Ibadan Annual African Literature Conference, Ibadan, 27.7.-1.8.1981.

Kalmanash, J. and W.A. Skeath, "Aspects of Psychiatry in Malawi", A paper presented at the 2nd Pan African Psychiatric Conference, Dakar, March 1968.

Kalmanash, J. and W.A. Skeath, "Some Aspects of Mental Health Planning with Special Reference to Malawi," Blantyre, 1968.

Kazadi, Ntole, Essai d' Etude Ethnolinguistique des Chants du Butembo et des Mikendi (Chez les Bahemba et les Baluba du Zaire), PhD, Université de Paris III, 1982.

Moyo, Steven, A Linguo-Aesthetic Study of Ngoni Poetry, PhD, University of Wisconsin, Madison, (micro–film), 1978.

Mphande, I.M., "The Mzukuzuku Chieftainship up to 1908: An Assessment of the Myths about its Origins and Role in the History of the Northern Ngoni," History Seminar Paper, University of Malawi, 1976.

Mudimbe, V.Y., "Les 'deux' littératures africaines", Afrika Studiecentrum, Leiden, 20.–24.1976.

Nazombe, Anthony, "Spirit Possession Songs and Social Tension: A Comparative Study of Vimbuza and Nantongwe" Conference on Literature I, Society in Southern Africa, University of York, 8–11.9.1981.

Ngandu Nkashama, P., "Méthodologie pour une poétique africaine", Afrika Studiecentrum, Leiden, 20.–24.1976.

Nsuka zi Kabwiku, Chants de Deuil Ntandu. Présentation et Description, PhD, Université de Paris III et INALCO, Paris, 1976.

Okpewho, Isidore, "The Oral Performer and his Audience: A Case Study of the Ozidi Saga", Sixth Ibadan Annual African Literature Conference, Ibadan, 27.7.-1.8.1981.

Òsúndáre, N., "Poems for Sale: Stylistique Features of the Content, Form, and Performance of Yoruba Ipolowo Poetry", Sixth Ibadan African Literature Conference, Ibadan, 27.7.–1.8.1981.

Rassner, R.M., "Narrative Rhythms in Agiryama Ngano: Oral Patterns and Musical Structures", Sixth Ibadan Annual African Literature Conference, Ibadan, 27.7.-1.8.1981.

Redmayne, A., "Chikanga", National Archives, Zomba, 1968.

Ricard, A., "Sur les modes de transmission des textes oraux et écrits", Afrika Studiecentrum, Leiden, 20.–24.1976.

Sekoni, Ropo, "The Narrative Narrative–Pattern and Audience Experience of Oral Narrative Performance", Sixth Ibadan Annual African Literature Conference, Ibadan, 27.7.-1.8.1981.an

Soko, Boston J., "Le role des ancêtres dans la création du Vimbuza", Colloque, 12.-17.6.1982, Centre International de Rencontre de Cultures de Tradition Orale: Cultures de L'Oralité, Université de Bretagne Occidentale, Brest.

Soko, Boston J., "Le Vimbuza comme mouvement de résistance contre la christianisation: 1920 – 1963", Laboratoire d'Anthropologie Juridique de Paris, Université de Paris I: Panthéon-Sorbonne, 2éme Session du Colloque Sacralité, Pouvoir et Droit en Afrique, 25.-27.5.1981.

Soko, Boston J., "The Vimbuza Phenomenon: Disease or Art", University of Malawi, Research and Publications Committee, Occasional Papers, March 1981.

Timpunza-Mvula, E.S., "The Pounding Song as a Vehicle of Social Consciousness", Conference on Literature 1, Society in Southern African, University of York, 8–11.9.1981.

Vimbuza, Minute Book of the M'mbelwa Native Association, 8.1.1920, National Archives, Zomba.

Records

International Library of African Music, Sound of Africa Series, Rhodes University (S.A.). (Disques sur les Tumbuka Henga).

Rouget, G., "Possession à Madagascar", Disques OCORA OCR 83, col. Musée de l'Homme, Paris. (Musique Vezo, Mahafaly et Masikoro–Mikea).